SOCCER MADNESS

SOCCER MADNESS

Brazil's Passion for the World's Most Popular Sport

Janet Lever
California State University,
Los Angeles

WAVELAND
PRESS, INC.
Long Grove, Illinois

For information about this book, contact:
    Waveland Press, Inc.
    4180 IL Route 83, Suite 101
    Long Grove, IL 60047-9580
    (847) 634-0081
    info@waveland.com
    www.waveland.com

With love,
to the family of
Dr. José Carlos and Eduly Ross,
and to the memory of Peter Reichard

Contents

1995 Preface

"Planet Soccer" became a slogan and a reality in 1994 when countries like the United States, Japan, and China finally joined the league of nations united by their interest in international soccer. That year viewers in 188 nations--virtually every country on the globe--saw Brazil defeat Italy in the first penalty-kick shoot-out in a final game of the World Cup. Because that World Cup tournament was the first to be played in the United States--and the first to be played in a country without a strong soccer tradition--it symbolizes the growing interest in what has been called "the beautiful game."

The globalization of soccer culture through promotion efforts in both Third World countries without thriving organized sports as well as First World countries with numerous deeply entrenched spectator sports is not accidental. Rather, expanding the market for the sport to all corners of the globe was consciously designed and executed. Because of the success of the plan, understanding the cultural and sociological importance of soccer is more important than ever. This book is in part about the significance of global participation in the international sporting community--especially what it means for the United States finally to be initiated into the world of soccer.

Soccer Madness is being reissued just as the United States prepares to launch its most carefully planned and financed national soccer league. The future of the league is undetermined, but it is hoped that domestic games will help Americans further cultivate an understanding and appreciation of the sport. As new fans identify with favorite players, they also gain greater interest in the performance of the U.S. national team in international tournaments. Because of pride in nation, fans united by their mutual interest will quickly become fans united by their passion. At that point they will not only be bound to other American fans, but also become bonded to people around the globe who share the passion for soccer.

This book is also intended to give students and sports enthusiasts a solid case study of the meaning of sport and fandom in a single country where soccer is intertwined with national identity--Brazil. *Soccer Madness* is about how that Third World nation came to be the greatest soccer power on earth, and what that source of pride means to Brazilians. Understanding the role of sport in that society provides a unique window through which we can see the people, culture, and politics of one of the largest and most important nations in the developing world. But beyond the case of Brazil, examining the success of soccer yields insight into the cultural achievement of spectator sports in all modern societies.

The World Cup and Soccer in the United States

Soccer, football, futebol, fussball--whatever you call it, the kicking game is unquestionably the world's most popular team sport. Over one billion people watched the final match of the 1994 World Cup, the only true global championship for professionals in a team sport. The cumulative audience for all 52 matches was over 32 billion viewers. What is most remarkable about the '94 Cup is that it was held in the United States--the only major country in the world *without* a Division I professional outdoor soccer league. The North American Soccer League (NASL) was formed in 1966 but folded after the 1984 season.

The Fédération Internationale de Football Association (FIFA), world soccer's governing body, has excluded countries without professional soccer from hosting the World Cup, but in 1988 FIFA awarded the honor of hosting the 1994 championship to the United States anyway. There were several reasons for the exception. FIFA officials had been impressed with the large soccer attendances of the 1984 Olympic Games held in the United States FIFA preferred not to hold two consecutive Cups in Europe, and there were no other suitable contenders outside Europe with adequate stadia facilities. The U.S. infrastructure was so superior that 24 cities could make official bids to be one of the nine venues for the tournament. FIFA also acted to bring

Americans--and their potential television and merchandising revenues--into the international soccer fold.

As a condition of the award, the U.S. Soccer Federation (USSF) promised to launch a new top-level professional soccer league. Initially it was hoped that Major League Soccer (MLS) would be in place by the time of the Cup, but failure to raise the targeted $100 million in start-up capital caused repeated delays. Ten to twelve U.S. cities will field MLS teams beginning in 1996. Cities awarded teams to date are Tampa, Chicago, Boston, Columbus (Ohio), Los Angeles, New Jersey (Giants Stadium), San José, and Washington, D.C., and Long Island (N.Y.). About $5 million in seed money came as a loan from the USSF. With over $40 million as its share of World Cup profits, the USSF Foundation can do much more than in the past for the general advancement of soccer in this country.

Although the World Cup is the globe's most-watched sporting tournament, the fact is that most Americans had not even heard of the event prior to its staging here. A Harris poll taken a few months before the opening game revealed that eight in ten Americans still were not aware the World Cup would be played here. Most didn't know the World Cup involved soccer; many confused it with the America's Cup yachting races. By the start date, media attention helped the World Cup achieve better name recognition, yet a Gallup poll found six in ten Americans had no intention of watching a single game.

Although the majority of Americans claimed no interest in the World Cup, there was an enthusiastic minority willing to spend from $25, to see a first-round match, to $475, for the final game (ticket agencies resold the best seats for $1250), and ticket sales moved briskly. Demand exceeded supply even though 65 percent of 3.65 million tickets were reserved for the domestic market. American soccer participants and supporters were given priority access to early-round tickets, and the later-round tickets were sold in a lottery-style drawing. No doubt a reflection of Americans' soccer naivete, 44,132 people came to watch the match between Nigeria and Bulgaria. An early game between two low-ranked teams would have been played in a near-empty stadium in any country with a soccer tradition.

Under the direction of Alan Rothenberg, who also heads both the USSF and the MLS, World Cup USA '94 was a commercial success even before the games began, having sold over one million more tickets than the previous attendance record set four years earlier in Italy. As foreign fans and media began to arrive, economists projected that the World Cup would give the U.S. economy a $4 billion boost.

In the beginning of the month-long tournament, poking fun at the low-scoring games became a nightly ritual on America's late night television between rival talk show hosts Jay Leno and David Letterman. Letterman wisecracked that World Cup viewers were yawning in a hundred languages. Leno informed us that Dr. Kevorkian had a new suicide machine: "With this one he shows you soccer matches until you're bored to death." Letterman eventually came around to recognize the popularity of the games by having as guests Andres Cantor, the Univision announcer who became known for his prolonged shouts of "go-o-o-l," and U.S. defender Alexi Lalas.

Prominent sportswriters likewise were joking about a sport where the lone referee acts also as timekeeper and can add on time for moments lost to injury or infringements, so only he knows when the game will end. They joked about the histrionics of players feigning injuries, scoreless ties, or the lunacy of ending a game with penalty-kick "shoot-outs." One didn't have to be famous to get a jab in print; as one Los Angeles citizen stated in his letter to the editor (*Los Angeles Times*, June 25, 1994, C3): "Soccer: a primitive form of hockey played by Neanderthals before the invention of skates and ice."

Although foreign press and visitors were in our midst, America's spokespersons did not try to hide our ethnocentric view that our team sports are superior and we don't mind playing them alone. Upon first exposure to world-class soccer, we haughtily endorsed our self-exile from the World Cup community of nations, thereby accenting our "Ugly American" image abroad. Our early public reaction was a bold reminder that Americans have different sensibilities and remain cultural isolationists in spite of our world leadership role. It should have come as no surprise that Americans wouldn't understand all the excitement around the World Cup, for we had no frame of reference. Until the World Cup, we had not experienced a true world championship of a professional team sport. The Super Bowl and NBA Championship are national events; at most, the World Series and Stanley Cup involve two nations.

But the games played on, and both exciting and tragic events claimed Americans' attention. First, there was the U.S.'s historic 2-1 win over Colombia, considered one of the top four teams. Then Colombian star Andres Escobar was assassinated by a hail of gunfire outside a restaurant in Medellin when he returned home after causing his country's embarrassing defeat by accidentally deflecting a pass into his own side's net.

Then the U.S. played the colorful Brazilian team on the Fourth of July, a game that got the highest TV ratings--9.3 nationally--to date for a soccer match. (For comparison, the ratings for the same summer's baseball All-Star Game were 15.7.). By the time the 24-country playoff had been whittled down to four, many Americans were caught up in the excitement of the nationalistic rivalry. In contrast to only one million viewers for the 1990 final match, nine million Americans (in 24 percent of homes with TVs turned on) watched the 1994 finale on ABC, plus another 1.6 million saw it on Univision, the Spanish-language network.

Henry Kissinger, former U.S. Secretary of State and chairman of the '94 Cup organizing committee, had been instrumental in bringing the World Cup to America. He was straightforward about his motive (*Newsweek*, July 16, 1990, p. 65): "We're on a missionary enterprise. . . . We've got to make this sport as popular in the United States as it deserves to be." Soccer tournaments are genuinely international events. FIFA, headquartered in Switzerland, now has 191 member nations, making it the world's largest international federation. By contrast, there are 195 National Olympic Committees recognized by the International Olympic Committee (IOC), which is not a federation; recognition simply means a country's athletes are eligible for IOC competitions. At this time, the United Nations has 184 member states and six non-voting recognized countries.

Because patriotism engenders fanatic interest in international play, soccer is better able than anything else in modern life to tap our deepest sense of "roots." When teams represent the groups that give us our identity--for example, those that center on our national origins or ethnicity--they arouse the most passion. The 1994 World Cup was a successful spectacle in part because it tapped the sentiments of America's immigrant population. Newspapers were filled with stories about the thousands of Irish, Italian, Argentine, Swedish, German, and Greek immigrants who have been living in America for twenty or thirty years, yet showed up at stadia draped in their home country's flag, singing patriotic songs. The World Cup provided an opportunity to step out of America's old melting pot and savor one's distinctive origins.

This special occasion to reaffirm who we are was not restricted to the foreign-born. We discovered that first-, second-, and even third-generation Americans had not forgotten their homeland. Italian-Americans, to name just one ethnic group, were as enthusiastic as native Italian tourists in the stands. Italian roots gave them a soccer power to cheer for, and the Cup gave them an opportunity to honor their heritage. In fact, FIFA itself recognizes that roots stretch across generations. National teams are not restricted to native-born players, but also may include those who had a parent or grandparent born in the country (eligibility criteria vary nation to nation). The 1994 Irish team, for example, had only seven players born in Ireland. Almost all of the rest were born in England, where their families had migrated looking for jobs. In fact, 20 of 22 of Ireland's teammates play on English teams, but they honored their heritage by playing on the Irish national team. Players with dual allegiance must choose a country, for once a player has played on a national team in an official match at any level, including youth teams, he/she cannot play for another country, ever.

The World Cup was also a splendid occasion for America's newest immigrants to enjoy solidarity with others who missed the homeland. Most conspicuous were the thousands of Mexican-Americans who came to the Rose Bowl draped in red, white, and green flags. A pre-Cup exhibition game between the U.S. and Mexico was played "before a tremendous crowd of 91,123, including the estimated 1,123 who didn't come to cheer for Mexico," wrote Mike Downey in the *Los Angeles Times* (June 5, 1994, C1). Other sportswriters, too, raised the question, "which was the home team?" Romanians in Hollywood and Koreans in "Koreatown" also got an occasion to cheer for their national teams from the old country. Angelenos without a hyphenated identity enjoyed the rare occasion to display patriotism, streaming into the streets of Pasadena wearing red, white, and blue face paint.

Playing soccer can also alleviate homesickness, linking immigrant adults with each other while making them feel at home in the U.S. It is estimated that 2,800 teams bearing the names of ancestral villages and states in Mexico, El Salvador, and Colombia participate in 40 Latino adult soccer leagues around Los Angeles. Soccer can help integrate immigrant youths, too. In one work-for-play program in Los Angeles, boys 13 to 18 spend a few hours a week on graffiti-removing teams in exchange for uniforms, equipment, refreshments, and transportation to participate in youth soccer.

In addition to those who live in ethnic enclaves, the enthusiasm of amateur soccer players from all-American suburbs accounted for the success of the first World Cup played in the U.S. The fact that this fan base is already large and growing provides another source of optimism for the success of the new MLS. Over 16 million Americans (a quarter of all players are adult, and more than one-third are female) at least occasionally play soccer. Soccer is America's fastest growing participant sport. High school participation has more than doubled since 1980, and there are now more varsity intercollegiate men's teams playing soccer than football.

Many are still skeptical that the nation's amateur players will purchase tickets to watch the professional players in the new MLS, or even watch them on TV. America is considered saturated by baseball, football, basketball, and ice hockey, as well as a host of sports for individual contestants. Not only do those sports have longer-standing traditions but they are better TV games. Soccer is ill-suited for TV because the field is so large, the players too spread out, and there are no time-outs to allow breaks for ads and instant replays. If the camera follows the ball, viewers miss the strategic patterning that sets professional soccer apart from the amateur sport. It is believed that Americans prefer higher-scoring sports and those that are faster and more violent. Besides, striking balls with the head instead of the hands seems weird to those who never played the game. To be fair, even soccer enthusiasts from Europe and Latin America are fed up with the overly cautious defensive-style play that has resulted in tedious, low-scoring games for the past twenty years.

Yet the MLS has a better chance than the extinct NASL because it learned from the latter's demise. The New York Cosmos had dominated the NASL because the huge ethnic and immigrant population provided a higher attendance base (sometimes outdrawing the Yankees and Mets) than in other cities. To correct this imbalance, the new MLS was originally designed to have a unique operating structure. Unlike other American sports leagues, which are a confederation of independent franchise owners, all of the teams and player contracts were to be owned by the MLS. Although owner incentives may cause MLS to fall short of its "single-entity" design, it should still achieve the goal of limiting disparities between large and small markets to ensure competitive teams, as well as cost controls, such as salary caps. The MLS would like to avoid both unequal resources and out-of-control costs, which contributed to the 1994 strikes in North American baseball and hockey.

The MLS is further advantaged by the growth in the number of soccer participants and foreign-born residents in the U.S., the vast publicity generated by the 1994 World Cup, and new opportunities for American players to develop their talents in foreign leagues before returning to play in the MLS. In a Harris poll taken after the World Cup, 53 percent of those who watched any part of the tournament said they were more interested in the sport (22 percent less, and 24 percent had no change of opinion). Capitalizing on soccer fervor and TV ratings that were 20-30 percent higher than expected, the MLS signed a three-year broadcast agreement that assures cable coverage of some regular games and ABC network coverage of the championship. However, when that same Harris poll asked about interest in a professional league with televised games, only 29 percent said they would like one while 69 percent said they didn't care. Critics charge that the delayed start of the MLS caused lost momentum, as the kickoff will be two years past the hoopla surrounding the World Cup.

If American fans are holding off support until the U.S. can field world-class competitive teams, they don't have to wait. Although the U.S. men's national team struggled to gain respectability by advancing to the second round of the World Cup, our women's national team is in the avant-garde, having won the inaugural FIFA Women's World Championship in China in 1991. The U.S. women showed marked superiority over their rivals, first outscoring opponents 49-0 in five qualifying games, then defeating Sweden, Brazil, Japan, Taiwan, and Germany on the way to winning against Norway 2-1 in the final game. Fred Barnes wrote in *The New Republic* (July 4, 1994, p. 15) the U.S. women's team plays, "a wild, all-out attacking brand of soccer that's thrilling to watch."

Even though seven key players retired after that victory, Americans have reason to be optimistic about the 1995 Women's World Championship in Sweden. The rebuilt U.S. squad defeated the Mexican women's team 9-0 in the first qualifying match. The U.S. team is also the favorite to win the 1996 Atlanta Olympic games, the first to feature women's soccer. American women play with a significant advantage. Although excluded from football, American girls have a long history of playing soccer in this country, at least since the 1920s when they competed at the elite Seven Sisters colleges on the East Coast. America's young women get a lot of experience and training in our schools. There are about 5,000 girls' soccer teams in interscholastic high school competition (fewer than play basketball and volleyball, but more than softball and field hockey), and soccer is the fastest growing women's intercollegiate sport.

Countries where soccer is the national game had largely excluded girls and women from playing. The English Schools Football Association was not allowed to "actively encourage" soccer for girls until 1990. In parts of Europe and Asia, however, women began playing the game seriously by the late 1960s and early 1970s. Improved standards of play aroused spectator interest by the 1980s. Women's soccer still lags in South America and Africa. Over twenty years ago I predicted that American women would initially conquer all competitors in soccer, and that prediction came true.

Soccer in Other Parts of the World

All major countries have professional outdoor soccer teams. Australia and Canada have semi-professional leagues, although interest in them still lags behind Australian Rules Football, rugby, and cricket in the former and American football, ice hockey, and baseball in the latter. Japan and China just joined the soccer community when each country formed a professional league, in 1993 and 1994 respectively. With no competition from deeply rooted team sports, soccer quickly became the most popular team sport in China, bringing to FIFA an enormous potential new fan base. China's new Marlboro League may promote more than soccer. China consumes one-third of the world's cigarettes, and Philip Morris agreed to underwrite the league, naming it after the company's flagship brand.

Unlike China, in Japan there was a great deal of competition from the very popular Sumo wrestling and baseball, yet the new J-League achieved commercial success in its first soccer season. Over 800,000 people requested tickets to the inaugural game, and every subsequent match also sold out. The media gave league games extensive coverage, as TV ratings surpassed those for baseball. Although broadcast at midnight, Japan's final World Cup qualifying match got a staggering 48.1 percent rating.

FIFA is consciously trying to expand its sphere of influence to all corners of the globe. Dr. João Havelange, president of Brazil's sport confederation since 1958, assumed the presidency of FIFA in 1974, then ruled it with an iron hand for the last twenty years. (He has not lost touch with Brazilian soccer either, for his son-in-law presides over the Brazilian Football Federation.) In 1982 Havelange expanded the number of World Cup participants from 16 to 24 to include more Asian and African nations. Nigeria, Morocco, Cameroon, South Korea, and Saudi Arabia (a country that had no organized sports programs until 1974) all qualified for the 1990 World Cup.

In 1994, at age 78, Havelange won his sixth four-year term with a platform promise to expand participation in the 1998 World Cup from 24 to 32 teams in an effort to include even more countries. FIFA is committed to staging the first World Cup in Asia in 2002; so far Japan is favored to beat South Korea's rival bid to be the host nation (South Korea has offered to sponsor it with North Korea, using the political ploy of enticing FIFA with a role in facilitating reunification). Nigeria is hosting FIFA's Under-20 World Championship in 1995. South Africa is due to host the premier African soccer tournament, the African Cup of Nations, in 1998 and has been proposed as a possible World Cup host for 2006.

Meanwhile, there have been noteworthy changes in soccer in countries where it has long been entrenched. There is an inglorious association between soccer and hooliganism in England. The country's worst-ever sporting tragedy occurred in 1989 when police misdirected thousands of Liverpool fans into an already-packed section just as a match had started at Sheffield's Hillsborough Stadium. Because the heavy fencing needed to keep the fans from the field did not yield, nor did the police recognize the gravity of the situation and release the safety gates, 96 fans were crushed to death while scores more suffered critical injuries. That disaster launched an investigation of British soccer and the resulting Taylor Report precipitated major changes.

For many the traditional way to view soccer had always been from the standing terraces of turn-of-the-century stadia; it was in these male-only terraces that the hooligans staged their fights. Earlier efforts to modernize the stadia had been met with resistance from traditionalists, but the Taylor Report mandated the removal of the terrace areas and the construction of bleachers, seats, or boxes throughout all stadia. This change (along with the installation of ladies' toilets) brought more women to the games which now provide a trendy outing for the higher classes. Many men from all social classes regret the loss of the masculine terrace culture, and some working class men defy the intent of the mandate by standing on the bleacher benches.

Mechanisms of crowd control changed drastically too, after the Sheffield disaster. Fences and barriers came down and were replaced with high-technology surveillance cameras. Criminal sanctions were stiffened such that hooligans were threatened with up to ten years in prison for violent soccer field crimes. The changes were successful, for arrests and violence related to soccer matches are down, and fan surveys show that hooliganism is no longer perceived as a big problem.

Unfortunately, league attendance is down, too. In part this is a result of the dramatically reduced stadia capacity with the transition from standing room to seats, as well as the accompanying increase in admission costs. But gate receipts were also affected by live TV coverage of regular league games. Until recently, viewers could watch only game highlights, but now a satellite service has acquired rights to 60 live games per year (for $534 million over five years) for its paying subscribers. Although British Sky Broadcast has only 1.6 million subscribers with receiving dishes (less than 8 percent of the TV market), many fans take advantage of the free viewing now available via satellite on large screens in the pubs. Growing commercialism in soccer also led the first division clubs to break away from the lower divisions to create a new Premier League; losing revenue from the top further contributed to the decline of England's smaller clubs.

Just as hooliganism is coming under control throughout the United Kingdom, youth soccer violence is gaining visibility in other European countries, such as Germany, Italy, and Holland. It is most troubling in Germany where it is linked with the growing neo-Nazi movement. As Friedrich Christian Delius wrote in *The New Republic* (July 4, 1994, p. 22), ". . . violent criminals . . . exit the stadium chanting, "Sieg Heil!" and then rampage against 'foreigners'. . ." As in Germany, racism and ethnic hatred mark extremist fans in Italy known as Ultras, often linked with outlawed right-wing groups. According to Ken Shulman in an article for the *Chicago Tribune* (February 3, 1995, p. 3), "It is not uncommon to see Ultras with shaved heads, marching beneath swastikas with their arms extended in a Nazi salute as they approach the stadium." Since 1979, seven Italian fans have died in stadium-related violence and thousands more have been injured. Shulman's article appeared after the latest incident because of the unprecedented action taken by Italian authorities who suspended the upcoming Sunday match for the first time ever (the games were played even during the Nazi occupation of Italy in World War II). Leaders are sending a clear message: stop the mayhem or we shut the whole show down.

Nevertheless, the overarching atmosphere at European matches is more like a carnival or party, rather than one of threat or intimidation. A group of popular culture scholars, under the editorship of Steve Redhead, write in *The Passion and the Fashion: Football Fandom in the New Europe* (Aldershot: Avebury, 1993) about the democratization of the sport. They describe the increase of women fans, the rise of independent supporters' clubs, and fan magazines (called "fanzines"). Yet they also foresee the opposite process, as emphasis on television rights and merchandising push soccer in the direction of American corporate-controlled sport franchises. They see the day coming when there are continent-wide super leagues controlled by international media moguls. Instead of passionate fans in the stands, they see a more passive, "respectable" audience sitting in executive boxes and all-seater stadia and in armchairs watching the game live via their satellite receivers.

Italy and Germany are the soccer giants in Europe. Remarkably, it was little Bulgaria, which had never won a World Cup match until 1994, that beat Germany to reach the semifinals. Writing in the *Times of London*, David Miller said, "There is an element of national celebration in Bulgaria's victory that few in the United States for the finals can understand. For the nine million population . . . this performance is a global representation of new liberties, a joyous statement of nationalism . . ." (as cited in the *Los Angeles Times*, July 13, 1994, W7). President Zhelyu Zhelev, in a nationwide broadcast, equated the soccer team's ascent to the fall of communism.

Soccer can be imbued with deep meaning on a much smaller scale. During the cease-fire in early 1994, after the long, murderous Serbian siege, residents of Sarajevo took a giant step toward normalcy when the home team beat the U.N. team 4-0 in the city's first live soccer match in two years.

Soccer's two other giants are Argentina and Brazil in Latin America. When people think about world-class soccer, they usually think about Brazil. It is the only country to have qualified for all fifteen World Cups and the only country to win four times. Brazil is the birthplace of many of the sport's most celebrated players, including the legendary Pelé, considered the most gifted player in soccer's history. The players' nimble attacking game combined with the loud, colorful, samba-dancing fans who travel by the tens of thousands to support the national team have made Brazil almost everybody's favorite second team, after their own. (One Brazilian fan's 53-day journey to the U.S. by motorbike was duly noted in the press.)

It was no different in 1994. Embracing the Brazilian team from the start, Americans jumped more squarely onto their bandwagon when the U.S. team was eliminated. Brazil won in 1994, but it was hardly the "dream team" that won the tri-championship in 1970. After tying the lesser Swedish team 1-1 in the first round, they barely beat them 1-0 in the semifinals and left the field while being booed by their own fans. The win in the final match against Italy was far from decisive, settled by a penalty-kick showdown after 120 minutes of lackluster, scoreless play.

After 24 years without a World Cup trophy, runaway four-figure inflation (over 3000 percent in 1993), and political scandal, the Brazilians were ready to celebrate any victory they could get. Close to 100 percent of the population tuned into the last games via television or radio. The country literally stopped for the final matches--Congress adjourned, schools closed, and businesses shut down. After the victory, people poured into the streets creating a noisy carnival of dancing and fireworks. There were no riots. Casualties included those in car accidents caused by inebriated drivers and people with high blood pressure who got sick from excitement.

When the players arrived home two days later, there was no national holiday declared, as there had been in 1970. But Brazilian President Itamar Franco received the team in Brasilia, no doubt with hopes of boosting his party's popularity ratings before general elections. He was borrowing a tarnished image, however, for the players themselves were soon caught up in a national scandal when they tried to bring in 18 tons of excess baggage (a second jumbo jet was needed to carry the cargo) without paying the estimated $1 million in duties. President Franco supported the players' privilege while the nation's tax chief resigned in protest, and, according to a newspaper poll, 79 percent of Brazilians thought their heroes should pay up like anyone else. In addition to the unauthorized excise tax bonus, each player was rewarded by the federal government with $150,000 for the victory. Star players were paid large lump sums for appearances in support of political candidates, and 17-year-old Ronaldo made an advertisement for the Brazilian army, encouraging young people to enlist.

The World Cup victory notwithstanding, Brazilian soccer has suffered a long slump. At the time of my original research in the 1970s, the clubs were on the verge of financial disaster due to skyrocketing player salaries. Things have gotten worse, not better. Brazilians' real wages have plummeted, and general admission to stadia climbed from $1.75 to $7.00. Attending local games, once a way of life, has become a luxury. Broadcast rights are small, because only important away-games are televised (and occasionally a sold-out home game). Cable TV is just beginning, and to date, systems have only contracted for major championship games to show to their small elite group of subscribing viewers.

Clubs are dependent on advertising revenue from corporate sponsors who pay large monthly fees to have logos emblazoned on team uniforms, leading some to say the players have turned into running billboards. Not only are the players sporting product logos, but in a controversial ploy Brahma, one of Brazil's three leading beer manufacturers, turned fans into billboards too. The company purchased large blocks of field-level tickets and offered free entry to those who would hold up cards or a giant banner displaying the product symbol during a major televised game. For a bargain price, Brahma's visual message got 43 minutes of unpaid advertising, while a competitive brewery got only a few minutes of airtime for its expensive paid advertisements. Unfortunately, the clubs do not benefit from unpaid advertising.

Star athletes who can command $1 million on the global market cannot be paid their worth in Brazil. Many do not control their own contracts but have managers or personal bosses who get the bulk of transfer fees when their players are sold to another team. Whether free agents or pawns, the players have made an exodus, leaving Brazilian teams without their homegrown talent. Eleven of the 22-member 1994 national team play in Europe (including eight of the starting 11); by contrast, all of the 1970 team played on Brazilian teams. There is a vicious cycle: the more players leave, the worse the quality of regular league competition becomes, and consequently fewer fans are willing to pay to see their teams play.

A new law is just taking effect which may radically change the financial condition of the soccer clubs. Until now the soccer clubs have been non-profit organizations The new law, designed to encourage amateur sport, says that any club that sponsors at least three Olympic sports (including soccer) can show a profit from certain fund-raising activities. As a result, soccer clubs have opened their own bingo salons and get to keep a small percent of the profits to support Olympic sports. Although full-service gambling casinos are forbidden in Brazil, bingo salons are allowed and are booming. Many clubs have hopped on Brazil's bingo-fever bandwagon.

There are other changes on the Brazilian soccer scene that are similar to changes in parts of Europe. Brazil's greatest soccer crisis stems from the rise of violence between rival teenage fan groups which the press has likened to gang warfare. At least six people have been killed in fights and shootouts after games. Members of fan clubs with up to 40,000 members have brought knives, bottles--even homemade bombs--to the games. Disturbances on the streets and on the trains and buses have become routine. Fans in Rio and São Paulo are staying away from stadia in record numbers; average attendance has dropped to fewer than 10,000 fans in stadia built for 150,000. The great Pelé--just appointed "Extraordinary" Minister of Sports--has pleaded with the people of his country not to ruin the sport: "Soccer must be a party to the fans and not a tragedy" (as cited in the *Chicago Tribune*, December 6, 1994, p. 1).

By contrast, stadia in smaller cities like Belo Horizonte and Curitiba have improved the party atmosphere such that they are now more welcoming of girls and women than in the past. Brazil even has accepted women as referees and line judges for men's professional competitions, including the national championship games. However, women are not supported as players. Early attempts to cover women's soccer on television failed. They have virtually no support from Brazil's big soccer clubs (except occasionally being allowed to train on their grounds) and are restricted to amateur leagues and pick-up games. It was not even a true national selection of All-Stars that competed in the Women's World Cup, but rather mostly members of RADAR, the champion team from Rio, who represented the country.

Over the years some soccer fans have switched allegiance to other sports, such as professional volleyball and basketball, two sports in which Brazilians excel. Both the men's and women's teams took some important international titles. For example, the men's volleyball team took home the gold medal from the 1992 Olympics and won the 1993 championship of the World Volleyball League; in 1994 Brazilians won the women's world basketball championship.

Further, the real heroes during soccer's lean years were Brazil's Formula One racers. First, Emerson Firtipaldi was named World Driving Champion in 1972 and 1974 (he is having a successful second career in North America where, in 1989, he became the first non-American winner of the Indianapolis 500 since 1966). Then

Nelson Piquet took that honor in 1981, 1983, and 1987 and Ayrton Senna in 1988, 1990, and 1991. Senna, the three-time champ, tragically died in a racing accident just a month before the World Cup began. When these three outstanding Brazilian drivers captured eight Formula One World titles, racing became more important than soccer for many of their compatriots. Even poor Brazilians could watch their race car drivers reflect glory on the troubled nation on free TV. Brazilians say that when Senna died, the country experienced unprecedented national mourning. In Brasilia, the World Cup winners hoisted a yellow crash helmet to the welcoming crowds and dedicated their victory to Ayrton Senna, Brazil's true national idol.

After the 1994 World Cup victory, the FIFA World Cup trophy was paraded in front of the people in major cities all over Brazil, with enormous security precautions taken for its safety. The precautions were warranted. The original World Cup--the one designed for the first tournament in 1930--was called the Jules Rimet Trophy after the FIFA president who created the world championship. The trophy itself had a turbulent history. During World War II it was hidden in a shoe-box under the bed of the Italian Football Association vice president so that it wouldn't fall into the hands of the Nazis. It reappeared in 1946 after the hostilities stopped. Then, just before the 1966 World Cup in England, the trophy was stolen from a public exhibition. Scotland Yard failed to find the trophy, but a mongrel dog named Pickles sniffed out the treasured cup in a South London garden a few days before the games began.

Early FIFA tradition established that the first country to win three World Cups would get to keep the Jules Rimet Trophy in perpetuity. The 1970 final match between Brazil and Italy was hotly contested because both sides were two-time champs. Brazil won and put the cherished historic cup on display at the Brazilian Football Federation in Rio de Janeiro. In 1983 the Jules Rimet Trophy was stolen and never recovered. There were no ransom requests, and some authorities believe that, since it was made of solid gold, it was possibly melted down. Whether it became a prized, albeit hidden, possession of a crazed fan or was destroyed by a selfish criminal remains a mystery. The Brazilian branch of Eastman Kodak, in a master public relations stroke, beat competitors (including arch-rival Fuji, an official sponsor of FIFA) to the idea of paying for an exact reproduction of the Jules Rimet Trophy and donating it to the Brazilian people. It is available for public viewing in Rio. The present-day FIFA World Cup is on loan to the victors until 1998. Bearing responsibility for the present-day FIFA World Cup, Brazilian authorities display its replica, too, while securing the authentic trophy in a federal bank vault until the next World Cup.

Acknowledgments

I am indebted to many individuals and organizations for materials and information used to write this new preface. Keith Cooper of FIFA and spokespersons from World Cup USA '94 and Major League Soccer were all forthcoming with their help, as were the fine librarians at the resource center in the Amateur Athletic Foundation of Los Angeles and at RAND. Many interesting details presented here were gleaned from the stellar coverage before, during, and after World Cup '94 by the *Los Angeles Times* staff. For updates on the status of soccer in Europe, I thank all participants of the 1994 International Symposium on Youth, Violence, and Sports held at the University of California in Santa Barbara. For the update on British soccer, I especially thank John Williams of the Sir Norman Chester Centre for Football Research and John Fulgoni of World Cup USA '94. For updated information on the most loved sport in Brazil, I thank my dear Brazilian "brothers," Carlos Eduardo Ross and Dr. José Augusto Ross, who were aged 12 and 10 when my adoptive family took me to my first Brazilian soccer match 27 years ago.

1983 Preface: A Personal Note on the Origins of This Study

My study of Brazilian soccer developed unconventionally—research is often serendipitous. The circumstances of data collection (including some understanding of the field researcher's identity) are important to a full assessment of the findings; too few writers share these details of the investigative process.

For more than a decade, I have been following Brazilian soccer and collecting materials for this book. I was first exposed to international soccer in England, the summer after my sophomore year in college. My brother had arranged a clerical job for me at Macy's foreign shipping office in London in 1966—the summer England was to host the World Cup, the international soccer championship that is held every four years. I had never heard of the World Cup, nor had I ever seen a professional soccer match. My contact with the game was limited to junior high school, where the girls played soccer in gym class while the boys played American football.

I quickly learned what the World Cup meant. Although soccer is a British invention, 1966 was the first time England had hosted the Cup. The upcoming event seemed the *only* topic of conversation. I followed the competition as a way to get my unfriendly co-workers to talk to me. The locals were optimistic about their team's chances to reach the finals; many talked frankly about how its strong record was England's shining light during a time marked by continuing loss of world power and a depressed economy.

Tourists poured in from foreign countries to support their teams and to watch the highest quality and most intense soccer played anywhere. Many Latin Americans came in ocean liners and lived on board during the month-long competition. Unlike the rich, who came by air and used the sporting event as an excuse for a long holiday, these ship-dwellers were working-class and middle-class people who had saved for years to make the trip. Most of these ships housed Brazilians who had come by the thousands. Their national team had won the Cup in 1958 and again in 1962 and was hoping to sweep three victories in a row. The first country to win three times would retire the Jules Rimet trophy. The Brazilian press and sport establishment thought the 1966 team was the best ever, and Brazilian fans expected to witness the coveted tri-championship.

There were several early upsets in the tournament. The weaker Hungarian team defeated the reigning champions. The Brazilian star Pelé was tackled brutally in the game against Portugal, forcing him off the field, and the team folded without his leadership. After first-round losses to Hungary and Portugal, Brazil was disqualified before the quarter-finals. BBC-TV showed the Brazilian reaction to the embarrassing defeats: men and women in Rio de Janeiro openly wept; one ship-dwelling fan attempted suicide by throwing herself overboard; Brazilian flags were lowered to half-mast and buildings were draped in black crape; angry mobs burned players and coaches in effigy. America has devoted sport fans, but I had never witnessed such a reaction to loss. I was impressed and baffled at how a sport could mean so much to a nation.

I also saw the reaction to victory. England not only went all the way to the finals, but won its first World Cup in overtime against West Germany. Fans created bumper-to-bumper traffic and lined the streets for a celebration that suspended British reserve for two days. I tucked away these vivid images when my summer ended.

The following summer, because of my Portuguese language studies, I was invited to join an exchange-student program in southern Brazil. I went with a group from Miami University in Ohio to Curitiba, then a city of 500,000 two hundred miles south of São Paulo. In addition to completing coursework at the local university, I needed to write a term paper for my own school (Washington University in St. Louis) to get academic credit for the summer. Fortuitously, on my first weekend my host family took me to a soccer match. I was one of about ten women in the crowd. The BBC-TV images flooded back; I had my topic for the term paper. I translated popular magazine articles on Brazil's soccer cult, and I talked about sports with everyone I met.

On a visit to Rio de Janeiro a sportswriter arranged for me to conduct a pregame interview with a professional player. Females were not allowed in the locker room, so I accompanied him down a long hall and up a flight of steps. I was unprepared for the floodlights that announced I had come onto the playing field, in full view of some fifty thousand spectators awaiting the start of the game. While the sportswriter got a human interest story, a radio announcer put me and some unfortunate goalkeeper on the air. The interview was very short and I have repressed the details of my exit from the field.

My sociology professors in St. Louis were genuinely excited about my written report. They asked questions I could not answer, and easily talked me into dropping out of school for a semester and using my tuition money to fund a return trip to get the answers. I could do the study as a senior honors thesis, they said, and still graduate on time. My parents (who also lived in St. Louis) were less enthusiastic about the prospect of a classroom without walls. For a home-cooked meal, my professors were willing to persuade them. By October 1967 I was back with my Curitiba family.

The focus of my research changed repeatedly, and the tasks of refining my topic and selecting appropriate methods were mine alone. My professors did not write. In three months I received one terse supportive answer to my frantic queries, "What do I do now?" "Do what you can; we're not expecting a doctoral thesis."

In what time remained, I focused on soccer as a route of social mobility for Brazilian athletes, preparing to interview as many active and retired players in Curitiba as I could, then to interview selected Rio and São Paulo players for comparison. If it could be arranged, I would interview the most successful player of all, Pelé.

From the beginning, there were advantages to being a female investigator. The novelty, which never wore off in Curitiba, provided opportunities for a closer look at soccer: I was interviewed on several television shows, invited to cover the games with radio commentators and journalists, and even asked to inaugurate a new soccer field at a local country club, where I was presented with a silver plaque inscribed to the "imperialist Yankee sent to spy on Brazilian soccer." I was granted interviews with any players I chose, although the coaches tried to steer me away from those they felt were "too coarse to talk with a girl," and though I had to make special requests to speak with black athletes. Club directors allowed me to attend their meetings, took me out drinking afterward, and talked freely in front of me. Directors from one club discussed bribing a referee; others admitted bribing opposing players to throw crucial games. These men either did not take me seriously or underestimated my improving language skills and drinking capacity. Owing in part to simple maturation and a raised consciousness, I would never again play "mascot" to make research easier, but I have never underestimated its payoff potential.

My gender and the novelty of my study helped me realize my ultimate goal—meeting Pelé. The president of the local soccer federation introduced me to the president of São Paulo's soccer federation, who in turn wrote me a letter of presentation to Pelé. When I arrived in Santos, the port city in the state of São Paulo, club officials warned me that Pelé was besieged by interview requests, many from persons holding letters of introduction as good as mine, and sometimes had to refuse. But, as I learned later, he agreed to the interview because I was American (a nationality known not to care about soccer) and female (even Brazilian women showed little interest in the sport at the time)—a surprising combination that had to be seen to be believed. Pelé (then twenty-seven) was very polite, patient with my broken Portuguese, and informative in his responses. That introduction led to an enduring friendship of which I am very proud.

I returned to St. Louis and wrote my senior honors thesis. My professors prodded me to shorten it for publication in a social science magazine, *Trans-Action*. I began graduate studies at Yale, then returned to Brazil for a third time in August 1969, through a foundation exchange program funded by multinational corporations. While in Rio, I visited the Brazilian national team then competing to qualify for the 1970 World Cup. By attending games and talking to sportswriters in nine Brazilian states, I began to understand regional variations in soccer. Although I felt up to date on the soccer scene, ultimately the trip was a personal disaster. I returned from northeastern Brazil with an unidentifiable tropical fever that put me in Yale–New Haven Hospital for forty-five days. I vowed never to return to Latin America.

But the fates tempted me again. The following summer Ian Taylor, a British sociologist who writes about soccer "hooliganism," offered to share his two press passes to the World Cup games in Mexico. He had read my *Trans-Action* article and wanted me to interview fans in Spanish and Portuguese. It was there and then that Brazil finally accomplished its tri-championship. More than a victory for Brazil, the tri-championship demonstrated the supremacy of Latin American soccer. Mexicans took over the streets just as the British had done in 1966.

The fan interviews that Taylor and I conducted amid the chaos renewed my interest in sport and popular culture and made me want to explore the place of leisure activities in people's lives. Articles on the sociology of sport discussed the effects of sport on athlete's lives; systematic studies of fans were conspicuously absent from the literature. I submitted a proposal to the Foreign Area Fellowship Program, suggesting I begin to fill the vacuum.

Despite my fear of another fever, I proposed Brazil as the locus of my fan study. I knew that people there felt deeply about sport. I wanted to hear Brazilians describe what the tri-championship meant to them. Besides, fandom would be difficult to measure in the United States, where someone can be a fan of football and hate baseball or love college basketball but be bored by the professional game. The task would be simpler in any number of countries, including Brazil, where soccer is the only professional team sport. I got the fellowship and returned to Brazil for a thirteen-month stay beginning in September 1972.

On that last trip I learned that there were also negative consequences to being a female investigator. I was "stood up" with frustrating frequency (sometimes as often as five times by the same person). But I persisted and got interviews with top league officials, club directors, coaches, referees, sportswriters, radio and television commentators, and fan club leaders. I attributed the casual disregard for my appointments to my gender and my five-foot stature as much as to the Latin temperament, and I was distraught by the resulting delays in my research calendar. Once, to be taken more seriously, I dressed in business attire and presented a card that read "Dr. Janet Lever." I abandoned the effort after hearing the receptionist announce, "There's a *doutorinha* [little doctor] here to see you."

Others went far out of their way to help me. My various experiences leave an enormous number of people to acknowledge. The

contribution of many are noted throughout the text; others deserve
to be singled out for special thanks. I owe a lasting debt to Joaquim
Coelho, my Portuguese professor, who arranged my first invitation
to Brazil, and to Helen Gouldner, Joseph Kahl, and Dorothy Meier,
my professors at Washington University, who encouraged me to take
the beginnings of this research seriously.

I am fortunate to have had the love and support of two families:
my own American family and Dr. José Carlos Ross, his wife Eduly,
and their seven children in Curitiba.

For my last trip to Brazil I thank some very special friends for
their good company, good food, and moral support: Tom and Rae
Flory, Barbara and Sam Santos, Guilherme da Silveira, and the late
Peter J. Reichard; and I thank the Foreign Area Fellowship Program
(FAFP) for its funding. I especially thank Professor Albert O.
Hirschman for his continued enthusiastic support of this project
from the time he reviewed my FAFP proposal to his recent review
of this manuscript for the publisher.

For their aid to my understanding of the Brazilian soccer system, I thank sportswriters José Inácio Werneck, João Máximo, Nelson Borges, and Artur Paraíba. For strategies of conducting social
research in Rio, I thank Wanderly Guilherme dos Santos. For entree
to local factories, I thank Louis Wolf Goodman.

I owe more recent debts of gratitude to certain Brazilians com-
mitted to advancing soccer in the United States: Professor Julio
Mazzei (who has served as both technical director and coach of the
New York Cosmos), Miguel de Lima (head scout for the Cosmos),
Carlos Alberto (the former captain of the 1970 Brazilian World Cup
championship team who came to the United States to play with the
Cosmos), and the great Pelé, who still finds time to answer my
questions.

Some European and American materials presented here are
part of a larger comparative work on sport and society for which my
colleague Stanton Wheeler and I have been gathering data for several
years. Professor Wheeler has generously allowed me to borrow freely
from those materials we found together. Let me also thank him for
his close critical reading of early drafts of this manuscript and for
endless hours spent sharing our ideas on the role of sport in society.

I am indebted to Howard S. Becker, who has been so giving
of his time and wisdom. In addition to editorial advice and assistance,
Professor Becker also made substantive critiques of several drafts of
this work. I received valuable critical advice from other readers,

whom I thank: Jay Coakley, Tom Flory, Robert K. Merton, R. Stephen Warner, and Harold L. Wilensky. I have also benefited from my students' responses to this manuscript.

I thank the staff at the University of Chicago Press for their editorial support and confidence in this book. And I thank Elizabeth Pereyra and Nancy Klein for their patience in the preparation of this manuscript. I am grateful to my clever friend David Standish for the title of this book, and to my friend Barbara Nellis for keeping my soccer library current.

I acknowledge the talents of my "samurai" editor, Fran Rosen, who did lots of abracadabra. Sharing the "motif" motif, Franny mixed the hard work of the final revisions with moments of real delight.

BRAZIL

Amazon River

AMAZON
LOWLANDS

Belém

Fortaleza

ARID
NORTHEAST

Recife

NORTHEAST
COAST

WEST
FRONTIER

Salvador

Brasília +

SOUTH
AMERICA

BRAZIL

INDUSTRIAL
MIDDLE
STATES

Belo Horizonte

Rio de Janeiro

São Paulo

Curitiba

SOUTHERN
STATES

Pôrto Alegre

0   500   1000

Scale of Miles

The Paradox of Sport: Integration through Conflict

Sport belongs in the world of play and leisure, yet business elites, mass media, and government and political leaders recognize its potential for making profits, disseminating propaganda, and eliciting pride. Organized sport prevails virtually everywhere and has developed over the past half-century from a relatively minor element of culture into a full-blown social institution.

An indicator of the importance of sport is the sheer amount of time and affect people the world over devote to it. A cynical sport commentator once said, "We all agree to *pretend* sport is important,"[1] but judging by the emotional displays of those watching or playing a closely contested match, people are not pretending.

When survey researchers inquire about the appeal of sport, the overwhelming response is that games are entertaining and provide a break from real life.[2] Sport stands apart from routine reality; contests offer excitement and drama because the outcome is uncertain. Luck and injury intervene, so an announcer can justifiably say, "on any given day, any team can beat any other team." The action is live, not scripted. Each contest is unique, unrehearsed, and finite, and the resolution, when it comes, is clear-cut. Unlike the chaos of ordinary life, sport offers us structure, with rituals signaling the beginning, middle, and end. Sport's symmetry gives us a sense of unity and completion within boundaries that are visible and enforced.

Contests can be more engrossing than other forms of entertainment. Unlike other performances, sport lies within the realm of

1

personal experience for most of the audience. Most fans have played the games, are knowledgeable about rules and strategies, and can share the athletes' pleasure in accomplishing difficult physical feats. Fans appreciate both the skills and the human spirit required to excel at the highest levels of competition. Given the violent nature of sport, fans also value the bravery required of their athletes, who are risking injury. Their physical strength, grace, and courage make professional athletes the male sex symbols of society.

The excitement and drama of sports invite active spectators who cheer and shout. Their affection and loyalty make sport a genuine emotional outlet with few equals in the world of adult entertainment. The audience's exuberance after home runs, goals, or touchdowns not only shows appreciation of effort and skill, but is rooted in the fans' personal involvement in a team's fate. Obviously fans prefer the pleasure of winning to the suffering of watching their teams go down in defeat, but even suffering can be appreciated as an indication of loyalty and caring deeply about something. Fans frequently use the word "love" to express feelings toward their teams and favorite players, and the word "hate" to show contempt for select rivals.

When asked why they enjoy sports, people rarely refer to their special relationships with other fans. More often, they see themselves as spectators of an event, not as part of the spectacle. Fans recognize the satisfaction they get from supporting a winner, releasing emotion, and witnessing violence on the field or a skillfully played game. Yet a large part of the euphoria of sport spectacles is created by the mass of humanity that has come together to share an event; many fans report physical responses—chills, flutters, butterflies—at the sight of crowds pouring into the stadium seats before the contest begins. Whether acknowledged or not, camaraderie between fellow fans, be they neighboring strangers in the stadium or friends surrounding a television set or transistor radio, adds to the joys of sport.

The Role of Sport in Society

Open enjoyment of the game does not negate the serious social consequences attached to widespread fandom. Likewise, speculations on the larger social significance of sport must not deny its sheer entertainment value. Nevertheless, the serious consequences of sport for society remain largely unexamined. Intellectuals, viewing play and games as trivial and inconsequential, feel little need for scientific scrutiny of the light side of life. Journalists and philosophers have contributed interesting speculations more often than social scientists have provided empirical data.

The careful examination of the role of sport in society remains minimal despite growing recognition that avocations, like occupations, are salient bases for identification in modern life. Not only do people devote more time to playing, watching, and discussing sport than to any other organized activity in public life, but the media, big business, and government manipulate that interest in sport to serve their own interests. Organized sport, as a major social institution, has consequences for any society. Sport can be used and sport can be abused. We need better understanding of the phenomenon to make the distinction.

Sport affects society in many ways, but this book is devoted to a careful exploration of its most important and universal consequence: *Sport helps complex modern societies cohere.* Creating order amid diversity is a problem that pervades modern thinking. All societies have conflict; cleavages and antagonistic factions are inevitable because of scarcity, injustice, and prejudice. All societies are also integrated to some degree, or they would cease to exist. Despite hostility and divergent interests, individuals, kin groups, towns, cities, and regions somehow get connected into a single national system. Of course the degree of integration in any society varies; a well-integrated society is one whose members are able to act together to achieve their collectively defined goals.

Sociologists have been justly criticized for their inattention to the central issue: What mechanisms are used to make a society whole? What makes society greater than the arithmetic sum of its parts?[3] Spectator sport is one mechanism that builds people's consciousness of togetherness. Paradoxically, sport helps bring the whole together by emphasizing the conflict between the parts. Sport is the perfect cultural reflection of our Janus-headed existence: it becomes the arena for conflicting interests while cultivating a shared outlook as the basis for order.

Its unique qualities enable sport to accomplish this antilogical feat. According to Anatol Rapoport, the feature distinguishing games from other forms of conflict is that the starting point is not disagreement at all, but rather the agreement of opponents to strive for an incompatible goal—only one opponent can win—within the constraints of understood rules.[4] In other words, conflict is not the means to resolve disagreement, but rather the end in itself. Sport is struggle for the sake of struggle, and it is this unique motive that explains the unifying power of its conflict.[5]

Sport, then, is the play form of conflict. Athletes and teams exist only to be rivals; that is the point of their relationship.[6] In the world of sport, there should be no purpose beyond playing and winning. Unlike rivals in the real world, who have opposing political, economic, or social aims, sport competitors must be protected, not persuaded or eliminated. In fact, a strong opponent is more valued than a weak one.

We tend to think of conflict as a problem that needs to be solved. But in its play form the benefits of conflict are made more apparent. First, conflict is more exciting than harmony. Second, the staging of conflict demands collaboration. Both sides must agree to the same set of rules, standards of acceptable play, and authorities. Cooperation becomes a product of sport rivalry through the desire to test skills, spirit, and the favors of fate. Not even heated rivalries or questionable victories disrupt the relationship, for the structure of sport requires repeated meetings. Only one team can win a single game, but the conflict retains its playfulness because sport as process is not zero-sum. The vanquished today may be the victor tomorrow— or, if not tomorrow, next season; the rankings are momentarily clear-cut, never final.

Besides, sport victories are merely symbolic. Prestige may be gained or lost, but no goods exchange hands and no soldiers are killed or imprisoned. We continue to interact because sporting conflict is materially inconsequential. As columnist Pete Axthelm said after the surprising U.S. victory over the Soviet Union in the 1980 Winter Olympics, "Beyond the happy rhetoric, our hockey triumph didn't validate our system any more than defeats in other years had undermined our way of life."[7]

If sport simply expressed the paradox inherent in all social interaction, it would serve well as an interpretation of our lives. But its utility extends beyond metaphor. Although sports can display contrived conflicts, such contests are usually dull. Spectator sports engross us most—and make their integrative contribution—wherever they dramatize social divisions that are real and meaningful. The "foundation stone" of nearly every variety of spectator sport, according to sportswriter Michael Roberts, is "the linking of the participant's destiny with the fan's, in terms of a common city, nation, race, religion, or institution of higher learning."[8]

The organization of sport determines which loyalties are tapped. U.S. sport teams most often represent schools and cities. The territorial monopoly that limits a city to one team in a league is unknown outside the United States. Cities elsewhere have more than one professional team in a sport, and those teams reflect special characteristics of their fan populations. A few of the most notorious rivalries in the soccer world illustrate the point: in Lima there is racial rivalry between Alianza Lima (blacks and mestizos) and Universitário Lima (white Creole); in Buenos Aires there is ethnic rivalry between Boca Juniors (Italians) and River Plate (English and Spanish); in Rio de Janeiro there is class rivalry between Flamengo (working class) and Fluminense (elite); in Glasgow there is religious rivalry between the Celtics (Roman Catholic) and the Rangers (Protestant).[9] Its teams are less known, but in Tel Aviv there is political rivalry between the Hapoel team, sponsored by the Labor party, and the Maccabi team, sponsored by the party of the moderate right.[10]

If rooting for a sport team or a particular athlete can reinforce one's sense of membership in all these salient status groups, then the scene is set for sport to accomplish its divide-and-integrate role. The Celtic fan may feel his Catholicism most strongly when facing the opposing Protestant Ranger fans, but they are literally standing on the same ground. To be rivals, participants must acknowledge their membership in the same system. The bond between the Celtic and Ranger fans will be further reinforced whenever their athlete-idols join together in a national team to represent Scotland.

Sports contests can symbolically represent any of these groups that claim people's solidarity, but they will arouse the strongest passions where they are linked with the status groups that arouse the most passion. Typically, our strongest sentiments are reserved for our primordial groups, those groups into which we are born, whether they center on language, custom, religion, race, tribe, ethnicity, or locale. Primordial sentiments represent a "consciousness of kind," and that consciousness is pervasive and easily tapped—unlike class consciousness, which usually needs to be cultivated.[11]

The resilience of primordial attachments is seen as most problematic in new and industrializing nations. Anthropologist Clifford Geertz describes this problem as the clash between primordial and civil sentiments. Primordial sentiments are the basis for the cleavages and prejudices that inhibit unified action. Civil sentiments require subordinating obligations to primordial groups for obligations of citizenship. Being a citizen of a respected nation offers a modern basis for personal identity, yet the more traditional bases for a sense of self typically conflict with the state's need for overarching political unity.[12]

For people in developing nations, political unity is essential to achieving their collective goals of a rising standard of living, more effective political order, greater social justice, and a bigger role in the world system. But, as Geertz observes, primordial sentiments become exaggerated during modernization as status groups fear losing power to a new centralized authority or, worse, being dominated by rival primordial groups. Geertz predicts that a more perfect union between multiple groups will be most successful where the goal is the modernization, not the obliteration, of ethnocentricity.

Geertz differs from most other intellectuals in his respect for primordial sentiments. Most think of them as "retrograde" and irrational. Old-fashioned primordial sentiments have been accused of inhibiting class solidarity and getting in the way of progress. But Geertz, seeing them as the roots of personal identification even in modern society, says they remain essential and deserve to be publicly acknowledged.

Typically a hindrance, primordial sentiments can be harnessed to aid national evolution. They are easy to mobilize because they are so apparent and powerful. In fact, Geertz says that universal suffrage makes courting the masses by appealing to their primordial sentiments irresistible to the political factions trying to solidify their power. Geertz's analysis highlights the channeling of ethnic differentiation into "proper" political expression (such as territorial subunits and political parties), but he recognizes that political outlets are not the only way to preserve primordial sentiments while furthering civil unity. He laments that other channels remain obscure.[13]

This book focuses on the case of soccer in Brazil to demonstrate that large-scale organized sport presents an alternative mechanism for using primordial identities to build political unity and allegiance to the modern civil state. Sport's paradoxical ability to reinforce societal cleavages while transcending them makes soccer, Brazil's most popular sport, the perfect means of achieving a more perfect union between multiple groups. Local soccer teams publicly sanction and express the society's deepest primordial sentiments, while the phenomenal success of the national team has enormously heightened all Brazilians' pride in their citizenship.

Brazil is a strategic site for a study of the serious consequences of sport. Insofar as the aim of this research is to demonstrate how sport helps complex modern societies cohere, it was imperative to select a site where integration is problematic. Although Brazil's problems of social order are not as great as those of many emerging nations (for example, India is divided by twenty-six major languages and six hundred local languages),[14] they are nevertheless significant. Brazil is a huge country with a diverse population, separated further by strong regional differences, poor communication, and a low level of education. Having one of the fastest rates of urban growth in the Third World, Brazil faces an acute problem of assimilating diverse groups of newcomers to cities where inadequate housing, transportation, and other public services have already been pushed to their limits. National integration is a top priority of the military government that has made Brazil the world's fastest-developing new industrial country.

Brazil's similarities to other Third World countries may permit generalizations about the role of sport in developing nations. Rapid urban growth characterizes major cities in Asia, Africa, and Latin America.[15] And national integration is considered a prerequisite for development everywhere. The use of sport in Brazil may tell us something about its role in other developing nations that emphasize large-scale sport and about the advantages of building small-scale sport programs (like those featuring certain inexpensive individual sports prominent in the Olympics) where they do not already exist in Third World nations. New and developing countries profit greatly from sport's ability to transcend rifts between groups and create a unified and positive national image.

Brazil is a strategic site also because of its proud record in international soccer, the world's most popular sport. Brazil is the only country to have qualified for all twelve World Cup championships, has accumulated the highest points total, and was the first country to win the cherished trophy three times; three of the world's five all-time highest goal scorers (Friedenreich, Flavio, and Pelé) are Brazilian; and Brazil boasts seven of the world's largest stadia, Rio's Maracanã (capacity 220,000) being the largest.[16] Along the way, Brazilian fans have gained global recognition for their loyalty and enthusiasm. Brazil's soccer accomplishments have earned it the respect of the global sporting community and fostered its citizens' pride in their nation.

Soccer is a phenomenon of major importance in Brazil, and one clearly worthy of study. Brazil is by no means alone in its passion for sport. The United States, the Soviet Union, Australia, West Germany, England, Italy, Argentina only begin the list of other countries where athletes are given very special status and where the masses care about their success. Highly developed sporting institutions do not exist everywhere, and it is not my goal to isolate conditions favorable to sport's growth. Instead, I am asking, Where sport is full-blown, what role does it play? If no significant role can be determined in Brazil, then one is not likely to be found in a society with lesser regard for its sporting heritage. If a significant role is found in Brazil, this may shed light on the role it plays in other sport-dominated cultures.

The Brazilian case is easily generalized on the basis of structural features that its sport institutions share with other countries the world over. The common pattern is due to the rapid diffusion and early centralization of soccer. Brazil fits the norm in having soccer as its sole professional team sport, and in having more than one club per city—nonprofit organizations run by volunteers. America's business approach to sport is the exception rather than the rule. Of course culture, historical circumstances, and geography combine to give Brazil's sport system a distinctive flavor. That is to say, if one looks closely one finds the organization of sport (even a universal sport like soccer) to be variable.

To isolate and probe the Brazilian case is to relate the peculiarities of sporting institutions to the distinctive features of that society. By focusing on the differences between the Brazilian system and those set up elsewhere—especially the very different system found in the United States—one can begin to answer the important question of how the *particular* way sport is organized affects the way fans relate to athletes, to each other, and to their communities. The idea of examining differences, then, is to draw conclusions about the organizational features that maximize social benefit as well as sporting entertainment.

Sport: An Expression of Sociability and Collective Spirit

Sport is able to perform its divide-and-unify role on multiple levels. Whether we examine it at the world, national, or local level, spectator sport gives dramatic expression to the strain between groups while affirming the solidarity of the whole. Sport promotes connections from the largest level of universal communication to the smallest level of the momentary bonding of two strangers. Events or sentiments that heighten allegiance at one level usually do so at the cost of diminishing allegiance elsewhere. Sport remarkably builds solidarity in multiple levels simultaneously. Recall those Celtic and Ranger fans who are reinforced in their different Catholic and Protestant identities at the same time as they are reminded of their mutual citizenship in Glasgow, Scotland, and—in the case of international play—the world.

Sport accomplishes this feat by paralleling the intricate weave of government agencies in organizational structure. Small towns, even rural areas, are linked to each other and to big cities for state and regional championships. Major cities are knit together into national leagues and are reminded of one another during regular competitions. Nations that play the same sports are drawn into relationships with one another through continental and worldwide federations that stage international contests between representative teams; nationalistic feelings are fanned while people are simultaneously united into a global folk culture.

While organizations as diverse as the Catholic church, the Lions Club, and professional or scientific societies stretch from local to international levels, sport is different. It provides a common frame of reference, meanings, and rules that transcend cultural, political, and language barriers. Sport provides the excuse for regular and routine meetings, both of administrative representatives around a conference table and of player representatives on the field. Those representatives have agreed on universal standards of performance and scoring to regulate, as far as possible, impartial officiating. In the end, a sport pantheon of stars and a series of special events make up a set of global symbols that constitutes one of the few elements in a folk international culture. High culture—opera, ballet, and the visual arts—also creates international stars, but they unite elites around the world. Only popular culture can promote universal communication and shared experience for the masses.

Before focusing on the Brazilian case study, let's explore some general attributes of sport that ideally suit it to the task of bringing people together in any society in spite of, sometimes even because of, their differences.

Sport at the Interpersonal Level

Sport has long been recognized as grist for conversation between persons who may have few other interests in common. Sport, like the weather, is a subject the cabby can discuss with his customer in the cashmere coat. Like the weather, the sporting scene can be followed day-by-day or more generally, comparing this "season" with past seasons. The differing evaluations of teams or players and the problematic character of game outcomes can sustain sport conversations a great deal longer than talk about the weather. Clear-cut resolutions in sport contests give debates an empirical edge as opponents contest one another frequently—almost daily in some sports. Sport conversations can have the tone of light-hearted debate or take the form of constructive dialogue, with each party adding to the knowledge of the other: "Who got the most . . .?" "Well, I read once that . . ." "That's interesting. Did you know that . . . ?" The special significance of officials' calls, complex rules, human error, and historical comparison become the bases of sport talk. The uninterested bystander appropriately fears that the discussion could go on endlessly.

Some argue that sport fandom is a waste of time because, win or lose, the material circumstances of a fan's life do not change one iota (unless he has placed a wager on the outcome). Were we to apply a strict means/ends analysis, we would miss a major appeal of sport. Sport is a play form of association that is appreciated for its lack of consequence. Sociability around sport and game rituals is an end in itself.[17] People talking sport, though they may appear to be arguing, are having fun. It is a pure form of banter. Neither party expects to change the opinion of the other or, more important, to affect the outcome of a single game by his talk. Although both care about the outcome of a game, there is the understanding that, in the "real" scheme of things, which team becomes champion is irrelevant.

The air of unreality is also reflected in the suspension of status differentials between fans in a stadium or sport bar. Fans rarely exchange names or personal information, even though they may talk to each other throughout the game. Neither wealth, occupation, nor formal education counts in this artificial world. Everyone is entitled to a point of view, and one runs little risk of being rebuffed when voicing an opinion. People atuned to a sporting event are expected to talk back. "You're never lonely in the ballpark."[18] Sociability between those in different social positions can be awkward, but fans implicitly agree to focus on the game and not on each other.

In stadium and bar encounters, fans are expected to suspend personal moods and enter the social mood of the crowd; this suspension makes sport good escapist entertainment. Usually that social mood is festive, at least while victory still seems possible. People say there is a party atmosphere. Joining in the expression of group emotion is mandatory; a spectator who remains emotionless in the wake of a tie-breaking run or goal by the home team seems odd. Exley, in *A Fan's Notes*, describes hating the man next to him in the stadium who cheered good play on both sides rather than becoming involved in the fate of one team.[19] As theologian Michael Novak advises, "the mode of observation proper to a sports event is to *participate*—that is, to extend one's own identification to one side, and to absorb with it the blows of fortune."[20] Imagine poor Pope Paul VI's dilemma when, it was reported, he watched the 1970 World Cup final between Brazil—the world's largest Catholic country—and his native Italy and would not allow himself to cheer for either side.[21]

The communion of strangers at a stadium or a sport bar is more than just an inferior substitute for family gatherings. There is a special joy in sharing emotion with strangers. Standing in McSorley's Bar in Greenwich Village during the 1978 baseball World Series, I heard a New York Yankees devotee say, "We're all fans here. We have something in common. We love the team." He embraced total strangers each time a run brought victory closer.[22] It did not matter that many were not native to the city, enthusiastic support of the Yankees declared that they belonged.

Focusing on the game eases social interaction between friends as well as strangers. The simple progress of the game serves as a guide for interaction. The fan who is a student of sport history, performance statistics, or strategies can take pleasure in displaying and exchanging that knowledge. So many aspects of sport are a matter of record that fans can claim to be eyewitnesses to significant events; friends who have witnessed historical moments together feel a special bond.

Sport holds an important place in family life too. The implicit agreement that all fans are peers also suspends normal authority roles. As with social class or race, generational differences too can be put aside, easing talk between a boy and his father. A man's ten-year-old son may be following the teams so closely that he can answer his father's questions about current standings, while the father can reciprocate with his historical perspective. This not only suspends authority, it has the potential to *reverse* it for a brief moment. Since many parents find it difficult to have two-way conversations with their offspring, such temporary suspension of authority must seem a blessing.

Insofar as teams have long traditions—sometimes stretching back for a century or more—and loyalties are often inherited, sport can also connect a man to his father. Sport roots people not only in places, but also in the past. Christopher Lasch said of "the culture of narcissism": "to live for the moment is the prevailing passion—to live for yourself, not for your predecessors or posterity."[23] Sport is one of the things that help us preserve our sense of historical time. At a minimum, it offers continuity in the personal life of the fan who has favored a team from childhood to adulthood.[24] As another patron of McSorley's Bar commented, "You watch a rookie blossom; you watch him grow up. It's like family."

Sport in the Community

Communal societies, small cities, and towns do not have the integration problems of complex modern societies or metropolises. Nevertheless, they inevitably contain factions that are separated by mild to bitter antagonisms. Even in communities where people know each other, they are usually divided by their kin affiliations and relative social power, and sometimes by race, ethnic, or religious differences too. Sport can serve to dramatize the strain between these factions, but it can also elicit a temporary truce while all parties are reminded of their commonality.

We can look at one of the simplest forms of sport to isolate its elementary ingredients. Anthropologist Clifford Geertz has described cockfighting in Bali. Geertz says the fights absorb the Balinese not because the cocks represent a bet to their supporters, but because they represent competitive status groups and allow them to "allegorically humiliate" one another. Backing a cock with a bet is a way to express allegiance to one's kinsmen or solidarity with one's local village. "Home games," fights between local cocks, exacerbate factions between kin groups, while "away games," between an outsider cock and a local cock, mend ruptures between the villagers. While both assuaging social passions and heightening them, the fights primarily function "in a medium of feathers, blood, crowds, and money, to display them."[25]

Whether sport can perform its dual dividing and unifying roles within the community depends wholly on the organization of its sport. In hundreds of American towns with no professional team to represent them and just one high school each, the school teams serve only to unify the townspeople. Sport teams are usually the community's most visible representative to the outside world; sometimes a team is the *only* collective symbol of the town. By carrying the town's name, the team reaffirms the community's existence against rival towns. People's sentiments toward their communities are strongest when they feel threatened by outsiders, even symbolically via sport challenges. The team's participation in state or regional tournaments lets the townspeople enjoy the feeling of solidarity while providing one of the few occasions for association with neighboring townspeople.

Robert and Helen Lynd, in their description of "Middletown" in the 1920s, provide what is probably the most-cited example of the role of sport in these communities:

> Today more civic loyalty centers around [high school] basketball than around any other one thing. No distinctions divide the crowds which pack the school gymnasium for home games, and which in every kind of machine crowd the roads for out-of-town games, North Side and South Side, Catholic and Kluxer, banker and machinist—their one shout is "eat 'em, beat 'em Bearcats."[26]

The Lynds even attribute the election of the new superintendent of schools to his having "put Middletown on the map as a basketball town."[27]

Although dozens of community studies center on the world of work, family, or religion, the authors make at least passing reference to organized sports as one of the few activities that focus community social life. Reviewing these studies led Stone to conclude that sport is a salient part of a community's focus of conversation, publicity, and mass media. It unifies because of the intercommunity conflict it engenders and the intracommunity communication it establishes.[28]

High school and adult amateur sports continue to have a natural place in the organization of small towns. Recently the high school basketball team in Manchester, Vermont, won the state championship for the fifth time.[29] More people attended their final game than had voted in the town's previous elections. Because no one wanted to babysit, the entire town—men, women, teenagers, and small children—came to the gym. It was everyone's victory. As one local put it, "only the cats and dogs stayed home."

In communities like these, sport unifies by reinforcing the division between townspeople and outsiders. A community must have at least two rival teams before its internal divisions can be represented on the playing field. In a place like Bermuda, with multiple sports clubs, competitions among them can dramatize cleavages between local factions while bringing rival supporters together. The clubs, as places to go and drink, also focus daily life for the 59 percent of the adult black male population who are members.[30]

In any case, even if sport divides community members as well as unifying them, it is more than something that alleviates boredom and fills time. Sport promotes communication; it involves people jointly; it provides them with common symbols, a collective identity, and a reason for solidarity.

Sport in the Metropolis

Big cities are full of strangers. The overwhelming size and density of their populations cause inhabitants to develop an aloof, blasé urban attitude, with the consequence that most neighbors are strangers.[31] Population heterogeneity also contributes to the problem of social integration in the metropolis. Typically, immigrant groups of different races, nationalities, ethnicities, and religions accentuate the city's heterogeneity, while internal migrants introduce regional variations on culture. Evolving from distinctions in education, occupation, and status, an elaborate class structure adds another dimension of heterogeneity.

Huge and diverse populations make it difficult for urban-dwellers to sense they belong to an integrated society. Large-scale urban phenomena are difficult to study, yet we need to understand what means are used to confirm the unity of the metropolis and its collective spirit. Sport is one institution that holds together the people of a metropolis and heightens their attachment to the locale. The pomp and pageantry of sport spectacles create excitement and arouse fervor, doing for the people of the metropolis what religious ceremonies do for people in communal societies.

In one of the classic works in sociology, Emile Durkheim suggests that religion is less important as a specific set of beliefs and deities than as an opportunity for public reaffirmation of community.[32] Durkheim argues that the quest for moral solidarity is present even among those who practice the most primitive religion, totemism, which has nothing to do with gods or souls. People of a locality believe they are related to totems (typically animals, but sometimes other natural objects), which are symbolized by emblems that everyone bears. In spite of their lack of blood ties, tribesmen feel related to each other because they share a totem. Team worship, like animal worship, makes all participants intensely aware of their own group membership. By accepting that a particular team represents them symbolically, people enjoy ritual kinship based on that common bond. Their emblem, be it an insignia on a lapel pin or a scarf with team colors, distinguishes fellow fans from both strangers and enemies.[33]

The simile "sport is like religion" refers, simplistically, to people's blind faith in and devotion to their teams. The stadium acts as a cathedral where the followers come together to worship their heroes (a few of whom hold the status of demigods); some literally pray for their success. Durkheim admitted that secular events could be equally successful in reaffirming the common sentiments of a collectivity by creating sacred things out of ordinary ones. Sport spectacles belong to the world of the sacred rather than the profane;[34] fans who say sport provides an escape from "real life" in effect sustain this religious distinction. They are acknowledging that the sporting drama stands apart from mundane reality and allows them to transcend their concrete individual existence. Unlike the isolated entertainment of "escapist" movies and much more like the effect of a religious celebration, sport fosters a sense of identification with the others who shared the experience.

At least since the intercity rivalry of the ancient Greek Olympic Games, glory has been shared by the townspeople of the victorious athletes.[35] Across time and place, sport promoters, whether governments or team management, have told fans they can properly assume the team victory as their own. Even if all the athletes are mercenaries and not native sons, once they put on the uniforms that bear the group emblem they become that group's proud representatives. The rooting phenomenon works, says Roberts, precisely because people are willing to believe that "empty uniforms comprise a spiritual container whose meaning is constant, although the flesh filling the uniforms changes ceaselessly."[36] A hero who is traded will be sorely missed and may serve to establish some rooting interest for his new team, but the former archenemy who has come to replace him soon wins the hearts of the fans when he is instrumental in bringing victory to the home team.

Examining Durkheim's theory of ritual solidarity, Collins saw that the greater the number of people present and the more narrowly focused their attention, the more exuberant the mass mood.[37] Major sporting events draw together more people more often than anything else in modern life. Where else do we meet with 50,000 others? With the exception of papal masses, religious events draw no more than a few thousand at most. Rock concerts in the post-Woodstock era could draw as many as 100,000 people for their multiband shows, but now even bands with hit albums are having trouble selling 20,000 tickets; most bands now prefer to play several nights in a smaller auditorium rather than take the risks of promoting one big show.[38] In the auditorium people's attention is drawn to the front, toward the staged action; the spectator looks past thousands of backs of heads to see the principal actors. Sport is staged in the round, in the center of a stadium, so the spectator confronts the emotion apparent on the faces of other spectators and is made even more aware of the mass of humanity sharing the event. Both rock concerts and sport contests, while eliciting chants and cheers, narrowly focus people's attention to arouse their emotions and common sentiments. And devotees of a team or a rock superstar both feel a special bond when they meet others who share their passion.

In a time of increasing sophistication and skepticism, people seem reluctant to leave their private shells to enter the mass mood. Things that were once sacred now seem "hokey." And sporting events seem to be the last bastion of hokey. Fans will abandon so much reserve that they can scream "CHARGE" and join in songs like "Take Me out to the Ball Game" (in the United States) and "We'll Support You Ever More" (in England). A writer describing the Pittsburgh fans during a World Series baseball game against Baltimore said cries of "C'mon family" were heard throughout the game, and signs said "We're all in this together." "While it may be hokey . . . it's undeniably affecting."[39]

Of course, sporting and religious events are not the only things that promote a mass mood, yet other events that do so occur infrequently and haphazardly. Entrepreneur and philosopher Bill Veeck likens the shared experience and community support apparent in sport to the attitude triggered by disasters:

A pennant-winning team makes an enormous contribution to the morale of a city. Everybody suddenly becomes friendly. There is a feeling of common purpose that never fails to remind me of a city after a disaster. Have you ever noticed the camaraderie that comes over a city that is digging itself out of a bad snowstorm? People who normally wouldn't nod as they pass, talk to each other. Involved as they are in a common experience, they know they can speak to each other without being rebuffed. Just as important, perhaps, they have survived and they are digging themselves out, and so when they talk about how bad it was they are really congratulating each other on their fortitude. Just as with a snowstorm, there is that feeling of reflected glory in a successful baseball team. Cleveland is winning the pennant. The eyes of the whole country are upon Cleveland, upon us, upon me and you. *We're looking pretty good, aren't we, Mac?*[40]

But does the team's success make Cleveland a better place to live? Somewhat anonymous American cities like Cleveland, Pittsburgh, Philadelphia, or Kansas City are not renowned for the local chauvinism of their inhabitants. By virtue of having a professional team, they are distinguished from dozens of other cities as "major league" towns. A winning team, by attracting "the eyes of the whole country," figuratively puts a city on the map. Disasters like the collapse of two aerial walkways onto the crowded lobby dance floor of Kansas City's Hyatt Regency Hotel also bring attention to a city, but such publicity is considerably less welcome.

Sport victories give rare occasions to associate pride with one's hometown, which presumably *does* make it a better place to live:

Around Pittsburgh we went for decades without a winner in anything; inferiority matched the mood of the region. When the Pirates burst through as world champions, followed later by the Steelers, their success released pleasant feelings of vindication, and grounded a rectification of reality: it *was* a good region in which to grow up; national recognition was long overdue.[41]

Civic pride is not transitory. The spirit of the celebration lives in the memories of the participants and in the folklore passed on to those too young to have shared the moment.

Of course local pride is fostered by many things. People may be proud of a local product like steel in Pittsburgh, or even a particular style of rock 'n' roll in Philadelphia and Cleveland and blues in Kansas City. The city name may be associated with a fine orchestra or ballet troupe, or with a zoo of excellent reputation. Yet pride is heightened in a competitive situation—when people feel unified against outside "invaders," when they can assess national standing by looking at the daily paper—even if the conflict is only ritualistic, as in sports. Even people who are not usually fans are drawn into the mass mood as their team reaches the finals and outshines everything else as a media event. Team symbols help people create a collective spirit and identify with their greater metropolitan area.

Sport in the Nation

National integration has been a problem since the concept of nationalism developed more than three hundred years ago. When we think of a nation, we think of boundaries that include people of common descent, language, customs, and religion, yet the presumption of a homogeneous society is rarely confirmed in reality. For instance, self-determination dissolved the Austro-Hungarian empire, but no boundaries could be devised that would have put all members of a group into their own tidy boundaries. Problems of minorities emerged as unavoidable. Southeast Asia and Africa illustrate how nations were formed by the chance pattern of imperial conquest rather than according to the homogeneity of the people. Many nations include groups divided by the most basic prerequisite for communication—language. The Russian Empire included Turkish-speaking people; Canada is bilingual; Switzerland contains three languages.[42] The Congo Republic contained an estimated 250 tribal-linguistic groups.[43]

National integration is especially problematic for the developing nations. Poor transportation and communication keep regional differences strong. Foreign investments exacerbate divisions within regions by bringing modernity to the major cities of the Third World while leaving the hinterland a hundred years behind. National consciousness in these nations has been retarded by foreign domination of their political, economic, and cultural institutions. These problems are not easily overcome. Just as economic development is essential for a people's independence, so is cultural nationalism. National pride and self-consciousness can be a key instrument for change. Distinctive art, literature, folklore, and music provide a national self-image that helps integrate diverse peoples. Sport has played a crucial role in the development of cultural nationalism in many countries. Sporting victories grant the international recognition that helps developing nations shed their inferiority complexes.

Sport contributes to national integration by giving people of different social classes, ethnicities, races, and religions something to share and use as a basis for their ritual solidarity. Individuals sense numerous loyalties, some of which cut across one another; overarching goals can temporarily unite people in diverse groups and places.[44] State championships unite the provinces with the central city; national contests unite towns, cities, and regions; international competitions focus everyone's identity as national citizens. Everyone who resides within the national borders—the countryside as well as the cities—shares the event.

Sport's remarkable ability to bring diverse people of a nation together is perhaps best illustrated by the controversy over Argentina's hosting the 1978 World Cup championship. In 1973 the leftist Peronists decided to stage the World Cup in order to court popularity. When the right-wing military junta took over in 1976, they declared they would hold the Cup as planned—a decision also calculated to attract popular support. European journalists and others protested Argentina's political turmoil and distrusted its security safeguards. Protests mounted after the military head of the national organizing committee for the 1978 Cup was assassinated on his way to the first press conference. The protests were quieted when Argentina's infamous urban guerrillas, the Montoneros, issued a statement saying they would not disrupt the World Cup since they, too, were *hombres y mujeres del pueblo* (men and women of the people).[45] Left-wing socialists, right-wing militarists, even urban guerrillas can call a truce in the name of sport.

The World

Just as national championships reinforce the fan's identification with his hometown while reminding him of his membership in the society as a whole, international competitions reinforce nationalism while simultaneously uniting people into a global folk culture of idols and teams. Sport figures are more widely recognized than political or intellectual leaders or even performing artists. Brazilians who travel report that they are asked about Pelé by people who would not know where to find Brazil on a map.

Technological advances have helped realize the dream of universal communication. Most important, satellites permit live transmission of televised events that unite audiences around the world. Concrete special events extend the realm of our common experience;

what we see together makes us alike. And what we see can convey the pleasures and not just the sorrows of life. At the same moments in time, people virtually everywhere paused to experience the tragedy of John F. Kennedy's funeral, to observe the triumphant first step on the moon, and to share the joy of Prince Charles's wedding. The most recent example demonstrates how technology has expanded the integrative potential of certain events from national to global proportions. The worldwide audience for Prince Charles's marriage to Lady Diana Spencer was estimated at 750 million people in seventy-seven countries. It was a perfect video event for satellite transmission: it was planned far in advance and starred a central figure from the world's most famous royal family.[46]

This event can be compared with Queen Elizabeth's coronation in 1953, when viewers in Italy, Germany, Holland, and France got live reception, along with 53 percent of the population of the British Isles, while the rest of the world had to await film replays.[47] Two sociologists who analyzed that coronation called it "a great act of national communion."[48] Now the pomp and storybook aura of a royal wedding can provide a common vital object of attention for a momentary global communion.

No one really knows who is the most famous person in the world; contenders include Pelé, Muhammed Ali, John Lennon, and Prince Charles. But comparative data do exist for audiences of satellite-televised events, and the major international sporting contests draw together more spectators than anything else. The final game of the 1978 World Cup holds the record to date: more than 2 billion fans watched, including for the first time those in China and South Africa.[49] In other words, *nearly half the world's people shared a single event*. Estimates of the viewing audience for the whole tournament go as high as 20 billion.[50] To put this figure in perspective, the combined audience for two weeks of Olympic events was one billion people in 1976.[51]

Most Americans have missed the aesthetic and dramatic pleasures of World Cup soccer. The 1982 final was the first one broadcast by network television. It will be years before teams of native Americans take their place in World Cup finals. Our stance as outsiders is worsened by our image elsewhere as pirates who are luring other countries' best players with astronomical salaries that their nonprofit clubs cannot match. Our commercial clubs are under no obligation to release foreign players so they can participate with their country-men in the World Cup.

It seems strange that in respect to sport the United States is a cultural isolate. Clearly, America has contributed more than its share of entertainers to an international folk culture. Hollywood movies have created more of the world's sex symbols and heroes than films produced in all other countries combined. Now America's television shows are a major export. In the spring of 1980 an esti-mated 300 million people in fifty-seven countries watched the sea-son's last episode of "Dallas".[52] (British bookies took bets worth millions of pounds on who shot J. R. Ewing.) Shows like "Kojak" and "Bonanza" have enormous international followings. A bald col-league of mine, while on an excursion through the Australian bush, was called "Kojak" by an aborigine. Yet most Americans are not aware, and would not care, that the rest of the world sees our tele-vision shows. Television shows are national properties, even if others around the globe share an interest in their characters. There is no reciprocity; with the exception of a few British imports, we do not see what kind of television is created in other countries.

Sport is different because it is reciprocal. People in countries that share a love for the same sport also share respect for that sport's best athletes and for distinctive national styles of play. World sporting federations stage truly international events. Where Esperanto failed as the universal language, soccer as the premier world sport has laid a basis for global community by promoting common knowledge, shared symbols, and communication between people of different nations.

The Present Study

Insofar as the sociologist's primary concern is the social bond, and given that sport lies at the core of social life in modern society, then a central task for a sociologist should be to describe the nature of sport as a major cultural institution and to explore its importance. Not only the athletes, but those involved in the regulation, man-agement, staging, and viewing of a sporting event must be included in the scope of the inquiry.

Far too often those peripheral to the playing action have been left out of studies of sport. The derogatory appellation "jockstrap sociology" characterizes, to a large degree, empirical investigations of the sporting world. In reviewing a summary of research on sport,

I found that 72 percent of the studies cited were exclusively concerned with athletes—and those mostly adolescent and collegiate
athletes rather than professionals who serve as culture heroes. Another 15 percent were abstract discussions of sport as a metaphor or
mirror of society, stressing sport's support of the dominant social
values of a culture. The remaining 13 percent included 6 percent on
coaches and managers, 2 percent on government regulation, 2 percent on media influence, and 3 percent on fans. The fan essays deal
with violence at sporting events rather than with any constructive
view of the ways sport affects interaction between people.[53]

Political scientists and economists have avoided the topic of
sport almost entirely, contributing no major studies of the political-
economic impact of sport. Philosophers, theologians, and historians
have been more likely to turn their thoughts to sport, but their broad
conclusions have been drawn largely from "armchair" speculation.[54]
We need empirical studies of the place of sport in society if we are
to begin to understand its special cultural achievement. We have
anecdotal material on sport's power to unify the people of a metropolis or nation, but we need systematic data to specify how the
process works.

This book focuses on the world's most popular sport, soccer,
and on the country where it is most popular, Brazil, to show how
sport serves as both a structural and a cultural source of social integration. Paradoxically, this integration is achieved by reinforcing
the cleavages within society. I will use the case of Brazil to specify
how this divide-and-integrate feat is accomplished at every level from
interpersonal to international relations. Sport's ability to create social
order while preserving cultural diversity has meant that primordial
sentiments are able to promote rather than impede the goals of national development. The economic and political consequences of
sport, then, are crucial parts of the story.

The materials for this book come from a variety of sources.
During my four trips to Brazil, between 1967 and 1973, I observed
fifty to sixty soccer games. Most of the people I encountered informally—from the egg salesman to the commercial and political elites—
willingly "talked soccer" with me. On my first two visits, my formal
interviews were with professional athletes, and my information on
them was supplemented and updated on subsequent visits. On my
later trips I concentrated my interviews less on athletes and more
on top league officials, club directors, coaches, referees, sportswrit-

ers, radio and television commentators, and fan-club leaders. During all four trips I studied archival materials, including newspaper reports, attendance records, club memberships files, and financial statements.

These techniques yielded a rich combination of descriptive and numerical data that are helpful for understanding the central place of soccer in Brazilian life. Insiders on the sporting scene as well as others I spoke with offered keen insights into Brazil's soccer madness. Their perceptions, along with the "armchair" theories from academic literature and plain commonsense assumptions about sport, helped me construct hypotheses about fandom. After pretesting questions formulated to verify or reject these hypotheses, I interviewed two hundred working-class men in Rio de Janeiro during the final stage of my research. Only by gathering systematic information from the men themselves could I begin to learn how sport affects the type, frequency, and quality of personal interaction in the city; how many and what kind of men give sport a truly prominent place in their weekly routines; and how athletes and other public personalities compare as culture symbols for these men.

Since my last trip, I have kept up to date by corresponding with league officials, lottery agents, and other informants. I have also followed Brazilian newspapers, newsletters, and magazines and had contact with their correspondents in the United States. And I have learned a great deal from Brazilian athletes, coaches, and trainers who are here to participate in the American soccer boom.

The following chapters offer my idea of what a sociology of sport should be.

Soccer:
The Premier International Sport

The paradoxical role of sport is most dynamic at the highest level of competition. Fans sense allegiance to their country and a strong identification with one another, while at the same time such competition provides cross-cultural experiences. International contests, then, simultaneously reinforce ethnocentrism and unite nations into a global folk culture. Athletes fight for their nations' honor while admiring their opponents' skill, spirit, and style of play. As the world's most popular team sport, soccer creates a communal experience better than anything else in mass culture.

Americans have been excluded from this community of experience that bonds other nations, not only because we have just recently begun to play professional soccer, but also because our unique organization of sport makes us different. Americans take for granted several characteristics of professional sport. First, numerous sports are given national attention, and no one of them dominates the limelight throughout the year. Second, our sport clubs are big businesses owned by individuals and increasingly by corporate conglomerates who seek to make a profit. Third, team competition is organized between big cities, most having at best one major league team per sport. Fourth, live television coverage of team sports is extensive, and broadcast rights pay a large share of the sports clubs' expenses, including player contracts. Fifth, our high schools and colleges serve as a feeder system, providing athletes for this wide variety of professional sports.

24

But the American system is an anthropological oddity. The common features of sport in other nations far outweigh their differences. In most places soccer is the *only* professional team sport, and soccer season extends anywhere from eight months to the full year. Volunteer directors run the nonprofit sport clubs. Professional soccer clubs are hierarchically arranged in three or four divisions, with upward and downward mobility built into the system to keep it competitively alive. (Think of the baseball team at the bottom of the National League having to drop down to the AAA minors, replaced by the winning club from that division. Not only would the AAA contest come to life, but major league fans would have to support even low-standing teams to keep them out of the dreaded "basement.") Even small towns have a lower-division professional soccer team; major cities typically have four or more clubs in the top division. To protect this multiteam system, soccer authorities prohibit live televising of most domestic games. Insofar as team sports are little played in schools elsewhere, these soccer clubs must provide their own feeder system. They recruit adolescents, place them under contract, and provide professional training and high-level competition.

An international soccer federation controls both amateur-apprentice and professional leagues and unifies the soccer-playing nations by their common desire to test skills against one another. Lesser-developed countries are in a position to reap the greatest rewards from international sport. Where citizens lack confidence about their country's stature, fielding a respectable team helps promote a positive national image. A winning team does even more to dispel feelings of inferiority. One special feature of the play form of conflict is that David *can* beat Goliath. Long before economic and military strength back up political clout, sport offers a nation an opportunity for a high ranking in the world system.

International Tournaments

Nations have been drawn into relationships with one another through international competition since the beginning of organized sport in the mid-nineteenth century. Without doubt, the Olympic Games and the World Cup soccer championship are the two most important competitions that determine true world champions, and the two events are very different. The Olympics pit officially amateur athletes against one another in a potpourri of primarily individual sports like swimming, track and field, weightlifting, and gymnastics. The World Cup in soccer is the only global championship for professionals in a team sport.

The ancient Greek Olympic Games were revived by the inspiration of a French aristocrat, Baron Pierre de Coubertin, who was troubled by the growing commercialism in nineteenth-century sport and wanted to ensure the well-being of amateur sport. Only thirteen nations participated in the First Olympiad in 1896. The International Olympic Committee (IOC) now boasts a membership of 134 nations. The near-universal base of participation justifies the IOC's claim that the tournament determines true world champions in twenty-six events.[1]

In the past twenty-five years the Olympic Games have been debunked on the issue of the amateur status of their participants. Critics coined the term "shamateurism" to express their disenchantment with the IOC rule that excludes all but amateur athletes from competiton. The most blatant offenders are the communist countries that seclude promising athletes in their childhood and give them extensive training and special medical treatments. When they are ready for Olympic competition as young adults, in the USSR or East Germany, for example, athletes are luxuriously supported by the state and devote their full time to sport training. They perform minimal duties in their ostensible occupations.

Of course the communist countries are not the only ones to support their Olympic contenders. Whether funding comes from government sources, or from the proceeds of a sport lottery (as in Italy or Greece, for example), or from private donations (as in the United States), world-class athletes are subsidized, to varying degrees, so they can prepare to represent their countries in the Olympic competitions. The "shamateurism" debate is more hotly contested around the Olympic team events. In sports like soccer, ice hockey, and basketball that have professional status in some countries, the best players from those countries are disqualified from Olympic competition.

Like the Olympics, the World Cup has a global base of participation, but unlike the qualifiers that accompany Olympic team championships, the World Cup final is accepted as a decisive victory because it is set up to be a championship between professional athletes. Association football (abbreviated here as "soccer") is regarded as the national sport by more countries than any other.

The Fédération Internationale de Football Association (FIFA),[2] established in 1904 as the controlling body for world soccer, now has 147 member nations—an impressive number to coalesce around a single sport—13 nations more than are drawn together by the multisport appeal of the Olympics.

In fact, FIFA's membership is impressive by any standards. Only the United Nations, with 154 member countries, is larger.[3] The United Nations tries to peacefully resolve the real conflicts between countries, but the cleavages are so firmly drawn that global unity is impossible to achieve. A United Nations censure, like the one recently issued to Israel after its air raid on Iraq's nuclear reactor, has no real consequence. Nor did a reprimand in the World Court free American hostages from Iran. The emptiness of the gestures detracts from their moral authority. Ironically, integration is more easily accomplished through the play form of conflict; FIFA, for example, succeeds in creating a global collective consciousness by establishing a coherent and binding set of values and rules that its member nations must accept. A censure in the play world of conflict does have consequences. FIFA's power to exclude player clubs, even countries, from much desired international competition gives it the strength to enforce its mandates.

Like the Olympics, the World Cup is so big an event that it is staged quadrennially (alternating even years with the Olympics). So many play soccer that it takes two years and more than 250 preliminary games to determine the participants for the final competition. Preliminary competition is organized by continental zones to ensure that the World Cup is a global affair and not just a championship between the powerful teams in Europe and Latin America. Twenty-four nations participated in the 1982 play-offs in Spain. Besides the berths reserved for the host country and Argentina, the defending champion, there were thirteen countries from Europe, three from South America, and two each from Africa, Asia, and the zone made up of North and Central America and the Caribbean.[4] The tournament lasts one month as the entrants are whittled down to quarter-finals, then semifinals, until two countries meet in the championship match.

It is difficult to describe the magnitude of the World Cup to U.S. novitiates to the sport. Whereas the United States has been a dominant force in the Olympics since the very first modern games, it has entered only three World Cup competitions.[5] Americans show far more enthusiasm for the baseball World Series and the football Super Bowl—two sports that are not widely played internationally. Pretend those sports are played at top level elsewhere, then imagine those events, not as the season's finale but as the match that determines which team will represent the United States against the best teams of other nations. Even if the American reader can imagine an international competition involving the best professional teams in our favorite sports, that competition would be dwarfed by the World Cup.

The World Cup is not a club championship, like the Super Bowl, but pits national teams of all-stars—the country's best players at every position—against each other. Only native citizens can be selected ensuring truly representative teams. An all-star structure engenders solidarity within a nation better than an international club championship, where domestic rivalries may override patriotism. Truces are called as the best represent their country. After West Germany's 1954 World Cup victory over Hungary, a divided Germany was briefly reunited by the wild celebration on both sides of the Berlin Wall.[6] League schedules are arranged to permit professional athletes from all over a country to get together for lengthy training and elimination rounds. Like warriors preparing for battle, teams that reach the finals may be sequestered for one to two months, away from family and friends, for the fine-tuned conditioning that will fit the host country's climate and altitude.

At the international level especially, sport is mock war. To win a game is to "kill" one's opponent symbolically.[7] War and sport are alike in that both stir our loyalties and passions. Fighting enemies, representational or real, arouses our patriotism. Just as the spirit of war is brought into the game to intensify it, so too the spirit of the game has been brought into war to mock it, to make it less real, less terrifying. Paul Fussell tells how the English showed their sporting spirit during World War I by kicking a soccer ball toward the German lines while attacking. He contrasts these acts of bravado with the Prussians' dastardly use of chlorine gas.[8]

Sport offers an occasion for the display of civil religion. Where besides the stadium do we collectively sing our national anthem? The deeper the real antagonism between opposing nations, the stronger the patriotic sentiments of players and spectators alike. Pete Axthelm, describing the U.S. Olympic hockey team's victory over the Soviet Union, quoted the fan who said she "hadn't seen so many flags since the 1960s. When we were burning them."[9] One of my students remarked, "during Olympics, I undergo an amazing transformation from my usual liberal, antipatriotic commie-pinko attitudes to a flag-waving, slogan-shouting fanatic who sees a Red Menace in the outcome of the four-hundred-meter freestyle relay."

Nationalism is aroused by individual contestants but peaks over team sport. This is due, perhaps, to the momentum built during team games and the matching of only two countries at a time. In individual sport contests a number of countries are represented simultaneously, or seriatim, and our focus is diffused. In part, nationalism peaks because many consider collective action a truer test of a country's spirit than individual talent. To be sure, Americans experienced patriotic pride in the remarkable achievements of Eric Heiden, the skater who won five gold medals, but more intense nationalism was apparent during the USA-USSR hockey game in the same winter 1980 Olympics.

The difference in fan empathy is best reflected in a name. To extend the example, we say "Eric Heiden from the United States," and he clearly represents himself as well as his country—in fact, the rules of the Olympics emphasize individual rather than national competition, and point totals are only an unofficial way to declare one country the winner. The hockey team needs a collective name. Some individual players may merit special notice, but others remain nameless, and we refer to the entity as "the Americans." They symbolize us, and our strong identification with them is inevitable. More directly, empathy is greater where experience has been shared. Most youths grow up playing the national games, but only a few have ever tried to throw a discus or do acrobatics on a balance beam.

It is not surprising, then, that nationalism is most extreme at the World Cup, the highest level of competition in the globe's most popular participant and spectator sport. One analyst remarked, "The World Cup is really world war, organized, transformed, sublimated . . . like any other international conflict, [it] is a patriotic affair. . . . It's not the team that competes, it's the country."[10] Alan Ball reminisces about the 1966 World Cup hosted by England: "I didn't feel like I was playing *for* England, I felt I *was* England. . . . I could feel the power of the fans behind me. I win for them; they're a part of me."[11] The intensity of World Cup fever is so great that fans can literally cheer their national team to victory or jeer their opponents to defeat; evidence is that nine of twelve Cups have been won by the host or a neighboring country.

Critics of sport, especially soccer, often blame it for exacerbating international tensions. After all, the very point of sport is that one party emerges as the victor while the other is stung with the ignominy of defeat. When frenzied nationalism becomes linked to a team's destiny, sportsmanship can quickly dissolve into a win-at-any-cost philosophy. When flagrant cheating or frequent rule violations occur, the playfulness of the conflict breaks down. More often than not, the World Cup is marred by violence and expulsions, from early elimination games right up to the final matches. George Orwell accuses sport of perpetrating ill will, referring to international sport as "war minus the shooting."[12]

At least once in recent times, mock war has precipitated real war. In 1969 the World Cup play-off series between Honduras and El Salvador served as a catalyst for what historians called the "Soccer War." There was animosity between the two countries because large numbers of Salvadorans were crossing the border and taking jobs from Hondurans; the government of Honduras got revenge by nationalizing properties acquired by the Salvadoran immigrants. Riots followed both the first game in Honduras and the second game in El Salvador, and diplomatic relations were broken less than a week later. El Salvador's tanks rolled across the border two weeks after that. The fighting lasted a month, and casualties were in the thousands.[13]

Because sport acts as the symbolic statement of social conflict, the intensity of that conflict determines whether it can be played out ritually. That the game metaphor broke down during the "Soccer War" is one reflection of how intense the animosity between Honduras and El Salvador had become. The most intense competitions often involve nations that share borders; the entire history of their conflict is drawn into the contest. Similarly, English, Scottish, and Welsh teams have refused to play in Northern Ireland because the hostilities there go beyond playful characterization. The Arabs have long refused to meet the Israelis on the playing field, and now Pakistan and India have taken the same position. In fact, FIFA had to place Israel in the European zone in order to find willing opponents. The countries most in need of the integrative benefits of sport are the least likely to get them.

Sport's ability to transcend language and cultural barriers for an attentive world audience makes its mix with international politics inevitable. Hosting the World Cup or the Olympic Games always provides a colorful stage for propaganda; this use of sport is most likely to elicit protests when the spoils go to an authoritarian regime, as was the case with the Nazi Olympics of 1936, the 1978 Argentine World Cup, and the 1980 Moscow Olympics. The slaughter of the Israeli athletes at the 1972 Munich Olympics stands as the most tragic example of the contamination of sport with politics.

Many suggest eliminating flags and national anthems in an attempt to minimize politics in sport. But others find redeeming virtue in the connection—for example, praising the American boycott of the 1980 Moscow Olympics as a riskless but effective way to censure the Soviet invasion of Afghanistan. That boycott had numerous historical precedents. Egypt, Iraq, and Lebanon withdrew from the 1956 Melbourne Olympics in protest of Israel's move into the Gaza Strip, and Spain, Switzerland, and the Netherlands pulled out to protest the Russian invasion of Hungary.[14] Some who understand Argentina's soccer madness believed that the threat of exclusion from the 1982 World Cup might have halted the Falklands war.

The political impact of these boycotts is unclear, but there are other instances of sport exchanges where the benefits are more certain. In 1971 an American table-tennis team traveled to Peking; what was soon labeled "Ping-Pong diplomacy" is credited with paving the way for détente and Richard Nixon's historic 1972 trip to China. The "basketball initiative" in April 1977 enabled the largest group of Americans to visit Cuba since Castro's takeover in 1959.[15]

Even a single athlete can make a difference. Black American Arthur Ashe accepted South Africa's invitation to play professional tennis on condition that he travel freely, without censorship, that the spectator stands be integrated, and that he not be asked to accept honorary white status (the government's way around apartheid regulations). In his autobiography he says, "Arthur Ashe is not going to topple a government, but the very nature of sports is such that I believe that progress can be made in this frivolous area first."[16] Sportswriter Michael Roberts agrees that just threatening to bar sport-crazy South Africans from tennis, soccer, cricket, and rugby matches "probably carries more weight than all the arms embargoes, economic sanctions and liberal handwringing put together."[17]

The spirit of international goodwill may be best served when an athlete competes against an impersonal standard of achievement rather than directly against other competitors. Roone Arledge, president of ABC sports, described his thrill in televising the 1963 USA–USSR track meet held in Moscow at the time of the first arms agreement talks of the cold war:

> Khrushchev and Harriman were negotiating day and night, but at the very end of the meet, the two of them came out to Lenin Stadium to watch Valery Brumel, the great Russian high jumper, try for the world's record. It was getting dark and a light rain had begun falling. Brumel was down to his last attempt. He sprinted toward the bar, leaped and made it. There was a momentary lull as 90,000 people waited to see if the bar would topple. It didn't, and the crowd exploded. I turned our cameras on the chairman's box and Khrushchev and Harriman were jumping up and down, screaming, hugging each other. That was the single most important image I have ever broadcast. Two old men. Enemies who spoke different languages and couldn't even agree on a way to prevent the world from blowing itself up. Yet there they were, embracing like brothers on world television at the simple act of a man jumping over a bar.[18]

The Rival Team Sports

Soccer is the only team sport that has a global championship for its professional players. Contests between professional athletes from different countries are common in individual sports like tennis, golf, boxing, and auto and bicycle racing, but contests in other team sports involve mostly amateurs.[19] A brief history of the other popular team sports explains their amateur status and, in most cases, their limited global diffusion.

Rugby and soccer are variants of the same game, so their histories are equally long. But the kicking game had much wider appeal than the handling game. Rugby retained its aristocratic flavor and amateur status, while soccer was quickly adopted as the game of the people and became professionalized. Foreigners who came to England for an elite education took the game of rugby back home with them, and it is now played as an amateur sport in France, Italy, Rumania, Canada, South Africa, Australia, Argentina, Japan, and the Fiji Islands, as well as elsewhere in the United Kingdom.[20] Although there are international matches that command attention in the countries involved, like the biannual one between England and

Wales, no single championship event unites the far-flung nations that play the game. Professional rugby in England, Wales, and France is not taken nearly as seriously as the amateur game.

The rules of amateur rugby are far more complex than those of soccer, which is sometimes called "the simplest game."[21] Rugby rules pertaining to certain game situations were ambiguous in the late nineteenth century. It was assumed that the gentlemen players of the elite schools and clubs could fairly and honorably resolve questionable infractions one by one, as they arose. Any breach of agreed-upon rules was believed to be unintentional because a gentleman's code of behavior was in effect. Absence of codification worked in Victorian England, but it was intolerable in other rugby-playing places like America and Australia, where frontier spirits thrived.

In those isolated places there were no experienced players to turn to for explanation. The need for order necessitated both rule changes and innovation, and the game of rugby quickly evolved to unique forms of football in both Australia and the United States.[22] The development of indigenous forms of sport meant that all future championships would have to remain national events. Rugby became "football" in the United States, and Americans called the worldwide kicking game "soccer" to avoid confusion. For the same reason, I have followed the North American practice in this text, albeit with apologies and recognizing that the kicking game is aptly known as "football" throughout the rest of the world.

The American game of baseball, also of English origin, has its roots in the British game of rounders.[23] Transmission of the game to other countries occurred in various ways, including missionary contact, and baseball is now played in Japan, Cuba, China, and several Central and South American countries. The Little League baseball championship became a national contest after Taiwanese children defeated American teams once too often. The championship for professional teams, absurdly called the "World Series," has always been closed to foreign teams.

The American games of basketball and volleyball were YMCA inventions designed to provide indoor winter sport. They were spread all over the globe through YMCA outposts and today are played worldwide. The competitions of the 108 member International Volleyball Federation, founded in 1947, are dominated by Eastern European and Japanese teams. Basketball is second only to soccer in number of countries involved. The Fédération Internationale de Basketball Amateur, founded in 1932, has 133 members.[24]

Basketball is officially an amateur sport in all countries except the United States. In recent years world basketball has become sufficiently commercial that the best players receive under-the-table payments for their services and are more aptly thought of as semi-professionals. American players who were not good enough or who have grown too old for their professional leagues are found on the starting rosters in many countries. Small towns in Europe often invest their resources in a basketball team because it is cheaper to field five quality basketball players than eleven quality soccer players.

Despite basketball's popularity, it has never become professionalized. For one thing, the number of spectators drawn to the game is not sufficient to pay even five athletes to do nothing but train and play. In major cities of Europe, for example, a major basketball game attracts 1,000–5,000 paying spectators, while major soccer games regularly draw 100,000. Soccer is still the national sport that boys just about everywhere grow up playing, laying a basis for their adult spectatorship. Basketball requires a hoop and a bouncing ball; soccer can be played by the poorest children in an empty lot with rolled-up stockings in lieu of a proper ball. Besides, soccer appeals to more participants because, like baseball, it is considered a "democratic" sport. Tall, short, stocky, or slim—anyone can play, unlike football, rugby, or basketball, where particular body builds give some a distinct advantage.

Basketball is likely to remain an amateur sport for some time because that is how the international organization institutionalized it. Professional players would be ineligible for Olympic competition and the Inter-Continental Cup sponsored by the Fédération Internationale de Basketball Amateur. Although the American Olympic Committee sponsors a fine team, the United States does not dominate the Inter-Continental Cup. The nation that invented the game provides paltry media attention to the event and sends a second-rate squad instead of the best university team or all-star collegians.

Cricket and ice hockey are two other British inventions.[25] The slow summer game of cricket is played in the United Kingdom, Holland, and Denmark and has spread to the warm climates of South Africa, East Africa, the West Indies, Australia, New Zealand, Sri Lanka, Fiji, and India.[26] Although there is an International Cricket Conference, the game is not centralized. It is professional in some places, amateur in others, and there is no single championship that unifies member nations.

Fast-paced ice hockey had immediate appeal, but was limited in diffusion to places with appropriate cold climates. The International Ice Hockey Federation (IIHF) was founded in 1908 to regulate amateur sport. In addition to its involvement in Olympic hockey, the IIHF stages annual world and European amateur championships contested by twenty nations but dominated by Canada, the Soviet Union, Sweden, Finland, and Czechoslovakia.[27] The Stanley Cup of the National Hockey League is a championship series for professional teams, but at most it involves only two countries, the United States and Canada.

In terms of the number of players, both male and female, field hockey is one of the world's most popular participant sports. Although it is an ancient game, with several independent roots, the British introduced the modern game around the world and institutionalized it as a strictly amateur sport. Played in more than seventy countries, field hockey draws large crowds only in India and Pakistan, two of the countries that dominate the sport in the Olympic games along with Germany, Holland, and Argentina.[28]

In most places soccer reigns as the only professional game. Where it coexists with other team sports, soccer's popularity far outpaces the number two sport. Soccer is also the number one sport in amateur participation. In Europe alone there are nearly 14 million amateur players registered with the national soccer associations;[29] there are fewer than one million amateur ice hockey players registered in the Soviet Union, Sweden, Czechoslovakia, Finland, Canada, and the United States combined.[30]

Whether the focus is the amateur or the professional game, soccer must be considered the premier world team sport. It is centrally organized for international play and fits all climates and body types. That is why soccer has been called a "sporting Esperanto— a form of human association which defies language and cultural divisions."[31]

Soccer's Lucky Story

The single origin of soccer, its incredibly rapid diffusion, and its early international centralization explain the similarity in the organizational structure of the sport, both amateur and professional, from country to country. Fortuitously, the height of the game's popularity in England coincided with the years of Britain's maritime, industrial, and imperial reign. In less than two decades, the British helped establish the game throughout Europe and South America. FIFA was formed in 1904 to standardize the rules and promote international contests. Later the Olympics and the new World Cup drew more attention to the game, and the sailors and soldiers of both world wars finished the job of spreading soccer to every corner of the earth.

Forms of kicking ball games were played in ancient China and Rome, and a riotous brand of soccer was played in the streets of medieval England during public holidays. But the game played today was invented in the mid-nineteenth century in the elite schools of England. Thomas Arnold, headmaster of the Rugby School, changed the very nature of sport from a barbaric celebration to an activity that educated boys in the virtues of hard work, discipline, and self-control. In 1845 rules were written for the game played at Rugby, to minimize violence and injury. The idea of organized games spread quickly, and by the 1850s the game was common in the schools and universities of the south of England and among the professional classes. But there were no standardized rules, and there was considerable disagreement between those who preferred the handling game (like that played at Rugby and Marlborough) and those who preferred a kicking game (like that played at Harrow and Eton). In 1863 the latter formed the "Football Association" to define a set of rules for the game we know as soccer. The Rugby Football Union was formed eight years later.[32]

Soccer remained an aristocratic recreation until the late 1870s, when it was taught to the emerging industrial working classes by clergymen, businessmen, and factory managers. Some of these sport missionaries had the same motive as headmaster Arnold, especially the clergy, who saw soccer as a way to combat urban delinquency in the squalid northern cities. For others the more immediate concern was their desire to play and win the game, and thus their need to recruit the best talent available. Soccer has been credited as one of the contributors (along with religion and civic pride) to the incorporation of the new working class into the mainstream of life in Victorian England.[33]

The Football Association encouraged the expansion of soccer just at the time industrial workers were given Saturday afternoons off. Puritan religious leaders abhorred Sunday recreations, and until then people had free time only on Sundays. Historian James Walvin concludes that "football emerged as an industrial game, not as a palliative to the grimness of industrial life, but largely because industrial workers, unlike others, had free time."[34]

The institutionalizing of Saturday-afternoon soccer served as recognition that "the workmen had a right to share in the culture and leisure enjoyed by others."[35] Soccer immediately became a recreational outlet for the urban masses. The humble recruits changed the style of play to suit their smaller physiques. The working-class game became one of close control, dribbling, and accurate passing. The soccer that developed in the industrial cities of the Midlands and the North soon surpassed the game of the southern middle and upper classes.[36]

Professionalism became the moral issue that exemplified the class conflict. By the 1880s, soccer could draw 10,000 paying customers for a match, and the clubs could afford to pay players to take the time to perfect their skills.[37] The leisure classes considered payment an affront to the traditions of amateur sportsmanship, but the working class players needed the money.[38] The gentlemen of the Football Association threatened to rescind the membership of clubs that paid players and thereby to eliminate them from the prestigious Football Association Cup competition. In return, the northern clubs threatened to withdraw en masse and set up their own competition. A compromise was reached in 1885, when the Football Association accepted professionals but prohibited them from serving on any committees or attending any meetings of the association. That is, the quid pro quo for professionals on the field was administrative control of soccer by amateurs.[39]

The aristocrats of the Football Association made sure that this paternalistic pattern extended down to the clubs as well. English clubs were organized as limited companies, selling shares to the public and run by a chairman and board of directors. The English Football Association prohibited directors from receiving any remuneration for services and limited shareholders' dividends to 7.5 percent. The idea was to keep commercial profiteers out and ensure that amateur sportsmen who loved the game would stay in control.[40]

The amateurs who ran the Football Association were from England's elite classes (to a large degree that holds true today).[41] The amateurs who assumed responsibility for the clubs were from the growing middle class and nouveau riche. It was the community's manufacturers, entrepreneurs, and successful merchants who established themselves as the benefactors of sport; rather than making money, they were expected to give donations or interest-free loans to the clubs during troubled times. They were also expected to use their outside positions to offer players part-time and postcareer employment so as to attract first-class talent to their clubs.[42] What they got in return was the pleasure of serving their communities, the power to control the teams they loved, and free publicity to attract new business and promote political connections.

The soccer clubs of England split between those that embraced the new professionalism and those that preferred to retain their "clean," dignified amateur status. The South remained a bastion of amateurism and the North expanded professionalism. The professional clubs, having salaries to pay, were more concerned about the haphazard scheduling of matches. In 1888 British soccer directors from the strongest clubs borrowed the American idea of league formation to regulate competition and increase attendance.[43] Although it was intended to be a national league, the founding teams were all from the industrial North and Midlands. It was five years before a London team joined the league and brought the improved standard of play to the South. The notion of sport as heavily financed and highly organized activity that attracts vast partisan crowds developed simultaneously in the United States and England, and it was soon exported from England to the rest of the world.

Professional soccer became the dominant spectator sport of urban England. By 1892, with the introduction of lower-division soccer, the contours of today's British system had already been set. One historical analyst finds it a remarkable example of the tenacity of traditional institutions: "The major clubs, their grounds, even their colors would be recognizable to a supporter of the 1890's. The rules which govern the game, both on and off the field, have changed less than those of any other major sport."[44] The class lines were set as well. The vast majority of soccer players, spectators, and officials were from the working class; directors, shareholders, and reporters of the game were drawn from the middle and upper classes.

While the British system was taking form, soccer was spreading like wildfire across Europe from the late 1870s through the 1880s. The speed with which soccer traveled from England to the Continent and established itself as the international game was truly remarkable. The game thrived everywhere that England traded or worked. As soccer historian James Walvin makes clear, the game developed from small, random beginnings, wherever Englishmen were anxious to play their new national game. The means of diffusion were many: students who had studied at English schools brought it back with them to Holland, France, Portugal, and Italy; the British Embassy staff displayed the game in Sweden and Denmark; British sailors in the Royal Navy exported the game to all the port cities of Europe; British engineers introduced soccer in Spain; and two Lancashire textile factory managers founded a club near Moscow where they were initiating local industry.[45]

European clubs and national football associations were formed on the British model, as were local leagues and Football Association Cup competitions. National controlling organizations were essential in arranging international competitions. In 1902 Austria beat Hungary. Then in 1904 Belgium and France played to a draw. Twenty days later the French called a meeting in Paris, and delegates from Belgium, Denmark, France, the Netherlands, Spain, Sweden, and Switzerland founded FIFA and installed a Frenchman as its first president. The timing of the meeting is striking considering that Spain, Sweden, and Denmark had yet to play an "international."[46]

The British Football Association, though invited, was conspicuous in its absence. The International Football Association Board, set up in 1882 by the football associations of England, Ireland, Scotland, and Wales, was to be the only body with authority over the rules of the game, and the British association felt FIFA was superfluous. Two years later England did join, but only on condition that the International Board remain responsible for the rules of the game. FIFA was to see that member countries adhered to the rules and that international matches were played by truly representative teams approved by their respective associations. Furthermore, FIFA institutionalized for the world the British Football Association mandate that a soccer club "shall not be used as a source of profit for its directors or shareholders."[47]

Meanwhile, British sailors had taken the game to the port cities of South America, and British officials who managed banks, railroads, and textile factories there established soccer in the social clubs of the major cities. The game took root firmly in Uruguay, Argentina, Chile, and Brazil, where there were active British colonies supervising an abundance of British investments. The pattern in these countries is identical. The introduction and growth of soccer in Brazil suitably describes the process in all these southern Latin American countries.

It is believed that British sailors brought the game to the port city of Rio de Janeiro as early as 1884. But the game did not take root until 1894, the year Charles Miller, the Brazilian-born son of the British consul in São Paulo, returned after playing first-division soccer while attending school in Southampton, England. Equipped with official balls and the established rule book, he helped set up clubs with the English Gas Company, the São Paulo Railways, and the London Bank. By 1898 the local Mackenzie College fielded the first predominately Brazilian team, and by 1902 there were enough clubs for a São Paulo league and championship cup.[48] Events proceeded similarly in Rio de Janeiro, where the first soccer teams were fielded by clubs that had been established at the end of the nineteenth century to promote regattas or cricket. A Rio league was formed in 1906.

This was the era when soccer was "chic." The game was restricted to the few who knew the sport and had access to the aristocratic clubs where it was played. New waves of European immigration expanded the clubs. The arriving Germans, Portuguese, and Italians formed their own teams to rival the British. Soon these players were joined by the sons of the local elite who had learned the game while studying or traveling abroad and had taught it to their collegiate friends at home. Even Flamengo, today's team for the masses, began with a squad made up exclusively of medical students. Young ladies from Rio's finest families came fashionably dressed to the clubs to admire the town gentry on the field.

But this period was short-lived. Industrial workers who began as spectators soon became players and formed their own district clubs. Many claim credit for the transition. Bangu, a textile factory run by the British, started its own team in 1904, allowing two Brazilians to play with them. More important, the factory workers were invited to watch the games.[49] Club historians claim that Flamengo brought the game to the common people because it was the only team to hold training sessions on an open field in plain view of neighbors and laborers returning from work.

Touring British teams stirred enthusiasm among the locals. The famous amateur Corinthians team, made up of Oxford and Cambridge graduates who had the time and means to travel, swept victoriously through southern Brazil in 1910. Ironically, the elite

Corinthians name was taken for a new club formed in São Paulo by a wall painter, a tailor, and some factory and railroad workers who, according to folklore, played in homemade uniforms of burlap sacking as Brazil's "first poor team."[50] In 1915 Rio's and São Paulo's metropolitan leagues had expanded and looked much as they do today. The three-stage transition of players from the British to the local elite and finally to the working class was complete. The fashionable ladies in the stands went home when the working people took over the game.

British clubs and naval teams continued to cross the ocean, mixing business with sport. The first intracontinental match took place in 1902 between Uruguay and Argentina for the Lipton Cup (donated by the tea magnate). By that time, both those countries had football associations. The impetus to form football associations in both European and Latin American countries stemmed from a desire for national championships. But in huge Brazil, where distances between cities prohibited a national championship, the equivalent of a football association formed because of the intense desire for international competition. The Brazilian Sports Confederation was established in 1914 to select a genuine national team for play against Argentina in a precursor to the South American Championship. In 1916 a South American Confederation was formed to make the championship official. By then Chile and Argentina had joined the FIFA, though no Latin American team had yet played in Europe. That changed in 1924 when Uruguay entered the Paris Olympics. The Latin style of play—fast, flashy, and full of tricks—was a revelation to Europeans, and the Uruguayans handily won the Olympic soccer tournament. They won again in 1928 in the Amsterdam Olympics, this time accompanied by teams from Chile, Argentina, and Mexico.

Accepting the Olympic competition as definitive was already problematic, for some leading soccer nations had openly endorsed professionalism, making their best players ineligible. Austria was the first continental European country to allow professionalism in 1924, followed by Czechoslovakia in 1925, Hungary in 1926, and Spain and Italy in 1929.[51] Under the leadership of its French president Jules Rimet, FIFA began a tournament for professionals to decide the world's leading soccer nation. To show that it was a *world* championship and in respect for Uruguay's Olympic wins, the first World Cup was to take place in Uruguay in 1930. With the World Cup established, there was no longer any need to resist professionalism so as to preserve player eligibility for the Olympics. Furthermore, contact through "internationals" provided a basis for countries with professionalism to pirate players from those without. Argentina, in 1931, was the first Latin American country to professionalize its soccer as a way to thwart the exodus of players to Europe. Brazil then began to lose its players to Argentina and was forced to permit professionalism in 1933 in spite of strong middle-class resistance. Brazilian players had been paid surreptitiously in any case, and legal contracts not only blocked players from leaving a country but also prevented internal movement from team to team. Other nations on both continents quickly joined the professional fold.

Professional soccer stretched to every region of the earth during the two world wars. In fact, so many countries joined FIFA that it was necessary to add an intermediate level between the national football associations and the world organization. The Latin Americans formed a Continental Federation early in 1916. The idea took a long time to spread, but in 1954 there started a Union of European Football Associations (UEFA) to oversee a European championship and the regional World Cup qualifying rounds. The Asian Football Confederation was also founded in 1954, followed by groups in Africa in 1956, North and Central America in 1961, and Oceania in 1966.[52]

Europe and Latin America play the strongest soccer; never has a nation from any other continent won a World Cup. The pattern of European versus South American confrontation was set early. Uruguay won the Jules Rimet trophy on home ground at that first World Cup in 1930. In 1934 Italy won it in Italy. Never has a European team won a World Cup staged in South America, and only once did a Latin team win on European soil, when Brazil took home the 1958 Cup from Sweden.

Although the Latins and the Europeans come together to play the same game under the same rules, cultural variation leads to pronounced differences in playing style. The World Cup is more than a competition between separate nations; it is a place to contest different interpretations of a game and to observe the symbolic manifestations of cultural clash. The Latin style is thought to show more flair and improvisation, with an emphasis on individualism and attack: "Brazilian football is a dance full of irrational surprises and Dionysiac variations."[53] Taken as an expression of national personality, Brazilian soccer is rhythmic, balletic, and cunning; Brazilians use their word *alegre*, meaning both happy and showy, to describe their style of play.[54] The Europeans are more controlled and methodical, priding themselves on efficient teamwork and defense. The victorious British team of the 1966 Cup was described as "unspectacular . . . attacking cautiously with the probing patience of a skilled surgeon."[55] The Russian and German styles are associated with strength and determination.[56]

On the surface, it seems surprising that soccer took earlier and deeper root in Europe and Latin America than in those places where the British had direct political control. Walvin suggests that imperial authorities feared that the huge crowds soccer drew could mobilize social unrest; Czarist Russia, where home crowds numbered 30,000 as early as 1890, clearly used that reasoning to suppress soccer in parts of Poland and the Baltic provinces under its rule. When imperial rule disintegrated in Africa and Asia in the postwar years, soccer flowered along with political and social freedom.[57]

More surprising to many was the failure of soccer in the white dominion countries like Canada, Australia, New Zealand, South Africa, and the United States; though the British had introduced the game early, it failed to take root. Walvin's explanation is simple and credible: where local sports were firmly entrenched, it proved impossible to dislodge them.[58] Latins and Europeans readily adopted the simple and cheap game in the absence of indigenous team sports, whereas America, South Africa, and Australia already had organized sports. By the 1880s and 1890s, when soccer was being exported around the globe, the United States could resist its lure because professional baseball and Ivy League football were firmly established. Similarly, South Africa already had cricket and rugby, and Australia had cricket and its own brand of football.[59]

Enterprising American businessmen introduced a professional soccer league a little over a decade ago after television led to an era of financial boom and expansion for spectator sports in America. It was a dismal failure. Only when Pelé joined it in 1975 did the North American Soccer League (NASL) have the superstar quality to attract paying customers. Although the league is still dominated by foreigners (most teams have only three North American starters—the minimum required by the NASL), soccer has become our fastest-growing spectator sport, doubling its fan following from 7 percent to 14 percent of the population in just one season.[60]

The recent soccer boom has begun to expose Americans to the game both as players and as spectators. Unfortunately, the business concerns of American soccer entrepreneurs have led them to modify the game: "shoot-outs" and "minigames" that resolve tied scores are our invention, and television executives are encouraging time-outs in what has been a nonstop running game. FIFA watches with interest these rule innovations in an environment not bound by tradition. Nevertheless, the price of changing soccer's rules and traditions will be prolonging America's isolation from the global sporting community.

Other features of America's soccer boom also accentuate our stance as outsiders. Whereas elsewhere the stands are filled with working-class men, American spectators are 45 percent female and 74 percent college-educated.[61] Whereas elsewhere the players are from the working class, youth soccer in America is a suburban movement. A million children are enrolled in soccer little leagues—already half the enrollment of baseball's Little League—and the game's popularity with adolescents has made it our fastest-growing college sport.[62] Foreign observers may be correct in their warning that American soccer players will never be able to compete with Europeans and Latin Americans until they forsake the college draft, in which teams select rookies from all the graduating players, in favor of the apprentice system common elsewhere.

As our young players become professionals and paying fans, American soccer will lose its foreign flavor. Right now American soccer embodies a meshing of cultures, whereas soccer elsewhere symbolically dramatizes the clash between different nationalities. The New York Cosmos, for example, have players from fourteen nations kicking the ball "that knows no language," as described by the team's technical director, Julio Mazzei. Even the soccer organized for United Nations employees divides nations by continent, whereas U.S. soccer turns cultural strangers into teammates.

America's distinctiveness will pose a glaring problem when we fully join the global soccer community. Right now professional soccer franchises in the United States lose money for their owners. When soccer becomes a commercial success, we will be in violation of the venerated FIFA regulation against profit making. The business orientation of American sports is seen as a contradiction to the spirit of sport worldwide and adds to our image as a money-minded people. An owner's ability and willingness to abandon loyal fans and move his team to another city with a better market for his product is probably the feature of the American system that most shocks foreigners. Our sport system reflects our national character. One can draw conclusions about a people through their sport because it usually fits into a whole cultural pattern.

National character becomes set early and is repeated through history, although manifested in different ways. Baseball's National League was founded in 1876 as a profit-motivated organization. At the very same time America's commercial instincts delayed the dedication of the Statue of Liberty. In 1875 its French sculptor, Frédéric Auguste Bartholdi, conceived the statue to symbolize America's welcome to millions of immigrants. The statue was to be a gift from the people of France, but international public interest brought donations from "ordinary folk and dignitaries alike" from all over Europe. The Americans were asked only to supply a fitting location and a pedestal. But public apathy prolonged fund-raising for years. Americans did not see any commercial or practical utility in the project, and the symbolism alone did not move them. Art exhibitions, auctions, musical entertainments, prizefights, and repeated editorials by immigrant publisher Joseph Pulitzer were needed to raise funds, while the disassembled, crated statue waited for its pedestal.[63] In this story, as in sport, Americans showed themselves to be business-minded, whereas the French were early internationalists, not only with their conceptualization of the statue but also in their initiation of the modern Olympics, FIFA, other international sporting federations, and the World Cup.

Europeans have been able to disassociate sport and commerce because of their spirit of noblesse oblige. Domestically, wealthy volunteers run everything from the local clubs to the national football associations. Internationally, everyone from the delegates to FIFA's Congress to the president and members of the Executive Committee serve for honor—only the full-time secretary general at the Zurich headquarters is salaried.[64]

Professional soccer has always been dependent on volunteers at the top. Most clubs have been losing money for years owing to escalating player salaries, rising costs, and the growth of competing leisure industries (especially free television) that diminish game attendance. For example, only six of the English League's ninety-two clubs were in the black after the 1977 season, the rest being $30 million in debt.[65] But soccer clubs do not have to declare bankruptcy because they are not a commercial product. They are supported by a never-ending supply of philanthropists willing to throw good money down a "bottomless well of hope."[66] There are plenty of people who will give money "to get close to the game, who want to be part of its excitement, who want a say, however slight, in its control."[67]

While the money and volunteered time of the directors saves soccer clubs from bankruptcy, their amateur mentality has also taken part of the blame for the commercial failure of the clubs they run. The world over, these directors are successful entrepreneurs who are said to use their hearts more than their heads in making policy for their clubs. Furthermore, these men lack skills in sports administration and management of athletes, and they resist hiring public relations experts who would attract people's recreation money.[68]

The directors' donations can keep their clubs solvent as long as competitors for their best players operate under similar economic restraints. They cannot raise player salaries to the astronomical levels paid in American sports or compete with exceptional countries like Spain where live television coverage is permitted. Broadcast rights have given Spain's clubs a financial advantage that has been used to lure the world's greatest stars, like Holland's Johan Cruyff, with irresistible contracts.

FIFA's regulations restrain the pirating of national heroes through a reserve clause that makes a player the property of his club until it agrees to release him for prohibitive transfer fees. A player cannot circumvent either the reserve clause or a disciplinary suspension by leaving his country to play for a foreign team. A proper certificate of transfer, signed by his national football association, must be filed with FIFA before he can play elsewhere. Another FIFA regulation forbids the employment of agents that would facilitate player transfers.[69] An International Federation of Professional Footballers is launching an attack against this infringement of players' freedom, but it is weak relative to the awesome powers of FIFA.

As to the regulation against profit making, neither FIFA's president nor its secretary general cared to answer my questions about the impending problem of America's business orientation to sport. They may choose to ignore the infraction when it occurs because America's entry into the World Cup, which would be accompanied by lucrative broadcast contracts from American networks, would go a long way toward resolving soccer's financial crisis. The lines between America's professional-business and the rest of the world's amateur-volunteer orientations to sport may begin to blur as soccer faces a shotgun wedding to television in other countries and as American promotional gimmicks are borrowed owing to economic necessity.

While American clubs exhibit sport merchandising for the global sports community, foreign stars exhibit soccer virtuosity to Americans. Ironically, FIFA includes the United States with under-developed countries as it carries out its mandate to aid soccer's growth. Similarly, Coca-Cola granted $5 million to global youth soccer and earmarked much of the money for the United States.[70] Real world status differentials can be suspended, sometimes even reversed, in the play world of sport.

Sport serves as a leveler between nations. Whatever their relative political status, nations meet as equals in the sport community. Long before they can compete in other spheres with the most powerful nations of the world, developing nations can demonstrate superiority in sport, as Brazil did in 1970 with its definitive tri-championship. Spontaneous carnivals erupted in the streets of the capital cities all over the continent as other Latin Americans joined Brazilians in celebrating a victory over the Europeans in something everyone agreed was important. I joined the street parade in Mexico City, where the final game had been played, and saw numerous signs that read, "MEXICO—World Soccer Champion—by Friendship."

Four years later, Dr. João Havelange—who had been president of Brazil's sport confederation since 1958—campaigned for the presidency of FIFA and won. The election marked another way the international sporting community acknowledged Brazil's leadership in soccer. Dr. Havelange is the first non-European to hold the esteemed position of highest power in FIFA. Fulfilling a campaign promise, Havelange has expanded the number of World Cup participants from sixteen to twenty-four so that more nations from Africa and Asia can join the global event.[71]

Sport and Social Integration in Brazil

Internal unification of highly industrialized nations like the United States has profited from advanced technology—especially air transportation and coast-to-coast television and telephones. Brazil has been taking advantage of abundant natural resources to industrialize rapidly, and federal investment in highways, railroads, and telecommunications has begun to link faraway regions, but the task is enormous. In a nation like Brazil, sport's contribution to social integration is special because it can precede technology's contribution and even promote modernization goals. The success of soccer in Brazil has been a force for pulling together its several parts and unifying them through national pride.

Brazil is an enormous country divided by marked regionalism and by a culturally and racially diverse population. The fifth largest nation in the world, Brazil makes up half of South America in land mass. Its 116 million people constitute half the population of the continent. Sheer distance obstructs communication between different parts of the country; Brazil's dense jungles and mountainous terrain impede transportation even between neighboring states. Relative isolation and ecological diversity have produced strong regional identities expressed through heated political rivalries. These tensions overlap with ethnic and racial divisions between the different groups who were conscripted or lured in by the special labor demands of each region.

Brazil can be divided into six major regions:[1] In the Northwest, the Amazon valley is covered by the densest tropical rain forest in the world. Scattered tribes of American Indians lived in this vast jungle and mixed with Portuguese colonizers who came in search of forest products such as Brazil nuts, rubber, palm, and hardwoods. Most of the population lives along the Amazon, although primitive Indian tribes are still found deep in the interior. One of the current government's most ambitious and painstaking projects is building the Trans-Amazon Highway to prepare that vast territory for exploitation and development.

Brazil's Northeast is dramatically different. Grazing has always been the basis of its economy. Portuguese landowners used native Indians to care for their herds, and the people today reflect centuries of Indian and Portuguese mixing. The arid backlands of cactus and scrub are plagued by severe droughts every eight to fifteen years. During those times, thousands must migrate or die. In spite of mass migrations, the region is still one of Brazil's most densely populated.

The northeast coast, with its fertile soil and regular rainfall, was the setting for the sugar and cotton plantations of the colonial period, when wealthy Portuguese families established an aristocratic estate system. The economy is still based on plantation agriculture, although crops are now more diverse. The strong black African culture that was brought in by more than 3 million slaves between 1600 and 1888 is reflected in the overwhelmingly black and mulatto population.[2] African heritage is seen in the regional cuisine, the *macumba* or *candomblé* religious cults (known as voodoo in other parts of the world), and in the African influenced samba that spread from the Northeast to become the special music and dance of Brazil.

The industrial Middle States are São Paulo, Minas Gerais, Rio de Janeiro, and Espírito Santo. Rio de Janeiro grew in importance as a port city that exported valuable minerals and raw materials to foreign markets. By the late nineteenth century and the early twentieth, world demand for coffee had made São Paulo the richest state, so independent that it made a serious attempt at secession. Rio de Janeiro and São Paulo both resemble American "melting pot" cities like Chicago, having drawn in many of the same European nationalities. The wealth from coffee and the opportunity for jobs attracted waves of immigrants from Italy, Germany, Spain, Poland, and Portugal, and also from Japan and the Middle East. The large city of

Belo Horizonte in Minas Gerais also reflects the influx of foreigners who came in search of gold and diamonds.

An estimated 5.5 million immigrants entered Brazil between 1875 and 1960, bringing modern Western culture with them.[3] Picturesque Rio de Janeiro best displays the racial mixing of European, African, and Indian bloodlines. The blend results in a unique Brazilian type, often of exquisite beauty, that makes Brazil world-renowned for its "racial democracy." There are rivalries between residents of Brazil's two giant cities: Cariocas (people from Rio) describe Paulistas (people from São Paulo) as driven by work and materialism, and Paulistas describe Cariocas as lazy sensualists who worship sun, beach, and beauty.[4]

The extreme South has a temperate climate. The southernmost state has a pampa (rolling prairie) with the gauchos that are usually identified with Argentina. The other states' fertile agricultural land attracted German, Italian, and Japanese settlers, whose influence is seen in modern farming techniques, crops, architecture, and language. Until all school classes were required to be conducted in Portuguese, these immigrant groups had put up strong resistance to assimilation. With the exhaustion of coffee lands in São Paulo, coffee farmers moved south to these states. Their temperate climate, with occasional killer frosts, cause the fluctuation in coffee supply reflected in the prices on the world market.

Finally, the "Wild West" frontier lies in the heart of South America. It resembles America's Wild West of yesteryear in its lack of law and order, outlaws, and boomtown mentality. The scant population comes from all parts of Brazil, lured by the hope of amassing fortunes with great cattle ranches or by gold discoveries. Though the vast grazing lands are not fertile, settling the interior is thought to be a prerequisite to fulfilling the nation's "manifest destiny." In that spirit, President Juscelino Kubitschek commissioned the building of the futuristic capital city of Brasília in the heart of the state of Goiás. Construction began before roads were built, so workers and materials had to be flown in at extraordinary costs that contributed to runaway inflation. Against all odds, Brasília was designed and built in less than four years, becoming the symbolic new national capital in 1960.[5]

The Ties That Bind

Most important to Brazil's sense of wholeness and special identity are its common language, its overwhelming Catholicism, and its heritage of cultural blend. Yet the same institutions that help make Brazil a single nation reflect the tensions between its regional and cultural divisions. Brazil is the only Portuguese-speaking nation among eighteen Spanish-speaking ones. Although its common language unifies Brazil's adopted immigrant groups and symbolizes its distinctive identity, there are regional variations in dialect, slang, and common usage. Cuisine can be regional, too, with northeastern dishes like *vatapá* (fish stew spiced with palm oil and coconut milk) and southern dishes like *churrasco* (a variety of barbecued meats). But there are also national dishes, served everywhere, like *feijoada* (black-bean stew served with manioc flour, collard greens, and orange slices) that exemplify Brazil's unique blend of Amerindian, West African, and European cultures.

Popular culture becomes especially important in developing nations, where a distinctive image can foster a nation's sense of unity. Products of a culture that earn international recognition go a long way toward accomplishing this integration. In the early part of this century Brazil was known to the outside world mostly as the producer of coffee and semiprecious stones, but since then other cultural contributions have been exported and appreciated. The melodic bossa nova—especially as composed by Antonio Carlos Jobim, João Gilberto, and Edu Lobo—gained a world audience. Brazilian authors Graciliano Ramos, José Lins do Rêgo, Erico Veríssimo, and Jorge Amado took their places in world literature. Carlos Niemeyer's designs for the federal buildings in Brasília were studied by architecture students everywhere.[6] Demonstrated by the recent box office success of *Dona Flora and Her Two Husbands*, *Bye-Bye Brazil*, and *Pixote*, new Brazilian films are expressing national culture to appreciative audiences worldwide.

If you ask Brazilians what best symbolizes their special culture, the answers typically are some combination of spiritualism, samba, and soccer. Each of these Brazilian creations demonstrates how regional practices can disseminate to unify a nation. They are the topics of conversation; they involve activities and organizations that attract diverse groups; and they provide common symbols of devotion.

Nominally, Brazil is unified by the Roman Catholic church; 90 percent of the population is Catholic. As is typical of Latin America, church services and activities involve more women and children than men, but almost all Brazilians share the symbols of the cult of the saints. Church leaders, however, do not act as symbols that people share. Only Dom Helder Camara, a radical priest who was once considered the number one enemy of the military regime, might be recognized by laymen everywhere. Nor does the church hierarchy—six cardinals within their own regional jurisdictions—present a unified Brazil. Besides, Brazil's religion is not as homogeneous as outward appearances suggest. The blending of African and Indian spiritualist cults with traditional Catholicism has produced a continuum of religious practices. Some Brazilians are strict Catholics; others identify themselves as spiritualists, but most practice some blend of both.

Umbanda (also called candomblé and macumba) was originally an African-Amerindian spiritual cult practiced by the slaves of the Northeast. To lessen the repression from whites who were threatened by the cult, slaves hid their gods behind the facade of Catholic saints. They turned Iemanjá, the goddess of the sea, into the Virgin Mary, Oxalá into Jesus Christ, and Ogum into Saint George, and Exu became Satan.[7] As the cult grew and spread to other regions, it incorporated aspects of European spiritualism and eliminated the more African rituals, such as animal sacrifices, in an attempt to become more respectable. Meanwhile, many whites accepted the supernatural power of the Umbanda gods and the spiritual leaders who put themselves into spectacular trances. Middle- and upper-class people, ostensibly Catholics, quietly practiced Umbanda.

After World War II, Umbanda groups sprouted in the major cities, especially Rio and São Paulo. Over the past three decades Umbanda has grown exponentially and now includes followers from all social classes. Official statistics show that, in a population of 116 million, 20 million are Umbandistas, many of whom are also practicing Catholics.[8] Many Catholics who previously hid their dual allegiance now publicly embrace the cult, but many more still practice it in secrecy, making the figure of 20 million an underestimate.

Instead of repression, the cult now gets state support. The secretary of tourism in the state of São Paulo sponsors the annual Festa de Ogum and Festa de Iemanjá; both festivals are celebrated as if they were national holidays. But apart from these two holidays, Umbanda does little to promote Brazil's unity. There is no national organization. Each locality has its separate set of special deities; even the principal icons are given different appearances in each region.

The most important festival of the year is called Carnival in Brazil, the Catholic Mardi Gras from the Saturday before Lent until the morning of Ash Wednesday. The Mardi Gras overshadows other religious and patriotic holidays and brings together Catholics and Umbandistas in a feast of samba. Even though the holiday is celebrated at least on a minor scale in most Catholic countries, the passions unleashed as Brazilians sing, dance, and drink for four days are not found elsewhere. The Portuguese holiday was a heavy, serious occasion; in Brazil, Carnival became festive with the color and life infused by the Africans recently released from slavery. Replacing the mournful slow *fado* melodies of Portugal were the faster, vital, exciting African rhythms originally brought to the Northeast, then down to Rio.[9]

Samba and Carnival grew together. The modern samba, uniquely Brazilian, is said to have been born in the *favelas* (shantytowns) of Rio at the turn of the century. Originally, sambas "were the purest folk music, a spontaneous, unsophisticated expression of life on the *morro* (hill), including its poverty, hard work and bitterness . . . only later, as carnival developed, was there growing emphasis on romantic love, on enjoying the carnival and on singing the praises of Brazil."[10] The Umbanda imagery mixed in samba songs again demonstrates Brazil's cultural blend.

The music presents a happy relief from a hard life. Rapid unplanned growth in Brazil's major cities has resulted in inadequate housing and in shortages of food, clothing, and sanitation. Many are forced to live in squatter settlements filled with ramshackle huts made of cardboard, tin, wood, and canvas. Typically situated on the periphery of the city, these suburbs for the poor are far away from employment sources, public transportation, and other city services like water and electricity.

In Rio, nearly 20 percent of the population (about one million people) live in shantytowns.[11] In contrast to other cities, some of Rio's favelas are built high on the beautiful hillsides that hug the finest neighborhoods inside the city proper. (These are the favelas romanticized in Brazilian movies like *Black Orpheus*.) Even with their breathtaking views of the beaches and bay, these hillsides are the province of the poor. The only way up them is on foot, and they are subject to mudslides during the long rainy season. Yet despite the dismal conditions, for favela dwellers, even more than the rest of the city's inhabitants, participation in Carnival is central to social life.

Since 1928, clubs called samba schools have represented Rio's favelas and other poor neighborhoods in a citywide parade with contests for the best songs, dances, and costumes. Every town and city has a celebration; but Rio's Carnival is by far the biggest. Starting in November, each samba school begins its internal competition among the local composers who wish to have their tunes chosen for presentation in the parade. The community, after weeks of partying and dancing to the compositions, votes for its tune and starts preparing the lavish costumes and dances for Carnival. Since the late 1930s, when the dictator Vargas boldly merged popular culture with political goals, samba school themes have been topics of national history, thereby promoting patriotism and mythology in what was a predominantly illiterate society.[12]

There are twelve first- and twelve second-division samba schools, and approximately one thousand *blocos* (blocks) that are less prosperous and less organized.[13] The best school in the second division gets to march in the parade the following year, and the last-place first-division school drops to the second division. The hope for citywide exposure keeps the spirit of competition alive in the second division just as the system of relegation and promotion does in the multiple-division soccer leagues.

From December until February or March the drumbeats heard from the hills stretch later and later into the night. The affluent who live in the high rises at the base of the hills cannot escape the preparations and mounting excitement for the coming event. As many as 4,000 from a single community may be involved in the presentation, even though participants must pay for plumed satin costumes that often cost a month's wages. In all, some 40,000 dancers perform before 29,000 tourists who come from all over the world, giving Carnival one of the highest participant/spectator ratios of any major cultural event. The parade begins in the evening and continues until midmorning.

Carnival is the only occasion for the poor to come down off the hills and in from the outlying suburbs to take center stage in the cultural life of the city. For those exceptionally talented singers and dancers who earn starring roles in the presentations, Carnival represents a chance to make a reputation and escape from poverty, or at least to enjoy special status within their communities. Established celebrities, including soccer players, join their favorite samba schools lending the weight of their stardom to help them win. All Brazilians, children included, dance the samba. The thousand blocos have their neighborhood parties on the street, while elite clubs hold private parties. Nationally distributed magazines devote a full issue to photographs of the parade and the festivities in the most chic clubs of Rio, so that Brazilians everywhere can enjoy the costumes of the *favelados* and the debauchery of the international jet set.

All year long samba music is ever-present on the streets and beaches, emanating from cheap transistor radios and makeshift bands. Dozens of percussion instruments are used in Brazil, such as chimes, triangles, and the *berimbau* made from tautly drawn catgut. But Brazilians also produce samba rhythms by tapping a glass with a spoon, shaking a half-full matchbox, pounding on an overturned metal ash can, or scraping keys across a crinkled surface. Favorite singers and musicians enjoy a celebrity rivaled only by that of soccer stars. Brazilian composers take their music seriously and submit it to public competitions for awards, prizes, and recognition. Thousands of songwriters try their tunes in an abundance of local, national, and international song festivals. Brazilians await the outcome of these contests as they do that of a soccer championship. Winners are guaranteed commercial success; lyrics are memorized by the multitude, radio stations give them substantial air time, and the songs become inescapable. Unlike the divisions between enthusiasts of blues, jazz, folk, country, rock, and classical music in the United States, Brazilians are unified in their regard for the samba, whatever else their musical tastes.

Athletic victories are especially good sources of international recognition and national pride because sports command the largest audience for popular culture events. Maria Bueno symbolized Brazil's greatness when she won at Forest Hills in 1959 and Wimbledon in 1960, and Emerson Fittipaldi did the same with his many championships in auto racing in the early 1970s. Yet heroes in individual sports rise and fade. It is through team sports, with their highly organized structure that precedes and outlives any particular set of athletes, that more than momentary unification of a nation is established.

The National Organization of Soccer

Sport promoted national integration in Brazil long before other social organizations crisscrossed the nation. It was not until the dictatorial regime of Getúlio Vargas, between 1930 and 1945, that a federal bureaucracy burgeoned and labor unions were formed. Even today these and other national organizations are weak by U.S. standards.

In Brazil only 15 percent of all workers belong to trade unions, political parties have been stifled, local business predominates over national corporations, and network television is still in its adolescence.[14] In contrast, the nation was unified by a federation of sport clubs by 1914. Today there are 5,024 registered soccer clubs involved in formal competition, more than 400 of which play in professional leagues.

The soccer club as a Brazilian institution dates from the end of the nineteenth century. Clubs proliferated so fast that leagues were founded in 1901 in São Paulo and 1905 in Rio, and by 1915 five more provincial leagues had been started in the North (Pernambuco and Bahia), the Middle States (Minas Gerais) and the extreme South (Paraná and Rio Grande do Sul). The club network soon encompassed the farthest reaches of Brazil. The first club in the Amazon, in Manaus, was founded by the British operators of the world's largest rubber plantations, and the last frontier was invaded when, in 1919, a soccer club was formed in the state of Acre in the remote northwestern region.[15]

In 1941 the club network was linked to the federal government as part of President Vargas's centralization program. A decree was passed creating a National Sport Council (CND) within the Ministry of Education and Culture, with the explicit directive to "orient, finance, and encourage the practice of sport in all of Brazil."[16] The National Sport Council has overseen Brazilian sport through several organizations including the Brazilian Olympic Committee, the Armed Forces Sport Commission, the University Sports Commission, and the Confederation of Brazilian Sports (CBD).

Although the CBD falls under the formal purview of the government agency, the reality is that the sportsmen democratically run their own show from the club level on up, with little interference from the CND. The CBD is a private agency run by elected representatives who self-regulate their sporting concerns. The CBD has not only controlled both professional and amateur soccer, but has used revenue produced by professional soccer to support most other sports at the amateur level.[17] Funds for the entire complex CBD operation come primarily from its 5 percent share of the gate at all interstate and international soccer matches.

Professional soccer clubs the world over (except in the United States) are organized as nonprofit institutions. Brazil's soccer clubs are publicly "owned." Fans can buy a "share" or "title" of club stock for between $500 and $1,500. Unlike corporate stockholders, these shareholders never receive dividends, but the titles can be sold, with a transfer fee, or passed on to heirs. That the latter is most often the case speaks for the emotional as well as monetary value of these slips of paper. Shareholders are entitled to vote in club elections and run for club office. Fans who can afford it, then, can purchase a voice in how their club is run. The greater the number of shares an individual or faction holds, the more votes are controlled. Insiders often lament internal politicking, referring to these bloc votes.

Volunteer directors are the backbone of the clubs. Typically, the dozen or so directors are elected by the one hundred councilmen who themselves were elected by all the shareholders of a club. These elections are often hotly contested by distinct factions with competing views on club management. To qualify as a club director, a man must be a shareholder, sometimes needing between ten and fifty shares. Additionally, making large donations to club coffers helps men get elected. As is the case in other countries, Brazilian directors are mostly middle-aged self-made businessmen who can afford to donate their time and money to the clubs they love. Directors say they run for office because serving one's club is a great honor; some see their position as "public service, just like carrying the flag."[18]

But there are also self-serving reasons that motivate directors to offer their time and money. If we think of a soccer club directorship as a second job, albeit unpaid, then we can generalize from the very common pattern of multiple job holding in Latin America. In a discussion of Brazilian careers, anthropologist Anthony Leeds tells how powerful Brazilian men hold several positions simultaneously because each one may serve as springboard for a more important one and therefore be useful in empire building.[19] Alliances with others in key social, political, and economic positions are essential. To foster such alliances the media constantly emit cues that convey information on a man's career and connections. Reciprocity between careerists and reporters is common.

Directors can easily use their soccer club positions to personal advantage. Sport gets daily coverage in the newspapers, and clubs come equipped with a stable of reporters through whom directors can gain notoriety and project their names. Because soccer is so visible in Brazilian society, directors are valued members of alliances, along with men representing the military, banking, the legal system, and government. This linking of oligarchies facilitates the operation of soccer clubs—for example, when loans are needed, building permits are to be expedited, or zoning regulations require change.

According to Leeds the object is to create a name, promote one's career, and project oneself into ever-larger spheres, ideally moving from local to state to the national scene. Soccer's organization provides the perfect trampoline. Some men rise through the ranks of their clubs, first as councilmen, then as directors, to become elected representatives to the affluent and powerful state soccer federations. Funded by 10 percent of the gate from all intrastate games, these federations prepare schedules, tabulate match results, appoint referees and linesmen and oversee their reports, register players and check their transfer documents, and serve a public relations function for press, radio, and television.

The personal advantage to representatives—who, like directors, donate their time—is the opportunity to join alliances with wealthy and influential men at the state or federal level. At the societal level, having formal networks that connect the diversified regions benefits Brazil. The informal alliances among commercial and industrial leaders, the media, and the military, banking, and government elites are also advantageous. Once united, whether for soccer or otherwise, a diversified group of the socially prominent can affect or promote other political and economic action.

An examination of the structure of the CBD further demonstrates the democratic character of Brazil's largest sporting institution. The CBD is divided into sectors to carry out its responsibilities. State representatives sit in the General Assembly of the CBD, which passes the sport rules (e.g., governing player transfers) and policies (e.g., approving Brazilian participation in international competitions) for the whole country. It also elects a president who selects his Directory to preside over the various departments of the confederation for a three-year term.[20] The directors then appoint a Technical Committee that includes a coach and training staff who select and prepare the Brazilian National Team; should the Directory be unhappy with the team's performance, it can dissolve the Technical Committee at will.

Independent of both the Directory and the General Assembly is a judicial department that interprets rules and metes out punishment for infractions. The Superior Court of Sport Justice is made up of distinguished lawyers and judges who serve, also as volunteers, concurrent with the term of the Directory. Although appointed by the General Assembly, the judges are independent and cannot be dismissed for any reason. Local and state federations have their own tribunals, and the federal court serves an appellate function as well as having jurisdiction over interstate and international sporting matters.

The Brazilian sport system, like others in Europe and Latin America, is democratic in the sense that elected representatives from the local clubs and leagues are voting members of the controlling bodies. The General Assembly (the legislature), the Directory (the executors), and the Court of Sport Justice (the judiciary) act as checks and balances to prevent the arbitrary use of power. This system boldly contrasts with the office of the commissioner in each of America's professional sports. American commissioners, although appointed and paid by the club owners, have a great deal of autonomy of action during their term (a commissioner can be ousted only if extreme abuse of power is demonstrated) and are mandated to place the good of the sport above any single interest. Ironically, a country proud of its democratic institutions allows what amounts to dictatorial control over sports, while numerous authoritarian regimes, like Brazil's military government, coexist with democracy in sport.

Sport and Politics

Sport and government more than coexist; their relationship is better described as symbiotic. In Brazil, politicians have spurred the growth of both spectator and participant sport; sport, in return, has helped politicians court popularity and has helped the Brazilian government achieve its nationalistic goals.

Brazil's modern history is one of social and economic change through authoritarian centralization. In 1930 Getúlio Vargas seized power when the Great Depression disrupted the world coffee market. Dramatically symbolizing the demise of the regional patriarchs, Vargas had the traditional state flags publicly burned. His administration's goals intertwined political unification, industrialization, economic nationalism, and social welfarism.[21]

During his reign Vargas helped create the modern steel and petroleum industries that laid a foundation for further industrial growth. He formed labor syndicates but kept them under strict federal control, excluding workers from any real government participation.[22] Nevertheless, Vargas's paternalistic labor legislation (e.g., minimum wages, eight-hour workdays, and child labor laws) brought him enormous popularity. Free elections were reinstated in 1945 after Brazil's fight against fascism in Europe embarrassed the leadership at home. Vargas endorsed his war minister, General Dutra, as his candidate. Five years later Vargas himself was elected president as the workers' candidate, but uncontrolled inflation and corruption disgraced his administration and led him to suicide in 1954.

After other civilian presidents failed to reduce the runaway inflation and mounting worker discontent, fears of communism led the military to stage a coup d'état in 1964. The junta immediately dissolved Congress and the political parties, annulled state elections, imposed press censorship, and suspended civil liberties. Its first president, General Castelo Branco, promised a swift return to electoral democracy, but the military regime was still in power as of early 1982.

To combat inflation, the generals instituted a program of economic austerity, including restrictions on credit and imports and a continuing currency devaluation. The government continued to welcome foreign investments and made its own investments in infrastructure and heavy-industry projects. Returns were immediate. Between 1968 and 1974 Brazil's economy grew at an average rate above 10 percent. That period of sustained growth, unequaled elsewhere, has been called the "Brazilian miracle." Though Brazil still supplies over 40 percent of the world's coffee, its economy has grown increasingly diverse and independent, with manufactures accounting for one-third of the country's exports.[23]

Although the military took full credit for the "Brazilian miracle," the program of economic nationalism and foreign investment started with Vargas and was stepped up by the civilian presidents who followed. The state runs the biggest steel and iron ore companies, as well as having oil, electricity, telecommunications, railway, shipping, and aircraft monopolies. The state-run Bank of Brazil, holding a quarter of all deposits in the nation, can direct the path of private enterprise through its loan policy. Brazil differs from the socialist nations in its combination of public and private enterprise, with much of the latter based on foreign capital.

But the growth enjoyed between 1968 and 1974 would have been impossible without the austerity measures backed by an authoritarian government. The military cut real wages and introduced forced saving to keep credit plentiful for industrial investment. In the decade from 1960 to 1970 the concentration of wealth in the hands of a few increased, though a general improvement in the standard of living and new opportunities for jobs in the expanding industrial sector camouflaged it.[24]

Brazil's development slowed considerably after the sharp rise in OPEC oil prices in 1974 led to an overwhelming balance-of-trade deficit and mounting foreign debt (now roughly $57 billion). The regime, then under General Ernesto Geisel, tried to minimize dissension by easing the authoritarian rule. But inflation grew worse. With yearly inflation now at 110 percent, protests from every social class have forced President João Baptista Figueiredo to step up political liberalization. Media censorship has been lifted, rights to the disfranchised have been restored, and congressional elections have been reinstated. The regime says it is now trying to deal with rising popular discontent (and simultaneously stimulate internal demand for goods) by efforts to redistribute wealth through progressive wage increases and new social welfare spending, but some economists say that the concentration of wealth at the top is increasing.[25] Evidence that the government still imposes limits on workers' rights is the recent sentencing of labor leader Luis Ignácio da Silva to three and a half years in prison.

Unofficial government policy seems to include the notion that soccer can be used to distract workers from their serious grievances. Wages lag hopelessly behind runaway inflation. In the absence of collective bargaining, the government's annual revision of the minimum wage is the most important factor affecting Brazilian pay scales. Each year on Labor Day, 1 May, a spokesman for the Labor Ministry addresses the nation to thank the workers for their contribution to the economic development of the country, to request that they continue to sacrifice for Brazil, and to announce the minimum wage increase. In 1973, while I was conducting worker interviews for this study, the labor minister announced a 16 percent increase making the monthly minimum wage a woefully inadequate $51.23.[26] To sweeten the pill, the Labor Ministry's Rio office gave away 15,000 free tickets to Maracanã Stadium for the big holiday game between Flamengo and Fluminense—ironically, the team of the masses against the team of the elite.[27]

The government has also turned its hand to ensuring that the poor will not be barred from soccer games by regulating maximum ticket prices for "popular" admissions in public stadia. In 1973, for local games Maracanã prices were 35¢ for standing room on the concrete tiers and $1.75 for the huge upper-deck bleachers area. Prices for reserved seats for the middle and upper classes are not controlled and can be more in line with the inflationary spiral.

The symbiosis between soccer and government predates Brazil's military regime. The power of alliances enjoyed by soccer's elite was shown in the ease with which club directorships could be used as stepping-stones into political careers, and vice versa. For example, Dr. Laudo Natel left the presidency of the São Paulo Football Club for the governor's mansion, and Sr. João Falcão simultaneously served as a state deputy and president of the São Paulo Football Federation.

These overlapping roles are still apparent. At the time of Brazil's preparation for the 1978 World Cup in Argentina, the president of the CBD, Admiral Heleno Nunes, was also presiding over ARENA (the official government party) in the state of Rio. The *Latin American Political Report* said this of Nunes's two hats:

> Though the party has relieved him from his political duties to enable him to concentrate on a victory in Argentina, it is impossible to separate the politician from the sportsman. He recently commented that "a win in Argentina will be very important for ARENA" and he has influenced the selection of the team. Coutinho had to include Vasco da Gama's center forward, Roberto, in the team pool at Nunes' behest. Even ARENA politicians conceded that Roberto's inclusion was dictated by the need to cull votes in Rio de Janeiro, where Vasco da Gama is the strongest team. . . . Nunes converted all the World Cup preliminary matches into political rallies with lineups of prospective candidates, ARENA banners and military bands.[28]

Brazilian politicians have long believed that soccer-related projects win them more popularity than important public works that require long-range planning and appeal to a more future-oriented constituency than they feel they have. Carlos Lacerda, while governor, retained the favor of his Rio constituents by filling in part of the bay to construct Flamengo Park, one of the city's few public athletic facilities. As governor of Minas Gerais, Magalhães Pinto won votes as well as immortality by building the 100,000-person Magalhães Pinto Stadium in Belo Horizonte.

Donations and favors to clubs could be used to garner popular support at any level, local to national. President Dutra gave a prime piece of property in downtown Rio to Flamengo, the club with mass appeal. A few years later, in the early 1950's President Vargas gave the club a huge, low-interest government loan so it could construct there a twenty-four-story building with a spectacular bay view. The club uses four floors for its administration and receives high rents from offices on the other twenty floors. Such wealth gives a club real competitive advantage. Political motives for such generosity are obvious; however, there are those who believe that Dutra was a true Flamengo fan who used his powerful position to help his beloved club grow and prosper.

Outright gifts from politicians to individual clubs are now forbidden, but merely stating that one is a faithful (fill in the name of the most popular team) devotee is still worth votes even in large modern cities like Belo Horizonte and Pôrto Alegre. (It helps to wear the club shirt during the speech.) Soccer sentiments, like the primordial sentiments they are based on, are easy to exploit politically because people are conscious of them and find them meaningful.

Even the military leaders who are not dependent on votes have benefited from their publicized devotion to Brazil's popular teams. Emilio Garrastazu Médici, whose term lasted from 1969 to 1973, was renowned as a fanatic fan of Flamengo and a patriotic supporter of the national team. His frequent appearance at Maracanã Stadium, without bodyguards, to watch his Flamengo team delighted millions. Médici's interest in Brazilian athletes extended beyond soccer. He claims never to have missed a minute of any televised auto race in which Emerson Fittipaldi was an entrant, and he sent telegrams or telephoned his congratulations in the event of a victory.[29]

Médici used his political clout to influence his favorite team as much as he used his favorite team to strengthen his political clout. He took advantage of his powerful position to interfere with the technical side of sport in ways not available to the average fan. Médici strongly encouraged the Flamengo directors to trade for Dario, his favorite player. Then, when Dario did not do well on his new team, the president arranged another audience with the Flamengo directory to request that they move Paulo Cesar to play "left point" to give more aggressive power to the front-line attack.

The association between soccer and political figures is important enough that politicians may claim to be fans even when they are not. The best illustration of this tactic was seen on the day the government released the name of Médici's "pre-elected" successor. The man chosen for the job was not well known to the Brazilian people. His photograph covered two-thirds of the *Jornal do Brasil* front page on 19 June 1973. The bold print under the photograph states, in order of importance, relevant characteristics about the man: "Gaúcho [meaning from the state of Rio Grande do Sul] from Bento Gonçalves [his hometown] 64 years old, fan of International in Pôrto Alegre and Botafogo in Rio, brother of two generals, married, with one daughter, Ernesto Geisel will be the 23rd president of the Republic." Introverted and intellectual, Geisel is not a soccer fan—a fact known in press and military circles. But not to cheer a team would set Geisel apart from other Brazilians. Identifying himself with a popular club was a simple way to state "I am of the people."

The symbiosis between sport and politics is perhaps best illustrated by the national sport lottery. The Loteria Esportiva (LE) was created in 1969 by the Department of Finance to produce much-needed revenue for government programs. Brazil's lottery is modeled after European sport lotteries. Federal governments around the world are cashing in on the enthusiasm for gambling, and sporting authorities appreciate the excitement betting adds to the games. Most sport lotteries are based on league soccer, but special ones are constructed for events like the Olympics, the Pan-American Games, and the World Cup. INTERTOTO, an agency headquartered in Switzerland, facilitates the exchange of information between lottery operators. The condition for membership is that public companies run the lottery and distribute net profits to social, cultural, or sport projects. In absolute money collected, Brazil's soccer lottery is the most successful of those in the twenty-three INTERTOTO countries: in 1977 it took in more than $367 million.

The basic model is the same in all countries where soccer pools are run. The bettors forecast a win, draw, or loss for each team included in the pool. The formula in Brazil is typical of many: thirteen games are listed, and the winner must select all thirteen outcomes correctly; the 31.5 percent of the gross returned to the winners is divided among the winners for that week. The world's single largest lottery prize to date went to a Brazilian backwoodsman from the state of Bahia who was the sole winner one week and turned in his ticket for more than $2 million in cash. At the other extreme, there was a week in which eleven of the thirteen games had logical outcomes, and 42,525 persons held winning tickets, leading an INTERTOTO official to marvel at how well the Brazilian man on the street knows his soccer.

After paying administrative costs and brokers' commissions, the Brazilian government's profits are split between the Department of Social Security (to support the aged, handicapped, and orphaned and the adult literacy and hygiene programs) and the Department of Education and Culture (for public parks, swimming pools, basketball courts, and other athletic facilities). As revenues soar, some profits can be set aside for other cultural projects, as is the case elsewhere. The German lottery subsidizes orchestras, art collections, and the restoration of monuments. Since the lottery began in Norway, $100 million of lottery profits has been spent on sport facilities, while $500 million has gone to support scientific research. In general, from 20 percent to 50 percent of a government's net lottery profit goes to amateur sport—either through direct subsidies to clubs to develop facilities and pay instructors or through public construction of stadia, swimming pools, basketball and handball courts, and bicycle velodromes.[31]

In addition to producing revenue, Brazil's sport lottery is instrumental in educating the citizenry and in bringing together the disparate regions into a single unified culture. The LE is now established in the largest 1,054 of 3,970 municipalities in Brazil, meaning that all municipalities with populations greater than 5,000 participate in the national lottery system.[32] Strict policy dictates that the games must represent *all* regions of the country, even though the best soccer is played in the southern states. Many of the semi-literate people in the Northeast cannot name the states or major cities of the South, and vice versa. Brazilian lottery players learn about their country while trying to amass their fortune. Seventy million blank lottery flyers are distributed weekly with the names of all the teams and their home states. Those who read newspaper summaries of the teams' recent performances before placing their bets get additional exposure to names and places.

Furthermore, the LE has been a source of pride because Brazil developed new betting machines that were so successful that Chile, Argentina, Paraguay, Peru, and Mexico purchased large numbers of them to operate their lottery systems, thus reflecting Brazil's cultural leadership in the Latin American community. When Brazil introduced the LE it could not just borrow a European system but had to develop an operation suited to Brazil's special needs. Initially, the Caixa Económica Federal (CEF is part of the Department of Finance) used electronic key-punch cards (familiarizing people with electronics), but it soon developed machinery that was efficient and could be operated manually in the many municipalities that have little or no electricity. The administration and brokerage of the LE and the betting machine industry created more than 20,000 jobs in Brazil.

The promotion of the sport lottery led to a direct change in the structure of Brazilian soccer. The government urged the CBD to establish a national championship so there would be lottery games all year long. In return for extending the soccer season from forty to eighty-five games, the Ministry of Education and Culture offered money to the CBD. Lottery money is used to subsidize the costly air transportation needed for teams to participate in a national championship and for the exorbitant expenses connected with preparing a World Cup team.

Other soccer-playing nations have long had national championships. Football associations in European countries were formed to oversee their national league competitions. But in Brazil, where transportation between distant cities was poor, a national competition between interstate clubs was impossible. Instead, from 1923 to 1963 there was a Brazilian championship between state selections. State all-star teams would be formed after the season to play a short series of special games. With all the wealth concentrated in Rio and São Paulo, their rich and powerful teams were defeated only once in the forty-year history of the competition. In 1950 the first major interstate club competition was formalized in the Rio-São Paulo Tournament, and its winner was considered the best club in the country. In 1967 this tournament was expanded to include clubs from three other southern states.

Advances in sport and technology go hand in hand. By 1970, air travel made it possible for the CBD to begin a real national championship, occupying the second half of the year. Initially this tournament included only seven states and a total of seventeen clubs. Each year the CBD ruled more teams eligible, and by 1978 the championship included clubs from all twenty-two states. Rio and São Paulo no longer monopolized the game, and the championship has been won three times by clubs from other states.

The president of the CBD stands accused of putting political interests ahead of the good of the game. Detractors among the soccer establishment and fans are worried that the national championship is lowering the quality of soccer in Brazil. The soccer season now extends to forty-nine weeks of the year. The Santos Club, for example, finished its last game of this year's state championship on a Wednesday and began its first national championship game the following Sunday. There is no off-season to rest, and the extensive travel exhausts the players. The travel burden falls disproportionately on the best teams because they draw huge crowds in the provinces. Even though their low-caliber teams deliver no spectacle, many of the provincial state leagues have been included for purposes of national integration and political support.

As was the case with the lottery, the military leaders hoped that the by-product of a national championship would be the greater unity of Brazil. Sport's paradoxical mission was to take advantage of the traditional regional rivalries to bring about a sense of a uniform culture, with soccer its "principal art form."[33] Exposing southern fans to teams from other states would serve the didactic purpose of familiarizing them with representatives from the vast reaches of Brazil. Fans from faraway provincial states now could actually see the great teams of Rio and São Paulo and take pride in their common citizenship.

The lottery and national championship no doubt furthered the government's goal of a unified Brazil, but nothing did more to arouse nationalistic fervor than Brazil's three World Cup wins, culminating in the tri-championship in 1970. And the military government took steps to share the spoils of victory.

It is likely that President Médici was behind the removal of João Saldanha as coach of the 1970 World Cup team. Although he had coached the Botafogo team for a while, Saldanha is best known as a sports analyst, and people were surprised when he was selected by the Technical Commission to pick and train the Brazilian Selection for the 1970 Cup. He got the team through the elimination rounds and qualified to play in the Mexico finals, but Saldanha was dismissed by the commission before the finals began. Some blamed Saldanha's short temper and fisticuffs; others said it had more to do with his uneasy relationship with Pelé. There is some truth in both explanations, but another reported account is more telling.

João Saldanha was an outspoken communist sympathizer in his youth, and that background hardly endeared him to the right-wing militarists who controlled the government. After Saldanha's appointment in 1969, President Médici invited the newly selected team for lunch in the palace, but Saldanha would not change his training schedule to permit them to go. Later in Pôrto Alegre an

Argentine reporter asked Saldanha why the player Dario was not in the first string. Saldanha replied that he already had Roberto and Tostão, who in his opinion were better. The reporter reminded him that Dario was Médici's favorite player. Saldanha laughed and said, "I don't choose the president's ministry, and he can't choose my front line." He was replaced shortly thereafter by Mario Zagalo. Claudio Coutinho, a retired army captain who had been a military physical training expert, was appointed to assist Zagalo.

The Brazilian government consciously exploited the tri-championship to link political with cultural nationalism. Right after the victory, Médici addressed the nation:

> I feel profound happiness at seeing the joy of our people in this highest form of patriotism. I identify this victory won in the brotherhood of good sportsmanship with the rise of faith in our fight for national development. I identify the success of our [national team] with . . . intelligence and bravery, perseverence and serenity in our technical ability, in physical preparation and moral being. Above all, our players won because they knew how to . . . play for the collective good.[34]

Returning from the Mexican World Cup, the team's first stop was Brasília, where the players received a presidential welcome from the proud Médici. The government declared the day of the team's return a national holiday so everyone could take to the streets in a mass celebration. In a generous mood Médici astounded the nation by opening the doors of the presidential palace to the people. Those doors had been closed since the coup d'état of 1964 and have not been opened again since that day in June of 1970 when the team returned; political observers called this the "miracle of soccer." At his lunch for the team, Médici bestowed on each player tax-free $18,500 bonuses from the government and the CBD. Photographs of the president holding the newly acquired trophy, surrounded by the national team, were published in newspapers and magazines circulated throughout Brazil.

After lunch the team flew to Rio de Janeiro, where they were greeted by close to two million ecstatic people waiting in the rain. The secretary of tourism coordinated a special Carnival parade of samba schools. Pelé, after describing the celebration of Brazil's first Cup victory in 1958, said the scene they found in 1970 was the same:

There was pure carnival in the streets: traffic diverted, the avenue jammed with people, shouting, singing, dancing, drinking, clogging any artery of traffic and not being particularly bothered by the honking horns nor the edging bumpers. There were regular carnival bands and many irregular ones; there was shouting, screaming, laughing; there were fireworks—it was a madhouse.[35]

Forty-four persons were killed and 1,800 injured during the two-day melee. Government leaders might have thought the casualties were a small price to pay for the strengthened allegiance of a whole nation. The major clubs from the major cities had contributed players to the winning team. Animosities were suspended for a time of alliance. In a vast land where communication is problematic, the team's contribution to national unity was of great value. Even illiterate peasants in the remote interior, listening to the games on their transistor radios, knew Brazil had earned the respect and admiration of the whole world. More important, the 1970 World Cup was the occasion to lease space from orbiting satellites that provided the first telecommunications link between northern and southern Brazil.[36]

After the initial celebration ended, President Médici continued to exploit the soccer triumph. Miguel Gustavo's marching tune "Pra Frente Brasil" ("Forward, Brazil"), written to inspire the World Cup team, became the theme song of the regime, played by army bands at all official occasions, and was aired on radio and television. Another government-inspired tune, "Marcha do Tostão" (Tostão was one of the 1970 Cup stars) begins with a breathless commentary from a World Cup match that rises to a prolonged howl of "GOOOAL" as Brazil scores and erupts into a "samba of victory to savour again the joys of Mexico."[37] The regime juxtaposed its nationalistic slogan "ninguém segura mais o Brasil" ("no one will hold Brazil back now") with a picture of Pelé in midair after a goal and plastered the new poster on billboards across the country. The tri-championship was to be taken as merely the first step toward realizing Brazil's manifest destiny. Popular polls showed near unanimity in the sentiment that it was soccer, not coffee or samba, that put Brazil on the modern map.[38]

Sport in the Metropolis: Rio de Janeiro

Brazilian cities, like American "melting pots," are filled with strangers who are very different from one another. Until World War II newcomers were mostly immigrants who introduced foreign cultures. Since the war, newcomers have arrived from other parts of Brazil, introducing regional variations too. Those who were born in the city have had to make room for others with strange ways. Nearly 40 percent of Rio's current population consists of internal migrants.[1] No formal institutions were set up to help these strangers adapt to city life. Many were aided by extended family or acquaintances who had come to the city ahead of them. Others sought help from the church, local charities, or their employers, if they were lucky enough to find work.[2] Soccer clubs have received little attention, but they were also important in helping newcomers adjust to city life.

The sheer number of people and the speed of unplanned urban growth put severe strains on the cities' infrastructure and on the psyches of their residents. In 1940, 69 percent of all Brazilians lived in the countryside and 31 percent in the cities; that ratio has now been reversed.[3] Brazil's two largest metropolises—São Paulo with 8 million people and Rio with 5 million—are models for mass society concerns and ideal places to explore how organized sport can help hold a metropolis together.

While allowing public expression of their diverse loyalties, fans' club affiliations also affirm their common belonging to the greater metropolis. Newspapers, radio, television, films, and now the sport lottery play a critical role in circulating shared images and information on local heroes and team standings. Insofar as soccer contests constitute main events in city life, residents who know about them feel like full participants. People need something to talk about, and soccer provides one of those common interests.

The Soccer Clubs

A popular saying in Brazil is that every town, regardless of size, has at least one church and one soccer field—"well, not always a church, but certainly a soccer field." The foundation of sport in Brazil, at both the amateur and the professional levels, is the private soccer club. In fact, towns and cities most typically have several soccer clubs. Baurú, a town in the interior of the state of São Paulo, had a population of 80,000 and two professional soccer clubs when Pelé was growing up there. Rio, with a population of 5 million, supports twelve professional soccer clubs. Four clubs field world-class teams (Flamengo, Fluminense, Botafogo, and Vasco da Gama), and the others range from clubs that rank respectably in the national competition to small community-based clubs restricted to the local championship.

Dividing a city's loyalties among so many clubs makes any single club less of a financial success than it would be if it enjoyed a territorial monopoly, as happens in the United States. Yet the multiclub pattern is the norm in the soccer world.[4] Brazilians, like Europeans and other Latins, protect the long-established rivalries between the big clubs and also the survival of the small clubs.

Professional soccer clubs, organized as nonprofit institutions, put their revenues back into the professional teams, the apprentice teams, and any amateur soccer teams that wear the club uniform. Given the near absence of athletic facilities in Brazilian schools, soccer clubs are important as the principal organizers of numerous other amateur sports.[5] Money from professional soccer is also used to train children, adolescents, and adult athletes for amateur competition in sports like rowing, basketball, volleyball, swimming and diving, and tennis. Collectively the soccer clubs serve as benefactors to thousands of talented children and teenagers who receive professional coaching and conditioning, medical attention, and sometimes housing and money for school.

Girls and women are very much involved in the clubs' organized team sport programs. In fact, Brazilian women's teams are recognized as among the world's best in volleyball and basketball. But girls are excluded from playing soccer. Boys are taught to kick a ball when they are about two; by age six they are already involved in pick-up games. (In Brazil, soccer balls come in several sizes to suit the growing child.) Girls are *never* involved in these games. Brazilians believe that their national passion is a man's game requiring masculine endurance and involving violent contact. The females I talked with took their exclusion for granted; my inquiries about their lack of interest were greeted with quizzical expressions or laughter.

Several people told me that it was against CBD regulations—some even said federal law—to organize girls' soccer. When I inquired in 1973, the CBD official laughed and said no such law is necessary, since girls playing soccer is unthinkable.[6] But in the late 1970s some women began to organize their own teams, so in March 1981 the federal government did pass a law forbidding sponsorship of female soccer teams and the use of athletic grounds for their competitions.[7]

Soccer clubs in Latin America, unlike most in Europe, are organized as social membership clubs.[8] Membership is open to fans as well as neighbors. Many members, however, rarely use club grounds but retain their memberships for occasions like victory dances or for the sheer pleasure of knowing they belong. Members are entitled to use the athletic complex, view the team's training sessions, and attend social gatherings. Most clubs accept as many applications as they receive, both for financial support of club facilities and for moral support of the team.

Clubs may offer dinners, dances, theater, movies, fashion shows, and picnics to family members. Women and girls are very active in the club's yoga lessons, bridge tournaments, and other recreational and social events. The number and type of sponsored events vary with the membership, the wealth of the club, and the team's success—winning means greater gate profits and more festive moods. But even modest clubs pride themselves on offering at least one gala festivity each month. After Carnival, the club often provides the *only* formally organized social event in the community that month.

Soccer clubs are low-cost and easily affordable to the growing middle class, although still out of reach for the vast lower class majority. The basic family membership costs between $15 and $50 initially, with monthly charges of $2 to $10. In theory, monthly maintenance fees will meet the expenses of the social sector; the reality is that in cities like Rio only two clubs make money on their social sectors. Clubs cannot raise membership fees to cover escalating costs without losing substantial numbers of supporters who could not afford a raise in dues. And large memberships are a source of pride. Increasingly, soccer has had to add subsidizing the physical recreation and social life of the middle class to its societal responsibility. The importance of this service is not to be underestimated. In a poor nation, only a tiny percentage of the population can afford high fees in private country clubs, and only a few large employers offer similar activities. Now that lottery revenues are paying for the construction of public athletic facilities, they will be more available to more people. Ironically, the soccer lottery will reduce people's need for the facilities of the soccer clubs.

Unlike commercial concerns that go bankrupt, soccer clubs survive deficit spending through the generosity of their directors, patrons, and fans. Wealthy fans who do not wish to donate the time required for a directorship can influence their clubs with money alone by becoming "patrons of sport." Patrons often initiate fund-raising drives, publicly present their large contributions, or offer incentive bonuses to the players for winning a particular game. Such offers may be made anonymously, but more often sportswriters announce the donor's generosity. Patrons are most important to the smaller clubs, where players' salaries are low and club incentive bonuses rarely exceed $50. A patron may offer an additional $100 a man to stimulate exceptional performance. Patrons of both large and small clubs may will a portion of their estates to their clubs, presumably so they can rest happily in the hereafter knowing they gave their clubs a competitive advantage.

When the directors decide to secure a star player, purchase a new property, construct a new facility, or simply alleviate accumulating debts, they initiate promotions such as lotteries, raffles, or membership drives. Hundreds of volunteers are needed for these projects, and the fans' contributions of time and money are noted and appreciated. But it is the directors themselves who are expected to make the first and largest donations. The late Amadeu Rodrigues Sequeira, then president of one of Brazil's largest coffee retailers, campaigned for the office of vice-president of Vasco da Gama by promising that, if elected, he would secure World Cup superstar

Tostão for the club. Tostão came at a record-high price—$520,000—
and it was Sequeira who made the first contribution, then personally
directed the fund raising for the balance.

The directors in control of the club make policy, hire key
personnel, and give personal loans or outright gifts to finance their
club in troubled times. Ultimately, the burden for fielding an unsuccessful team, trading a popular player, or hiring an unpopular
coach falls on their shoulders. They say they are willing to put up
with fans' anger and employee grievances because they love their
teams. But there are also many more pragmatic reasons directors
offer their time and money. Established businessmen, especially
those in sales, quietly admit that the public relations benefits of their
office compensate them. One Flamengo fan volunteered so much
time to his clubs that he was eventually elected a vice-president even
though he had no wealth. During his term in office he made so many
friends and contacts that his small business boomed and he accumulated a fortune. The public relations benefits come not only
through contacts made, but also from frequent media exposure,
visibility and prestige in the community, and the opportunity to
entertain business associates at matches.

Ego-enhancement rewards, like public relations benefits, are
universal. Hardaker, secretary of the English League, says, "it is a
fact that football has put a face on many faceless people."[9] One noted
observer in Brazil (who asked to remain nameless) remarked that
soccer also serves people who already have a public persona but wish
to change their image. He claims that a few directors in Rio and São
Paulo amassed their wealth through shady or illegal ventures and
bought their offices to earn respectability. But far more commonly,
directors are quite respectable nouveau riche businessmen and in-
dustrialists, and there are even a few men from high society. Special
alliances between these men at the local level, like those at the national level, can promote other cultural, political, and economic action in the metropolis.

Brazil's soccer club directors are not unlike some of America's
team owners, who, as rich and avid fans, are prepared to lose money
on the object of their passion. Sport losses would be offset by public
relations benefits for their other businesses. Beer barons like Jacob
Ruppert of the Yankees or Augie Busch of the St. Louis Cardinals
and chewing-gum magnate William Wrigley found that their intimate
ties to sport helped advertise their products as well as win community

approval. Corporate owners, increasingly becoming the norm, keep a low profile regarding their sports holdings and take advantage of neither the public relations nor the ego-enhancement rewards. Ego enhancement does still motivate individual owners like George Steinbrenner of the Yankees, who admits having wanted the celebrity status that comes with sport. He earned wealth but not recognition from his large shipping company, whereas purchasing the Yankees brought him overnight notoriety.

The principal difference between American owners and soccer directors rests on their accountability and professional orientation, not their motives. In the United States the owners' personal wealth is used to guarantee loans, and owners must apply sound business principles to team management. Because American owners are accountable, they place their clubs in the hands of real professionals and pay high salaries to men with specialized skills in sports administration and show-business promotion. In Brazil directors are less accountable. After their two-year term is over, they are free to walk away, passing on massive debts and expensive player contracts that they have signed in the club's name, not their own, to the next group of willing volunteers. Soccer commentator Armando Nogueira believes that most Brazilian directors do serve for love—personal advantages being incidental—and the very fact of the directors' passion for their clubs is also the root of the problem. They want to field a winning team at any cost. Rational and calculating in their own commercial ventures, directors decide with their hearts, not their heads, on important club business.

Rio's Intracity Rivalries

Rio de Janeiro provides a setting in which to explore the internal workings of soccer clubs and the role they play in symbolizing the real divisions within the city. Rio's twelve soccer clubs help break down the urban mass and integrate people into subgroups. Confrontations on the playing fields reflect the real-life antagonisms and jealousies between fan groups. In Rio, as in other Brazilian cities, the strongest rivalry is between social classes.

Rio's team of the masses in Flamengo; its symbol is a black vulture. Loyalties fluctuate according to team standings, but roughly one-third of Rio's population pledges allegiance to Flamengo, far more than to any other team.[10] It is said that more Umbanda rites are seen before Flamengo games than are performed for any other team. Flamengo is the most famous club in Brazil; requests for Flamengo shirts come from as far away as the Indian regions of the Amazon. Often migrants adopt Flamengo as their team when they arrive in Rio, because they have heard of it back home, thereby further swelling its huge following among the urban poor.

Flamengo has 65,000 card-carrying members (exceeded only by Corinthians in São Paulo with 150,000), but its fans number in the millions. They are despised by rival fans for their overwhelming numbers and boastfulness after victory and for the fervor with which they try to recruit new fans. However, they are also respected for their fidelity to the team and for their feeling of brotherhood toward other fans. Sayings like "when you meet a Flamengo, you meet a friend" attest to their communal spirit. Flamengo fans I spoke with claimed that, when they must choose, they prefer to do business with someone who cheers for Flamengo. I saw a beach vendor offer a discount to those who could show they were fans of Flamengo on the morning of a big game, although I presumed he was motivated more by commercial instincts than by sentiments of brotherhood. There is a folklore that people believe, like the story of a rich man's being robbed of all his possessions: finding a Flamengo membership card in the man's wallet, the robber, also Flamengo, returned everything.

Flamengo's greatest foe, Fluminense, thought of as the team of the elite, has the second-largest following in the city. The team's nickname is "white powder," referring to the powder used to lighten the faces of the aristocracy of an earlier era. Although both teams draw players from the lower class, Flamengo players are expected to act rough and crude; a more gentlemanly code is imposed on Fluminense players because of the heritage they represent.

Fluminense's social pretensions are best reflected by the fact that it is one of the few soccer clubs in the country that restricts its social membership. More like an exclusive country club than a soccer club, Fluminense rigorously screens applicants. The club's list of ineligibles includes criminals, persons with contagious diseases, and the handicapped, except those who were maimed while fighting for their country or while in the service of the Fluminense Club. Fluminense is so restrictive that its own players, although worshiped on the field, are treated as "employees" and are prohibited from attending most of its social activities.

Considered one of the most elaborate soccer membership clubs in the world, Fluminense is one of the two Rio clubs to profit from its social sector. White stucco buildings roofed with red tile, surrounded by lush gardens, form a compound in one of the central districts of the city. Fluminense has its own stadium that holds 25,000 people, massive gymnasium, tennis courts that accommodate more than 2,000 spectators, three swimming pools, steam baths, rifle range, and beautiful club buildings that house the administrative offices, library, trophy galleries, bar, restaurant, and ballroom.

Vasco de Gama represents the city's huge community of Portuguese immigrants and their Brazilian-born descendents. The team was well known in Portugal, so immigrants joined upon arrival. The club's ready-made community eased their entry by providing contacts for those who came alone and a place to socialize for those with extended family and friends already in Rio. Vasco is now one of Brazil's richest soccer clubs. The $20 million the club claims in assets has come mostly as gifts, in the form of city properties, from wealthy members of the Portuguese community. It has more than 2,000 "owner members" (*proprietários*) holding titles worth $2,500 each.

Vasco has 60,000 general members and the third largest following in Rio. It has fielded so many great winning teams that even those not of Portuguese descent have declared themselves Vasco fans. The Carnival celebration at Vasco's club grounds attracted 150,000 members and friends. Every Saturday night 5,000 teenagers come for their "Hi-Fi" dances. More than 2,000 watch players train before a Flamengo vs. Vasco match. In addition to the professional players, approximately 700 amateur athletes wear the Vasco da Gama uniform.

The Botafogo Club was started by college students in the affluent Botafogo district of Rio and attracted wealthy and politically powerful patrons who built a strong club based on modern management techniques. Botafogo has retained its appeal to the young, the urbane, the politicos, and the nouveau riche. Botafogo has supplied more than its share of World Cup players, so it attracts young fans from all over Brazil who attach themselves to the national heroes they see on television. Large clubs like Vasco, Flamengo, Fluminense, and Botafogo each have about 250 employees who care for the grounds, arrange the festivities, service the teams, and do the necessary clerical and bookkeeping work for the professional soccer, amateur sport, and social membership sectors.

The Botafogo organization illustrates the complexity of the soccer clubs. There is a division not only between amateur and professional sport, but also between land sports and water sports. Botafogo's aquatic division even features a yacht club in addition to swimming, diving, water ballet, water polo, and regattas. Soccer revenues are important to other sports. Even winning teams are usually not self-supporting. For example, only 4,000 people paid the $1 admission fee to watch Botafogo's men's volleyball team compete for its eighth consecutive city title.

Most of Rio's smaller clubs are named after the districts in which they are situated. Like the samba schools, these clubs are important links that hold the periphery to the central city. Since leisure alternatives are few in these communities, samba schools and soccer clubs offer the only organized social activities. They are also the only collective representation of community pride. When one of their teams beats one of the major clubs (and when such upsets occur, they often occur in the community's own small stadium), the whole district turns out for impromptu Carnival. Olaria and Bonsuccesso exemplify Rio's smaller clubs. Olaria is a middle-sized club with 18,000 members, most of whom live in the community. Over 13,000 of them own titles valued at $200 each. The club employs 80 people and sponsors 400 athletes, 78 of whom play soccer at professional and apprentice levels. Olaria offers one costly scheduled social event each month. Between 100 and 200 men show up to observe the team's daily training sessions. Bonsuccesso is a smaller club with 8,000 members, half of whom live in Bonsuccesso while half live in neighboring Leopoldina. Most members join for the facilities. Bonsuccesso offers the community a cinema, swimming pool, karate and judo lessons, ballet and yoga for women, and dances for teenagers. Having a fan following larger than its membership, Bonsuccesso's stadium fills to its 10,000-person capacity.

Because the state of Rio de Janeiro is really just the metropolitan reaches of the city, its soccer federation is made up exclusively of local teams. Elsewhere in Brazil, league championships are organized statewide. Even so, the most intense rivalries have been between the major clubs of the big cities.

Several things, in addition to the dramatization of conflict between local factions, account for the intensity of intracity rivalries. There are two battles for supremacy occurring simultaneously—one between the athletes and another between the opposing fan groups.

Picture Maracanã Stadium during a game between two major Rio clubs. A moat ten feet wide and ten feet deep surrounds the playing field so that fans cannot get at the players, the referee, or each other. There may be as many as 100,000 supporters facing 100,000 opposition fans seated across the stadium. Over the years traditional seating patterns have been established so that fan camps are concentrated, not scattered: during a Flamengo vs. Fluminense match, Fla fans sit on the right, Flu on the left; during Flamengo vs. Botafogo, Fla fans are on the left, and so forth.[11]

Other elements in the battle between the fans include visibility and loudness. Visibility is measured by the percentage of fans dressed in team colors or carrying flags. Bigger is better in Brazil. Some banners are so large that they are transported by truck and require the cooperation of an entire section of fans. To win the loudness contest, fans do not just try to outshout the other group; they bring samba bands to inspire communal singing and cheers. They also explode firecrackers and toss confetti each time their team scores a goal. Fans are drawn to the giant flags and mass of team shirts of fellow fans; these recognizable symbols focus interaction in what would otherwise be chaos.

Smaller team symbols identify both sympathizers and rivals outside the stadium. As a show of loyalty, Brazilians carry tokens of their allegiance all week long, not only on the day of the game. When I talked with men about soccer, more often than not I would be shown a key chain, lapel pin, or watchband with a club emblem.

Economic development is bringing changes that are reflected in the soccer scene, its loyalties, and its special rivalries. For example, newly affluent industrial cities like Campinas and Ribeirão Preto in São Paulo's interior are offering top salaries to players and fielding highly competitive teams, resulting in a genuine intrastate championship fight. Soccer's integration of interior cities with their capitals is becoming more effective now that the latter do not command all the power. Networks of commercial and industrial leaders who serve as directors for clubs in the boomtowns of the interior are being incorporated into statewide alliances. Of course, in sport integration comes with conflict. One dispute in Paraná's soccer federation led the interior cities to threaten to secede from the state.

Neither intrastate nor interstate games have the appeal of the traditional local rivalries that draw two sets of fans. Yet the national competition is growing in popularity. For shows of solidarity with one's city, fans of rival local teams have called momentary truces; for example, the other three major clubs sent their mascots to support Botafogo in the national finals against a São Paulo team. But Cariocas will not suspend animosity toward Flamengo. When it nears the national play-offs, fans from other Rio clubs come to the stadium to boo Flamengo and support the visiting team so they will not have to listen to Flamengo fans boast.

The lottery has changed the nature of intracity rivalries more than has the national championship. Monetary interests can supersede or conflict with old rivalries or even cause some fans to miss games they otherwise would have enjoyed. For example, the real fun for Flamengo-haters used to come whenever one of Rio's smaller teams beat the popular giant. Such upsets are rare, but they delight rival fans when they occur. Now, however, if that game is included in the week's lottery, logical bettors have to predict Flamengo to win. Some with bets on Flamengo claim they would rather read the results in the paper than listen to the game on the radio because they do not like being in the position of hoping for the victory of the "hated one."[12] Some faithful fans and staunch Flamengo-haters may decide not to play the lottery that week.

The Lottery and the Mass Media

There are aspects of the soccer scene that are remarkable for their ability to pull together the urban mass. Nothing does this as well as the sport lottery. People of all social classes and ages share the lottery games. And it is not just male soccer fans who bet. The lottery is the major exception to soccer's sexual apartheid. A Marplan survey showed that just about everybody—92 percent of Rio's adults—bets at least once a month, fully 62 percent betting weekly. Women bet nearly as often as men (90 percent of women bet at least once a month, compared with 94 percent of all men).[13] There are few occasions in modern urban life that prompt 92 percent of the population to participate in *any* single activity.

Some criticize the lottery for being a regressive income tax, insofar as rich and poor alike play the game. The Marplan survey shows that the rich are twice as likely to win as the poor because they play more often and for bigger stakes. For the minimum, a bettor gets fourteen marks, meaning he must select the winners of twelve games and can indicate win or tie for the thirteenth. For extra money ($86 is the maximum), richer bettors can purchase extra marks, meaning additional games can be marked win, lose, or draw. The more money invested, therefore, the fewer games need be predicted, so the greater the chances of winning.

But the critics are few because the huge revenues are used to promote social welfare programs and because the game is cheap to play; 58 percent of those in the lower class bet the minimum 20¢. Even the average bet of 69¢ is a small price to pay for the fun of a game and a dream kept alive by weekly reports of overnight wealth. When asked the open-ended question, "What's the easiest way to get rich quick?" 86 percent of Marplan's respondents answered the sport lottery, although the government also sponsors a numbers lottery and there is the popular illegal numbers racket, *jogo do bicho* ("animal game"). Playing soccer was always the hope of poor but talented boys trying to climb out of poverty; now, through the lottery, soccer takes the central role in a "rags to riches" fantasy for fans.

Insofar as sport is known for surprise endings, many bettors claim that familiarity with the teams may be detrimental.[14] Indeed, the backwoodsman from Bahia claims he won his $2 million by picking winning teams randomly. In the Marplan survey, 41 percent of the bettors said they make their choices by using logic, 33 percent said they choose randomly, and 17 percent said they bet their favorite teams to win. Men are far more likely to consult the expert opinion provided in newspapers and special magazines; women are more likely to discuss upcoming games with relatives and friends before making their choices.

Comparing lottery choices is a perfect sociable topic: stakes are low, potential winnings are high, feedback is almost immediate, and next week brings a new game. Even people who were not fans are now drawn into conversations about upcoming games. In addition to caring about their own team, fans now have twelve more games of the week to invest in.

Although infrequent relative to the weekly lottery, live telecasts of the Brazilian Selection bring literally everyone together. Ratings indicate that World Cup games capture nearly 100 percent of the television audience in Rio, not only for the final tournament, but even for the early qualifying rounds. Women are caught up in them as patriots more than as soccer fans. Everything comes to a halt for these games: the beaches are deserted, factories and shops close, traffic is reduced to a trickle. Everyone returns home, goes to a neighbor's, or crowds in front of appliance store windows to watch

television. There are also live telecasts when a team like Botafogo
plays an exhibition match against a foreign team like Colo-Colo in
Chile, and these games capture an impressive 60 percent of the
television audience.

The newspaper and radio are important in shaping the images
of teams and heroes that people talk about, even if they have not
seen the games. Winning goals of major league matches are frequently featured in front-page photographs, making even uninterested readers aware of the games.

In Brazil, detailed information is available in the three daily
newspapers devoted exclusively to sport that are sold throughout the
country: one is published in Rio and two (a morning and an afternoon
paper) are published in São Paulo. A daily paper devoted to regional
or national sporting news, with minimal coverage in the general
newspapers, has long been the tradition in nations with developed
sport systems. (England and the United States are major exceptions.)[15] Brazil is unusual in combining specialized dailies with extensive sport coverage in the general newspapers.

The Rio paper, *Jornal dos Sports* (*JS*), now forty-seven years
old, is the largest sports daily in Latin America. Its Monday circulation of 120,000 rivals that of the city's best-selling general newspapers. After a major Flamengo victory, its normal sales are boosted
a remarkable 40 percent, not only in Rio, but throughout the country,
indicating that popular teams like Flamengo (and the Corinthians
in São Paulo) are true national symbols. According to its director,
market surveys show that 81 percent of the *JS*'s readers are male
(51 percent between thirteen and twenty-five years old), with higher-
than-average education. (For their sake the paper also includes
school-related news as their only nonsport item; coincidentally, mass
college entrance exams are administered in giant Maracanã Stadium.)
Sales figures underestimate the readership, for an average of four
persons read each copy.[16]

Following the tradition set by France's sports daily *L'Equipe*,
the *JS* sponsors its own sporting events, making it second only to
the clubs as a promoter of participant sport.[17] The major event is an
age-graded soccer tournament for thirteen-year-olds to adult amateurs. The competition lasts six months and involves more than
31,000 players on 2,000 teams. The *JS* also sponsors soccer competitions for children under thirteen and gymnastic, track, and volleyball meets for female athletes. These tournaments are costly, but

they are justified by increased sales and the social service of promoting sport in a society with so few channels for organized competition. The paper's paternalistic role is better displayed in its requirement for participation in these tournaments. To enter, each player must pay $2, which is used to start a personal savings account; the organizers encourage added deposits, however small, throughout the championship.

Combining the *Jornal dos Sports* with one of the local papers gives the Brazilian fan more daily sports news than is available to his counterparts in either Europe or the United States. But the two most respected Rio papers, *Jornal do Brasil* and *O Globo*, offer so much sports coverage that they can compete with the *JS* for readers who buy only one paper. Each devotes approximately 15 to 17 percent of its news space to sport on an average weekday.[18] During special events much more space is allotted. For example, Brazilian papers devoted as much as 36 percent of their space to the month-long 1970 World Cup play-offs. After the tri-championship, the *Jornal do Brasil* put out an extra edition of twenty-two pages to report the final game and celebration.

There is so much space to fill that the sports page well reflects the multiple levels of sport, from local to international. Rio papers regularly cover the British, Spanish, Portuguese, German, Italian, Argentine, Uruguayan, and Chilean soccer championships. Although the bulk of international news is devoted to European and Latin soccer, the Brazilian papers also cover American superstars like Muhammed Ali (in boxing), Jimmy Connors (in tennis) and young Steve Cauthen (in turf). And attention is also showered on Brazilian athletes in any amateur or professional sport who do well in international competition.

Even though Brazilians are far less ethnocentric than Americans in their sports coverage, there is a high ratio of Brazilians to foreigners appearing in the photographs. I examined the *Jornal do Brasil* for two weeks and found that the ratio of natives to foreigners pictured in the news section was 1:1, in the arts and leisure section it was 1:2, and in the sports section it was 9:1. The news and entertainment sections reflect the fact that events and symbols are often set by the postindustrial nations. The reversed ratio in the sports section is indicative of the high level of development of Brazilian sport and the confidence in Brazilian athletes by world standards.

Even though Brazil is connected to a global sporting community, the sports page centers on local and national events. On Mondays *O Globo* has a column called "Brazil: North to South" that reviews the standings of the major state championships. Local events are fully covered, from professional down to the children's amateur rank. Although soccer and horse racing fill most of the space, other team and individual sports do get reported.

Brazilian sportswriters are willing to sacrifice a star's privacy to sell papers and fill the available news space. American journalists write less about private lives and more about what the players do on the field. In my interviews with Carlos Alberto and Pelé, both felt that Brazilian writers more often express personal prejudice against a player regardless of his game performance. Both agreed that subjective reporting and invading of privacy are not good for the players but no doubt serve to personalize and humanize them for the fans.

The Brazilian press recognizes the spectator as an important part of the spectacle. Fans are mentioned much more often than in American newspapers.[19] Of course, it might be said that Brazilian fans demand more press attention because of their frequent acts of violence: fights erupt in the stands after a group of Flamengo rowdies burn a Botafogo flag; a nineteen-year-old is beaten to death by two youngsters in a brawl over the relative worth of their teams; fans damage bleachers in Fortaleza as they stampede onto the field; a player is shot and killed by an angry fan during a district soccer game in the outskirts of São Paulo; a large crowd of disappointed Fluminense fans surround one of their directors in his car outside the stadium and demand the dismissal of the coach; fans relieve their sorrow by hanging in effigy the coach and members of the Technical Committee after the 1966 World Cup defeat.

Portrayed in a more favorable light, Brazilian fans are credited with contributing to team victory even in intracity matches where the notion of home-field advantage does not apply. Certain fan groups are cited for their loyalty, most notably the Corinthians of São Paulo, who define themselves as "people who suffer ninety minutes each week." They filled the stands despite twenty-three years without a championship. And newsmen give honorable mention to fans who stay until the end of a game in the face of lopsided defeat. Fans inspire individual players; a Botafogo player interviewed about his continuing slump made an appeal to the fans for a morale boost. Of course, fans also make news by turning against a player, by abandoning the stadium before the whistle blows, and for excessive booing. Fans from both clubs often join together to boo their teams during a slow, boring game, likely to be a scoreless tie. These events receive a lot of attention from journalists, who fear that a move toward the European style of defensive play will result in a loss of the aggressive Latin style that makes for good press and a great sporting event.

Sports also get substantial promotion from the radio, the dominant medium for live coverage of games. Roughly one-eighth of broadcasting time is devoted to soccer games, and half of all radios on in Rio are tuned to the Sunday afternoon games.[20] Spokesmen for the radio industry say it is impossible to estimate accurately the number of listeners, since so many gather around radios, indoors and out, but they do report that 85 percent of the sport audience is male. Sponsors pay relatively modest advertising fees to reach this vast male audience. Three sponsors—typically representing cigarettes, beer, and clothing manufacturers—pay $150,000 each for the rights to the city championship series (forty games), and another three or four companies will pay similar sums for commercial rights to the national championship (forty-five games). Additional fees may be collected for special competitions or Cup matches. The advertising revenues are pure profit for the radio stations insofar as they pay *nothing* to the clubs for broadcast rights. Club management accepts radio coverage as good publicity: hearing live games will get people interested enough to come to the stadium.

Somehow that same reasoning does not apply to television. In the mid-1950s television crews were allowed to enter the stadium freely, but by the late 1950s the club directors asked television to leave, believing that the rich who owned sets were the ones who had bought high-priced stadium tickets and that they now would prefer to stay home. The compromise that continues today is that league games are videotaped and shown at eleven o'clock that night. Given the late hour and known outcome, the ratings for these replays are low. The reasoning behind the late-night time slot: Brazilian families typically have one set, and it is assumed that the women control the channel selector and prefer soap operas to soccer. Scheduled after the women's bedtime, the games can be seen by the men willing to stay awake. The stations can afford to play to such a small audience insofar as they pay nothing for broadcast rights and have little else competing for late-night air time.

Here again the Brazilian pattern conforms with that in most other nations. In Brazil, England, and most other nations with highly developed sports, most of the three hundred to six hundred hours of television coverage per year comprises delayed-tape transmissions. Brazil's TV Globo three-hour Sport Spectacular, which features basketball, volleyball, and boxing, gets a respectable 25 percent of the television audience. The exceptions to the rule are the international soccer matches, which are shown live, but local games are protected by a policy that prohibits live televising of any games at the same time. Sometimes games from another state are shown in their entirety later in the evening. Besides the protective policy, technology limits live telecasts, since Brazil does not have its own satellite to bring city-to-city transmission. Using U.S. satellites, the New York Cosmos can be seen live on Rio television, but games from nearby São Paulo cannot. Live telecasts focus on sports other than soccer. At the peak of the careers of race car drivers Emerson Fittipaldi and Carlos Pace, entire Grand Prix events were shown live in Brazil.

England's media coverage is even more restricted. Radio stations are prohibited from announcing which of the day's games they will broadcast until fifteen minutes before starting time. BBC television is allowed to show only forty-five minutes of taped highlights following the Wednesday and Saturday league games, and the British get a grand total of *one* live domestic soccer match per year (the Football Association Cup final).[21]

The United States is again the oddity, with over twelve hundred hours of sport telecast each year, most of which is live coverage. Astronomical sums of money for broadcast rights are paid to U.S. professional sports leagues, then are divided and passed on to the member clubs to support the multimillion-dollar contracts of star players. The television networks get their money back by charging astronomical rates to their commercial sponsors. One minute of advertising on the 1981 Super Bowl cost $550,000, considered a fair value given the audience of 100 million potential consumers.

Even though financially troubled clubs around the world envy the television revenues that make American clubs rich, they defend their protective policy. Their rationale is twofold. First, the soccer establishment fears that, if top-ranked teams were televised, small clubs would suffer a fatal attendance loss, as did the minor-league teams of small town America when television broadcast baseball. Few realize that television revenue prompted the expansion of major-league teams, bringing the highest level of competition to audiences in more American cities. Second, league representatives and directors fear that even the big clubs would suffer diminished gate revenues if their games, or comparable ones, could be seen live on television. Despite the American experience of increased attendance through promotion of sports on television, the assumption is that in countries where people have considerably less disposable income, they would probably stay home to watch a free game.

Besides radio and television, cinema promotes soccer and creates fans too. A government mandate requires theater managers to show a fifteen-minute newsreel before the feature film. Producer Carlos Niemeyer, taking advantage of the characteristic of sport that fuses news and entertainment, includes seven minutes of stunning soccer photography as part of his roundup. The films are made for national rather than local distribution and feature teams from all over the country. The audience cheers its favorite teams and groans with the opposition's goals as if in the stadium. The Department of Finance, the sponsor of these newsreels, ends them with a celebrity, often a soccer star, urging viewers to start personal savings accounts.

The end result of all this media coverage is that soccer permeates the urban atmosphere. Like other major cities of the world, Rio is a city of apartment buildings. Almost every building in the middle-class neighborhoods has a doorman, and five out of every seven doormen listen to the games on the radio.[22] They shout and exchange insults while addressing one another by their soccer club identification: "Hey, Flamengo, you're lousy." Groups of adolescent boys listen to the game on transistor radios. As commentators scream "GOOOAL" the noise of fireworks rises above the stadium din. A fan who decides to forsake the stadium traffic and take a walk instead of seeing his team play in the afternoon game is aware of its drama every moment he is in the street.[23]

People who stay indoors do not escape the game either. Brazilian apartment houses contain numerous airshafts running the height of the buildings, through which sound travels unimpeded for ten stories, and most Brazilians play their radios and televisions at top volume.

According to Pelé, soccer games are an inescapable part of Brazil's small-town environment as well.

> [My mother] didn't have to listen to the radio to know how the game was going—every goal by Brazil would result in screams of joy from the front room, not to mention the explosion of fireworks all over town,

just as every opponent's goal would be greeted by a loud groan heard throughout the house.[24]

Because Rio has so many teams, local games are played on Wednesday and Thursday nights and Saturday and Sunday afternoons. During the local championship, there are six first-division games each week. In London, where there are four first-division teams, league schedules are arranged so that there are only two major games, one on Wednesday night and one on Saturday, to compete for spectators. According to João Saldanha, Brazil is exceptional for its number of good teams and loyal fans; he says it is the only country in the world where five games can be staged on the same day and each attract more than 100,000 people.[25]

Those living anywhere near Brazil's stadia cannot escape the traffic and crowds. The radio brings the drama of the local games to people everywhere in the city. Because of the lottery, fans are attentive to games from other states broadcast on the radio too. Groups of men and boys enjoy the game together on the streets, where no single person need take the host's responsibility. Brazilians value open expression more than closed reserve, and no taboos keep them from shouting or embracing when goals are scored.

Millions of lottery flyers announcing games are distributed weekly and are seen in virtually all public places; the movie theaters show highlights of the previous week's matches; on game days, fans often wear team shirts or colors as a show of solidarity. The popular *Jornal dos Sports*, with its first and last pages printed on pink paper, adds to soccer's visibility and is a signpost of fandom.

Soccer's Financial Crisis

Brazilian soccer is supported largely through gate receipts. Admission prices are considerably lower than their American counterparts (35¢ for standing room, $1.75 for bleacher seats, and $5 to $10 for reserved seats). Yet the enormous size of Brazilian stadia and the many games played by each team—eighty-five during a forty-nine-week season—meant that until recently the gate receipts were sufficient to sustain the soccer organizations. In 1980, twenty-four million people paid admission to see first-division games.[26]

The size and number of Brazilian stadia are an impressive indicator of soccer's importance, for Brazil ranks first in the world on both counts. Brazil has nearly 4,000 stadia with a combined capacity of 4,300,000 people. For comparison, total stadia capacity in the United States is 3,200,000, counting civic and private stadia, bowls, and ballparks.[27] (Latin American and European stadia capacities are often larger than American ones because so much space is devoted to standing areas and bleachers, which can be packed during important matches.) A large stadium is the greatest symbol of civic pride—a fact demonstrated in the extreme by the construction of a 35,000 person stadium in the southern city of Erechim—a capacity 10,000 greater than its population.

Enormous gates contributed to a healthy financial picture while player salaries were held low. However, after Brazil became established as the world's greatest soccer power with its successive World Cup victories in 1958 and 1962, European clubs offered huge salaries and signing bonuses to Brazilian stars. This raiding of national talent peaked with Brazil's 1970 tri-championship, and it continues today. The most recent publicized example is an Italian team's $5 million offer to Flamengo's Zico, touted as the new Pelé. Brazilian clubs raised the salaries of their many stars in defense. Escalating salaries, rising costs connected with both inflation and expanded playing schedules, and the growth of other leisure industries that compete for people's admissions fees have ushered in an era of financial disaster for virtually every major team in the country.

No one has acted on any of the suggestions for improving the financial condition of the clubs. Smaller leagues made up of the strongest teams might be one way to survive inflated costs and diminishing attendance; all the games would be major confrontations, with fewer clubs competing for spectator money. But conservative directors feel responsible for preserving the game the way it has been played, and the integration of large and small clubs has been a tradition of the soccer world.

The resistance to live television coverage of games is another reflection of this protective policy and conservative thinking. In 1977 TV Globo, the major network, experimented with live coverage of the São Paulo state championship between the popular Corinthians and their opponent, Ponte Preta. TV Globo paid $1,200,000 to the teams, one-third over what they could take in from ticket sales if they sold out their three-game final series. Two of the games sold out despite free access on television. TV Globo made a profit from advertising revenues and would be ready to broadcast more major games. But directors have not sold television rights to local games in the four years since the experiment, showing their deep-seated opposition to change.

The directors of two of Rio's major clubs are willing to adandon their protection of the small clubs to raise the staggering sums of money needed to finance modern sports teams. Even without selling live broadcast rights to television, some directors feel their clubs should be paid for television's delayed video showings and for the live radio transmissions of the games. But other directors have resisted a direct commercial orientation to sport and block the necessary unified action on behalf of the major clubs. These directors continue to make decisions that maximize pride rather than profits. The hundreds of men hawking team flags and souvenirs at the stadium gates pay nothing for the use of the club logo. Directors reason that the more flags waving from the bleachers, the higher the team's morale and the greater its chance to win.

The more businesslike approach to sport had been demonstrated to the Brazilian directors when Warner Communications' corporate fortunes were used to entice the famous Pelé out of early retirement and sign him to play for the New York Cosmos. The Brazilian press coverage of the Cosmos during the three years that Pelé played for them set the commercial example; Brazil's national hero exported soccer virtuosity to America while the Cosmos exhibited sport merchandising to Brazil.

The idea that broadcast rights are salable commodities was driven home forcefully during the finale of this cultural exchange—Pelé's last game, on 1 October 1977, where he was to play the first half with the Cosmos and the second half with the Santos, his Brazilian team. Radio and television stations all over the world made preparations to cover the game, paying Warner Communications a substantial fee for the privilege. Representatives from at least fifty radio stations throughout Brazil showed up in New York with the same intention, except that the request for a fee came as an insulting surprise—after all, Pelé was *their* countryman. Most departed in anger; only four stations stayed and paid. Finally the Santos team arrived, accompanied by their directors and local radio sportscasters. But the Santos station was not one that had paid, nor would it pay— it had *always* broadcast the Santos games. The club directors allied themselves with the radio executives and the sanctity of tradition over commerce; they voted not to allow the team to play unless the game could be carried to the fans at home, for free. Warner Communications was equally adamant: business is business. The cultural clash led to a stubborn stalemate while the whole world, unknowing, awaited the start of the game. At the last moment the São Paulo radio station, one of the four that had paid, came up with a face-saving solution: the game could proceed and its people in São Paulo would relay the play-by-play via long-distance telephone to the nearby city of Santos.

While the economics of big-time sport may force the rest of the world to copy the broadcast arrangement found in the United States, Brazilians may insist that television not break away from the action for the sake of commercial sponsors. Brazilians share with Europeans a profound respect for the critical variable of endurance in soccer and disdain the North American Soccer League's interruptions to accommodate the sponsors. They would advertise as they do now, with commercials before and after games and during half-time, and with announcers' reminders that the game is being brought to the viewer courtesy of whatever cigarette or beer, accompanied by a "crawl" low on the screen saying "smoke or drink our product." The crucial question about live television coverage of games centers less on the survival of the small clubs than on its impact on the major clubs. If a few more experiments demonstrate that people will go to the stadium in spite of free games at home, televised sport may save the best clubs from bankruptcy.

Long-term government loans have forestalled financial ruin for the Brazilian soccer clubs, but each year the clubs grow more indebted. Some clubs have had to sell valuable properties in the city to meet their payrolls. In 1976 Botafogo was forced to sell its stadium in the General Severiano property to pay its Social Security debts. The team suffered from having to travel long distances daily to a training field in an outlying suburb. Flamengo recently sold some of its real estate in order to keep Zico. Merging the proceeds from their sale with a donation from Coca-Cola, Flamengo's directors put together a creative $1.5 million package that makes Zico an ambassador for Coca-Cola as part of the deal.[28]

The sport lottery is one potential source of income that may alleviate soccer's financial troubles. The lottery takes its toll from soccer; it locks game schedules tightly and stimulates grueling seasons that players must endure. Upsets raise the suspicion that games have been fixed to manipulate the lottery outcome. There have been scandals in Europe, the biggest resulting in the two-year suspension of Paolo Rossi, who, three weeks after his return, led the Italian Selection to its tri-championship. There has yet to be a major scandal in Brazil, but incidents occur, as evidenced by the recent firing of three players from Ceará's ABC team who were accused of throwing a lottery game. So much money is at stake that the lottery invites interference.

Amateur sport and recreation have gained more from the lottery than the professional soccer teams that bear its toll. Professional soccer typically gets a larger share in most countries that have sport lotteries. In countries where public companies operate the lottery, between 2 percent and 12 percent of net profits are returned to the national football associations. In Brazil the CBD got this money and, after paying the expenses of the national team, used the rest to support amateur sport.

The financial crisis in Brazilian soccer has prompted a major restructuring of the organization of sport. Soccer authorities complained that reaching a strong, uniform policy democratically has been impossible in the CBD because some representatives care more about amateur than professional sport. Patrons of amateur sport make the same complaint in reverse. Professional soccer can best be managed by those who have assumed its guardianship as their sole responsibility. In response, the government's National Sport Council (CND) authorized the creation of the Confederação Brasileiro de Futebol, or CBF (Brazilian Football Confederation) in May 1979 to operate autonomously. Its General Assembly is made up of the presidents of all state and territorial soccer federations. Each of the amateur sports formerly affiliated with the CBD will now have independent confederations supported by the Ministry of Education and Culture.[29]

This restructuring should improve the financial condition of Brazilian soccer. The CBF will get a share of the gate at interstate and international games and be able to use it solely for soccer. The broadcast rights that are sold go to the CBF for the benefit of professional soccer, and this source of income holds great potential for future earnings. The CBF will continue to get lottery profits to support air travel for the National Championship and Brazil's World Cup teams. The Ministry of Education and Culture will continue to parcel out other lottery revenues for the support of amateur sport.

In other words, at the local level professional soccer will still subsidize amateur sport in the clubs, but at the national level professional soccer's support of amateur sports will be indirect, through lottery profits, as is the case in much of the rest of the world.

Sport in the Lives of Fans

Communication is the essence of the social process. Unlike most forms of conflict, which make interaction difficult or impossible, the play form of conflict prolongs contact by promoting communication. Soccer provides the most talked-about subject in the city, and the media's sport coverage fuels those conversations. The men in my study related to their friends, workmates, and neighbors through sport more than anything else. Soccer gives a common focus to their attention: they trade their special knowledge and insights about players and teams, argue about past games, and anticipate the next.

Soccer championships and the sport lottery focus interaction between intimates, acquaintances, and strangers. Cheering for the same team is accepted as the basis for a kindred relationship. During local championships, fans come face to face with opponent fans of different class, racial, or ethnic roots, and their differences are accentuated in the nonthreatening context of sport rituals. Their endless debates, in the form of friendly banter, bring them together because of their differences, not in spite of them. Although fans may cheer for opposing teams, their love of the game bonds them in a meaningful way.

Soccer promotes communal integration, but for whom? Sport does not have a central place in everyone's life. Among fans, some are far more passionate about their teams than others. My fan survey offers information on who knows the most about teams and players and who spends the most time and money following soccer. These

data will be used to address hypotheses drawn from the literature
on sociology of sport and also commonsense assumptions about those
who give sport a prominent place in their lives:

1. Are they society's loners or its well connected?

2. Are they those who were socialized into fandom, either by
playing the game themselves as youths, then staying close to it as
adult spectators, or by having relatives or friends who modeled passionate fandom?

3. Are they simply the ones for whom sport consumption is
easiest because they have the most leisure time, have the most disposable income, or live closest to the stadium?

Even lesser fans reap integrative benefits by following sport.
People need excuses for getting together and conversational subjects
that are easy and fun. In Brazil soccer, more than anything else,
gives men something to do and say. Like television personalities and
samba tunes, players, team standings, and lottery combinations are
an important part of the shared popular culture.

The Involvement of the Fans

Particular features of the organization of sport in Brazil affect the
way fans relate to each other, to their athlete heroes, and to club
management. Relative to fans in the United States, Brazilian fans
control the game—both on and off the field—by their dedication and
expressions of caring for their favorite teams.

A sense of involvement and effectiveness lies at the very core
of fan participation in Brazil. Fans are not passive spectators; they
influence the outcome of games and the management of clubs. Sport
commentator Armando Nogueira characterizes the relationship between teams and fans as a vicious circle: the team influences the
fans, who in turn influence the team. The team "lights the fire." The
team scores, fans get excited, and that helps the team score again.
Or, if the team is losing badly, fans leave the stands, further de-
moralizing the team.[1]

Fans assume the responsibility of giving their teams the
strength of their numbers, and face-to-face rivalry between two fan
groups gives special meaning to the familiar plea to "support your
team." Fans believe they can intimidate the referee into minimizing
unfavorable calls. Pointing their power toward a particular player,
they can inspire him to perform feats he rarely achieves or edge him
closer to blunder. The press portrays supporters as part of the spec-

tacle—with both good and ill effects. The press commonly blamed
the fans for the devastating 1950 World Cup loss to Uruguay when
Brazil was host country. The 200,000 people crammed into Maracanã
Stadium created what the writers labeled a "spirit of optimism."
They expected too much and made the players nervous, which led
to the decisive error. Fans unhappily accepted the blame.

Fans influence club management too. Those affluent enough
to be shareholders in their favorite clubs vote to force out unsatis-
factory directors. They participate in the democratic organization of
sport. Fans who cannot afford membership dues or club shares can
join one of several Torcida Organizada groups and still feel effective.
The organized fans stage angry protests when a beloved player is
suddenly traded or when they feel a coach should be dismissed.
Brazilian fans are visible, vocal, sometimes even physically threatening when they have grievances. Soccer may provide the one area
where they can sense efficacy: today they jeer, tomorrow the coach
is gone. Accepting no support from the club itself, they are com-
pletely independent of club politics. Members pay no dues; enthusiasm for the team is all that is needed. The groups raise money by
selling flags, shirts, and other souvenirs.

Brazil has no monopoly on involved fan clubs. In fact, supporters' clubs in England play an even more important role. Though
they are independent of the soccer clubs, supporters' clubs in England typically are housed very close to the stadium. They are open
seven nights a week, and fans casually drop in to drink, play darts,
or talk sports. Insofar as their soccer clubs are not membership clubs,
the supporters' club often becomes the focal point of a community's
social life and sponsors parties and dances. The directors' donations
and the sale of player contracts being insufficient for the professional
team's survival, most clubs also rely on contributions from supporter
groups. Members operate betting pools, bingo, and sweepstakes to
raise funds for the teams they love.

Fan clubs in countries like Brazil and England are successful
because they are organized around local teams and serve social func-
tions. Once solidarity has been built around team-related activities
and fans contribute more than just ticket money, they are more likely
to feel they have rights they can fight for together. A close look at
Botafogo's "organized fans" illustrates who belongs and what they
do.

Botafogo has four fan groups: Unifogo for fifteen- to eighteen-year-old boys, Femifogo for teenage girls, the Torcida Jovem (Youth Fans) for young men and women nineteen to twenty-two years old, and the Torcida Organizada (TO) for adult fans. Botafogo fans are generally younger than fans of the other three major clubs in Rio. The average age of the 822 official members of the TO is twenty five. Women make up 20 percent of Botafogo's TO. Organized fans offer both safety of numbers and protection by males of the group to females who want to see the games. Although women never serve as directors in the soccer clubs, a few have become leaders in the fan clubs.

For many years the president of Botafogo's Torcida Organizada has been a man, known throughout the city as Tarzan, who owns and operates a second floor wig shop in Rio's central district. According to Tarzan, members sit together at games, arrange to travel together to important matches in other cities, and have irregular meetings when something occurs in the Botafogo Football Club that upsets them. I interviewed Tarzan when he had just finished preparing a statement expressing group sentiments on a series of issues. The impetus for the statement was a press release from Botafogo directors laying the blame for the long streak of defeats on the fans. "Botafogo fans are the only ones that help lose games," it said, referring to fans' booing their own players and leaving the stadium early. Tarzan felt this was a direct attack on him and his group.

The manifesto began by asserting the fans' right to speak, precisely because they are independent of internal club politics. Their link to Botafogo is the "passion and love that enables them to endure wilting sun, rain, trains, buses, standing tiers and bleachers, as well as to work the following morning knowing that they will be the butt of their adversaries' jokes, just as they have been for the past five years."

It enumerated the following points:

1. We don't like player-director squabbles that result in the resignation of the director. We ask who runs Botafogo anyhow—the players?

2. Team trainings have frequently been delayed because the players are lackadaisical about their arrival time, resulting in poor conditioning of our team relative to others. The employees are damaging our team, and we're the ones who pay their salaries with our admission money.

3. We are particularly dissatisfied with Jairzinho (the highest-paid player on the Botafogo team, who also played on the 1970 World Cup team) because he feigns injury to get out of playing.

4. Finally, the irresponsible fiscal management of the current directory is saddling the club with huge debts that endanger club assets used as collateral. The loans are being used to buy players who are not panning out on the field.

They requested that the Directory appoint Charles Borer, their choice to run the professional football sector, as a show of faith that things would change, even though they recognized that Borer and the incumbent Botafogo president were enemies.

Tarzan's manifesto is an instructive statement of fans' rights and attitudes with respect to the cherished club, its directors, and its players. Unusual features of the Brazilian system—like open training sessions and voting privileges that come with membership clubs—make the fans feel especially involved and effective. The frequency of intracity matches increases the sense of fan responsibility. In return, fans expect to be taken seriously. In Brazil, all parties—the directors, coach, players, and press and the fans themselves—believe that supporters are important.

Tarzan's power extends far beyond his 822 fellow members. Commentator Armando Nogueira confirms that all Botafogo sympathizers at the stadium take their lead from the organized fans, who are visible in identical team shirts, displaying the largest flags and directing noisy samba bands and singers. Their influence is impressive, says Nogueira, because they can sway half a stadium of spectators against a player.[2]

Brazilian fans view players as employees not demigods—and not as just club employees, but *their* employees. Fans admire athletes; they view them as human, approachable, and presumably responsible. Brazilian soccer enthusiasts are not driven by blind love. Rather, their love is conditional; they recognize careless mistakes and complain. Vasco fans who were unhappy with their players' spirit burned their own flags at the stadium. Later that same year, when the team was eliminated from the championship finals, the fans gave the players a standing ovation to show their satisfaction with the changes in team spirit. The athletes said their greatest comfort in defeat was that renewed fan support.

Brazilian fans feel close to their idols. Club members may know the players personally. Even nonmembers have easy access to club training grounds, where they can view the player as a worker, not a performer. Workout times are published in the sports page. As many as 1,000 persons may attend the final training session before an important game; average attendance is closer to 200. It is significant that Brazilian fans are allowed "backstage." Tarzan's Torcida knows that players are delaying training because they are privy to information that fans elsewhere miss. Even in other soccer-playing countries, except for Spain, open practice is rare. In spite of inconveniences, Brazilian fans feel they should support their team by attending late afternoon practices. Besides, as part of the club family, they want to assess a favored player's injury and the general physical condition of the team.

Fans believe their rights are rooted in the personal sacrifices they make for their team. What they spend for tickets is nothing compared with the emotional distress of defeats and the humiliation of Monday-morning jokes by victorious fans. They make equally large sacrifices just to get to Maracanã Stadium.

The stadium, built before many Cariocas owned cars, has only limited street parking for those foolhardy motorists who enter the traffic caused by 200,000 spectators. Most fans spend more than an hour standing in packed buses and trains to get to Maracanã's gates and at least another thirty minutes in the line for tickets. Lower-class fans can afford tickets for either the standing tiers—between the moat and the reserved seating on the lower level—or the bleacher areas, which include the entire upper level. To secure a decent viewing position, men who choose the standing area must arrive sometime during the first half of the preliminary game (between the juvenile teams) and be on their feet for yet another hour before the main event begins.

Women are almost never seen on the tiers. At the beginning of soccer in Brazil, when the men on the field were bourgeois, it was fashionable for "ladies" to come to the grounds. But once the stands and playing field were no longer exclusively filled with "gentlemen," unflattering assumptions were made about women who would voluntarily enter settings of bad language and potential violence. Traditional and lower-class women still think that a daughter's presence at a soccer game will damage her reputation. However, newer stadia that afford more physical comforts and safety attract middle-class females, and their attending games as part of a teenage group is becoming more acceptable.

Men on the standing tiers pass time drinking beer. They cannot risk losing their places and have been known to relieve themselves in paper bags, then toss them back into the expensive reserved seating. The seats closest to the standing tiers are typically occupied by unsuspecting tourists. Brazilians, who know better than to sit there, see such acts as evidence of poor manners, not class warfare.

The bleachers are only slightly more comfortable, and the tropical sun can be insufferable. The bleachers also are mostly filled with men because, as in the standing tiers, brawls are likely.

Fans make financial sacrifices too. In 1973, when the minimum wage was $51 a month, an outing to the bleachers, with transportation and a snack, cost about $3. Enthusiastic fans average two trips to the stadium a month, spending 12 percent of their salary on soccer games if they earn the minimum wage and 6 percent if they earn twice the minimum (and that does not include their weekly lottery bets). Without television revenue, players' salaries are heavily dependent on the gate. Brazilian fans feel they pay the players out of their own small, hard-earned incomes.

If fans did not believe their presence affected the game's outcome, they could not justify the outlay of time and money, crowded trains, hours of standing, smell of urine, and risk of injury. According to Nogueira, lower-class fans are more fanatical because they must rationalize their very real sacrifices by exaggerating their love. Tarzan, for one, believes that fans who make sacrifices deserve something in return.

Tarzan's fourth grievance—irresponsible fiscal management—exemplifies another reason fans feel close to the soccer scene. Because the clubs are nonprofit organizations, fans can get accurate financial information. When Brazilian fans learn through newspapers that club real estate has been sold, they want to know why. When they read about an expensive long-term player contract, they wonder if it will be worth it. Typically, directors have an "open door" policy. If angry fans do not find them at the club grounds, they can find them at the VIP parking lot after the game. A large crowd of disappointed Fluminense fans surrounded the car of one director and demanded the coach's dismissal, and the president of Fluminense complained about hostile phone calls to his home from fans offering unsolicited advice.

Leaders of the organized fans can be involved in club affairs without having adversarial relations with the directors. The president of Flamengo's booster group, for example, fully supports club policy. Jayme Rodrigues de Carvalho has been leader of Charanga do Flamengo since he founded the group in 1942. Sr. Jayme was the first in Brazil to equip his members with uniforms and music—now standard practice for all. (Charanga refers to the musical support at the stadium.) He also wanted club flags. Since flags were not commercially produced in the 1940s, Sr. Jayme's wife sewed flags for sale to members. These methods were so effective that the Flamengo club paid his expenses to organize Brazilian fans at the 1954 South American Tournament in Argentina, for which his wife made the largest Flamengo and Brazilian flags ever seen—ten meters by eight. Brazilians, seeing the flags, went to that area of the stadium. After that, a Portuguese newspaper claimed that with the principles of his Torcida Organizada, Sr. Jayme had found a way for the fans to give a real advantage to their team.

Jayme Rodrigues do Carvalho, a low-level federal employee before his retirement, has spent his life in the service of the Flamengo Club and received no payment for his time, but he enjoys celebrity status. His trophy room at home stores the plaques and banners given to honor him: on the thirtieth birthday of Charanga, Tarzan presented Sr. Jayme with a plaque from the fans of Botafogo; Vasco da Gama elected him the "chief of the chiefs of organized fans"; he is an honorary member of all the soccer clubs in the city; Rio's State Federation honored him for his services to soccer's development; the organized fans from São Paulo's Corinthian Club gave him a medallion inscribed to "the faithful one"; and his greatest honor came when the local government gave him the rank of "special citizen." These trophies, he says, give him "nobility." With pride he announces that he has bequeathed all this to his son. He feels Flamengo has adequately repaid his hard work by granting him the status of shareholding member and remembering his birthday each year.

Service to a club brings community recognition, even a degree of celebrity to many fans. There have been famous fans in the United States. Most get fleeting media attention through some gimmick, like Hilda the Bell Ringer or Harry the Dancing Bear. In Brazil and other soccer nations, the route to recognition is more institutionalized through directorships, club patronage, and supporters' groups. Directors get so much exposure that they can run for public office, and leaders of the organized fans are popular personalities around town.

Even anonymous behind-the-scenes workers can become "fans of the month" or the focus of newspaper articles.

Some fans express their caring by making religious sacrifices for their teams. Spiritualist fans of Flamengo burn red and black candles (the team's colors) and perform other voodoo rites along the city's beaches. Santista, the masseur for the Vasco team, never enters the stadium on game day without his Umbanda charms. More elaborate offerings have been noted in the sports page: during the finals of the state championship in Amazonas, supporters of the Nacional team left a chicken, twelve black candles, a bottle of *cachaça* (a sugarcane-based alcohol), a spade, a cross, and little pieces of paper with players' names on them at the gate where the team was staying. They also left a cake as a present for the opposing team, but the players did not dare eat it.

Catholic fans also believe prayers and sacrifices can influence the outcome of a soccer game. Flamengo fans set red and black candles on the altars of Rio's churches. Sometimes, after important championship games, a man carries his team's banner while climbing *on his knees* up one of Rio's many hills capped with a religious shrine. Reminiscent of the classic Brazilian film *Pagador de Promessas (Keeper of the Promises)*, the man, in a desperate moment during the game, had sworn to some saint that he would pay that masochistic tribute should his team emerge victorious.

Soccer-related deaths are a sad testimonial to the deep involvement of Brazilian fans. After Flamengo lost the state championship in 1969, a club devotee jumped off a building shouting "Viva Flamengo." A writer covering the 1958 World Cup in Sweden claims to have witnessed a Brazilian fan's suicide from "sheer joy" when his country won the Jules Rimet trophy for the first time.[3]

Of course, Brazilians are not the only fans to kill themselves for their teams. In the 1966 World Cup a West German fatally shot himself when his television set broke down during the final game between his country and England. Nor have Americans escaped such bizarre ends. An often cited case is the Denver man who wrote a suicide note—"I have been a Broncos fan since the Broncos were first organized and I can't stand their fumbling anymore"—then shot himself.[4]

Cardiac arrest, in response to either winning or opposition goals, accounts for far more deaths than suicide. Although no cross-cultural records are kept on stadium-related deaths, they are believed to occur most frequently in Latin America. An Argentine stadium guard suffered a fatal heart attack when Holland tied the score late in the second half of the 1978 World Cup.

In the late 1960s I met a man in Curitiba, already a community leader, who successfully ran for the presidency of the elite soccer club that was then on the decline. He saw himself as the "messiah" who had come to lift his club to the state of glory it had enjoyed when his father was president. He was succeeding in his mission, but he died of a heart attack when the rival team made the winning goal during an important game. Rio's Flamengo Club had lost its president in a nearly identical situation a few years earlier. During championship finals, the Brazilian press publishes doctors' warnings to heart patients to stay away from both the stadium and their radios, or at least to eat lightly before the game. Armando Nogueira cautions, "cheering can kill you while playing cannot."[5]

Results of the Fan Study

Most fans never make religious sacrifices or engage in wanton destruction for their teams; most do not even join a club or its booster groups. Insofar as they do nothing to attract attention to their fandom, we know very little about them.

To examine the role sport plays in people's lives, I personally interviewed, in Portuguese, two hundred working-class men in Rio. I chose men as subjects because soccer is predominantly a male interest. The only other condition for inclusion was literacy because I wanted subjects who could be full participants in society. I explained to these men and their employers that I wanted to study how Brazilians spend their free time. (Soccer fandom was not singled out.) The subjects were excused from work duties for twenty to thirty minutes to talk in privacy, and they seemed happy and cooperative because of the break. (See Appendix 1 for the interview schedule.)

Social scientists call this a "convenience sample"—subjects were not selected randomly from the total population. Nevertheless, I took measures to assure that the composition of my sample resembled that of working-class males more generally. In factories, roughly equal numbers of unskilled, semiskilled, and skilled laborers were included. I asked the foreman to send in his entire section, one at a time, so that his own idea of who would make an appropriate subject would not bias my sample. In supermarkets and hotels, I

selected both manual workers and low-level bureaucrats. Men of
thirty-seven different occupations took part, but factory workers,
office clerks, salesmen, and doormen were numerically most important, in that order. Salaries ranged from the minimum wage of $51
a month to $300, with a median income of $100. By requesting
specific people, using the 1970 city census as my guideline, I selected
a group of men whose age, marital status, religious and racial distribution mirrored that of Rio's working class almost perfectly.

The men in my sample, like working-class males elsewhere,
do very little with their free time during the week.[6] After work they
go home and stay there.[7] They rest or watch television; 66 percent
report watching television most nights. Many men stay home on
weekends as well—sleeping, fixing things, or spending time with
their children. Some go to the beach an average of once a month,
and they go to the movies less often than that. Sometimes they visit
relatives or go on family outings.

Like most Brazilian working-class people, the men in this sample belong to very few voluntary organizations. A few reported belonging to the Auto Club of Brazil (which occasionally sponsors
parties). Only eleven men were current members of soccer clubs.
Even low dues are more appropriate to the middle-class budget.
Although 53 percent belonged to trade unions, the unions never met.
Membership was mandatory in most cases and primarily served to
provide medical benefits. Almost none belonged to neighborhood
groups of any kind. Church, one of the few voluntary organizations
that attracts people of the working class, draws far more women than
men. Whereas over half these men reported that their wives or mothers regularly attended religious services, only 22 percent said that
of themselves.

Most Brazilian men invest an impressive amount of time in
soccer relative to other leisure pursuits. Three-quarters of the men
I interviewed had gone to Maracanã Stadium at least once in the
previous month. Other than stopping for a beer on the way home
from work, soccer spectatorship is the most common activity that
gets men together away from home. Besides attending games of
professional teams, 53 percent reported attending a suburban soccer
game near home within the previous month, and more than two-
thirds of the men whose workplace sponsors a team also attend its
games regularly.[8] More impressive yet, 57 percent still played soccer

themselves during their weekend leisure time, many in organized leagues.

The centrality of soccer in the lives of these men is also reflected in what they read and talk about. Of those who read the newspaper, 56 percent said they read the sports page first—far more than any other single section. In fact, 32 percent said they supplemented their soccer news by purchasing the *Jornal dos Sports*. When asked what they talk about with their friends, a question I asked before inquiring specifically about sport, more people (43 percent) answered that they talked about soccer than cited any other topic of conversation. When asked what else they discuss, one man said, "more soccer." Most of those who first answered "soccer" followed with "the sport lottery."[9]

Almost all Brazilian men make sport at least a small part of their lives. Soccer provides these Brazilian workers with one of the few interests not related to work or family. Playing soccer is a source of fun and exercise. Watching suburban games focuses neighborhood gatherings, just as factory games focus the workplace. And Maracanã Stadium is one of the few leisure places these Rio men frequent with any regularity. Games and players are the main subject of their reading, the central topic of their conversation, and the object of their betting dreams.

Who Are the Fans?

While it is difficult, perhaps impossible, to measure the degree to which a fan really cares about his team, it is easy to chart how closely he follows a sport.[10] Does he put up with crowded trains and stifling bleachers to see his team in the flesh, or is he content to listen to the radio broadcast under a shady tree near home? Does he turn to the sports page first or, more extreme, buy the sports daily in addition to other news tabloids? Does he vaguely follow the local teams, or does he know the names of the players and teams from all over Brazil and other nations too? Seven questions that reflect the respondent's actual game attendance, mass media consumption of sport, and knowledge of players and teams were used to construct a fan score. The subject was given 1, 2, or 3 points for each question, resulting in fan scores ranging from 7 to 21.

The first empirical question to answer with these data is, How extensive is fandom in Brazil? Only one person of the two hundred interviewed had not watched his country's final game in the 1970 World Cup, and he was also the only person not to recognize Pelé's picture. Insofar as everyone but this man followed soccer at times, it is more appropriate to refer to those at the low end of the continuum as "weak fans" than as "non fans." For the convenience of discussion and presentation, the men have been divided by their fan scores into three groups: weak fans (scores between 7 and 12); average fans (scores between 13 and 18); and strong fans (scores between 19 and 21).

Typically, the *weak fan* has not attended a game in the past month. He does not usually listen to radio games except for those of the Brazilian Selection and some championship finals. He may glance at the sports page, but it is neither the first nor the second section he turns to. He recognizes photographs of Pelé and usually Tostão, veteran of two World Cups, but he does not know the well-publicized city star Jairzinho, who became nationally prominent with his performance in the tri-championship team. Hearing the name of four famous soccer clubs, two from other states in Brazil and two from Latin American capitals, he does well to place one of them.[11] This composite fits fifty men, one-quarter of the sample.

The *average fan* makes sport a routine part of his life. Typically, the average fan has seen his team play in the past month and attends a few important games featuring other teams during the year. He listens to the radio for major games of his team (i.e., when they play against another big club, but not the small ones) and to all Brazilian Selection and championship games. He turns to the sports page first or second, before moving to other news. He recognizes the photographs of the three World Cup players but has only a fifty-fifty probability of naming the lesser-known city player Afonsinho. And he also recognizes at least two of the four famous clubs from other places. This composite fits ninety-seven men, roughly half the sample.

The *strong fan* gives sport a central place in his life. In this study, the strong fan goes to two or more games each month and attends all major games of his own team and often the important games between other teams as well. He listens to every radio broadcast involving his team, even in play against one of Rio's smaller clubs. In fact, he listens to just about any soccer game on the radio when he has the chance. He invariably turns to the sports page first. He misses no more than one test item about players and teams and usually gets a perfect score. This composite fits fifty-three men, roughly one-quarter of the sample.

Data from my two hundred interviews indicate that virtually all men follow professional soccer. But who are the ones in this last group, the ones who earn the label passionate fans, or fanatics? (Brazilians who demonstrate excessive interest in their teams jokingly refer to themselves as "sick" fans.) The most common but untested hypothesis in the literature of both the sociology and the psychology of sport is that extreme interest is most likely to be shown by those who lead otherwise empty lives.[12] This view suggests that spectator sports provide surrogate kinship and community for those who lack objective ties to family, friends, and neighborhood.

A rival hypothesis can be constructed from the empirical findings of modern community studies. Axelrod, for example, showed that the number of primary ties (to kin and neighbors) and the number of secondary ties (to friends and workmates) are directly related, rather than the latter being a substitute for the former as is suggested by the mass society theorists.[13] Axelrod's findings fit a general viewpoint abbreviated as "the more, the more," which is a theory of mutually reinforcing ties. Thus, the rival hypothesis can be stated: The more ties one has to society (i.e., the more integrated one is), the more likely one is to passionately embrace its symbolic manifestations such as sports teams.

What kind of men are most likely to give sport a central place in their lives? All but one of the measures of societal integration demonstrate the validity of the "the more, the more" hypothesis. There is no evidence that it is isolated or alienated urban dwellers who compensate for their sense of lost community by forming fanatic attachments to teams and heroes. My data clearly indicate that those who are marginal to the social order are marginal to the soccer scene as well; those who are well integrated are likely to be integrated in *all* parts of the mainstream, including the centrally staged sporting rituals.

With respect to objective ties, men who have frequent contact with friends and neighbors are more than five times as likely to be strong fans as those with little contact. (See table A1 in Appendix 2.) Men with firm family ties are four times as likely to be serious fans as those with virtually no kin contact.[14] Just as primary and secondary ties are directly related, so do objective and subjective— or symbolic—attachments also reinforce one another, rather than the latter substituting for the former.[15] The more objective ties to friends, kin, or neighborhood, the stronger are one's subjective ties to the city through identification with its soccer teams.

Until now my thesis has been that soccer promotes societal integration for its fans. In the data presented here, however, the causal order is reversed. Because the common assumption has been that spectator sports are a substitute for authentic social experience, the questions were constructed to ask who are most likely to be the most committed fans—society's loners or its well connected? The answer is the latter. It is not that rooting for a team cannot fill an otherwise empty life; there are biographies of fans indicating that for some it does exactly that.[16] But the vast majority of strong fans are not marginal men, nor are most marginal men fans. Instead, fandom is for those who belong.

The notion of reinforcing ties is also supported by looking at the men's indirect ties to society via mass media participation. The more one watches television and reads newspapers, the more likely one is to score in the strong fan range. These findings are consistent with what is known about American leisure patterns. Meyersohn found that interest in television reinforces both other media consumption and other leisure activities.[17] The general idea is that individuals who have the energy and interest to pursue one leisure activity are likely to be motivated to pursue others as well.[18]

Although only 61 percent of the men had television sets in their own homes, virtually all reported easy access to sets in the homes of relatives and friends. The men who report daily television viewing are twice as likely to be strong fans as those who watch only once or twice a week. (See table A2 in Appendix 2.) The men's favorite programs include variety shows, soap operas (shown during prime time in Brazil), and old American gangster and cowboy films. The relationship between television consumption and fandom is not a reflection of watching televised soccer, for these men are far more likely to listen to the game live on the radio than to watch the late-night video replays, although many did report that when their team wins they later watch the replay. And a few soccer addicts claimed they would watch any televised game, even one they already knew had ended in a scoreless tie.

There is also evidence that strong fans are greater newspaper consumers than weak fans. It is not clear whether reading a newspaper merely correlates with fandom or is a consequence of it. Is the sport fan someone who is interested in everything around him and is therefore likely to buy a paper in any case, independent of his interest in sporting news? Or is it really his interest in the sports page that leads him to look at the newspapers for scores and then, perhaps, to scan other sections for news? My data are not the type that can support a causal connection; however, three facts about newspaper sales support the notion that soccer interest leads to news consumption, at least some of the time. First, since the start of the sport lottery, paper sales are sharply higher on Monday, the day the results of the previous week's games are published and the day the experts share their prognoses for the upcoming week's games. Second, sales also rise after Flamengo victories. Third, many of my respondents said they buy a paper only after their team wins.

Marplan surveys[19] show that roughly one-quarter of Rio's lower-middle-class residents read a newspaper daily; that figure is consistent with my findings for weak fans with nine or fewer years of formal education. However, a much larger proportion of strong fans, *regardless of their educational background*, report daily readership. Of men with five or fewer years of primary school, the strong fan is four times as likely as the weak fan to see a paper every day; with six to nine years of education, he is three times as likely; and even in the most educated category he is still one-and-a-half times as likely to be exposed to the news as the weak fan. (See table A3 in Appendix 2.)

Can we assume that a fan who buys a paper for soccer news will read other types of news as well? The fans I talked with said they did, and most listed crime reports or politics as the second section they read. Men who scored high on the soccer knowledge tests—again regardless of their education—were more likely to also recognize other popular culture figures, political figures, and the name of a controversial hydroelectric facility that had recently been featured in the news. Whether soccer interest leads to consumption of other news, or vice versa, the image of fans as persons who are integrated into their society is reinforced by this finding.

Are fans who are reading just the sports page at least getting exposure to names of other states and countries as a result of their interest in soccer? The men in my sample confirmed that they do learn about both the national and the global sport communities through the newspaper. Some even made it a point to tell me that they know much more about their country since reading about the sport lottery and national championship. Fully 75 percent said they regularly read the soccer news from other states (5 percent of those said they read about lottery games only), and 67 percent said they followed the sport internationally (12 percent of them said they read only about games that relate to the Brazilian Selection). In the knowledge test, 47 percent of the men correctly identified the famous River Plate team as Argentine. This reflects their knowledge of soccer, not geography, for most could not tell me where exactly Argentina is on the map. Compare this figure with the citywide Marplan survey that showed that only 37 percent of those interviewed could name Argentina's President Lanusse right after a publicity blitz announcing his state visit to Brazil.[20]

Information about the men's religious affiliations also supports the conclusion that fandom is for those in the mainstream—that people on the margin will be outside the soccer culture too. Whereas no difference in fandom was found between Catholics and Spiritualists, the thirteen men who said they were Baptists were heavily overrepresented in the weak fan category. Being Baptist in Catholic Brazil truly connotes outsider status. Baptist converts are serious about their religion and live close within the church community. However, their lack of interest in soccer cannot be attributed to time needed for church activities, because declared Spiritualists typically spend full weekends in ceremonial retreats, yet still find time to follow the games when they return.

When we examine religiousness apart from religious affiliation, however, we find the exception to the "the more, the more" hypothesis: the *more* religious attachments a man has, the *less* likely he is to be a strong fan. Those men who attend church regularly and think of themselves as devout are only half as likely to go to the stadium as less-religious respondents. (See table A4 in Appendix 2.) Soccer is only one of several mechanisms through which people are integrated into the larger society. Whereas mass media consumption and interest in soccer are mutually reinforcing, active participation in the church and the soccer world appear to be alternative routes to connecting individuals to their community.

The negative relationship between sport fandom and religiousness may be due to their similarities: both foster a sense of identification with others who share the experience; both involve commitment to an overarching, nonmaterialistic goal; and both employ communal rituals that produce a collective consciousness. Devotion to one may offset the need for the other. However, the difference between religious and sporting rituals may explain their appeal to two largely separate groups of men. According to anthropologist Claude Lévi-Strauss, religious ritual *conjoins* whereas sporting ritual *disjoins*. Religious ritual postulates an asymmetry between profane and sacred, faithful and officiating, dead and living, uninitiated and initiated, and so forth, and the ceremony brings about a union; whereas in games the asymmetry is preordained, insofar as the rules are the same for both sides, and the contest establishes the inequality of the winners and losers.[21]

Societal patterns suggest a much simpler explanation for the negative relationship. In Latin America active participation in the Catholic church is identified with women and children. More than half the respondents said their wives or mothers regularly attended religious services. Whereas many reported that as boys they had attended church regularly until age fourteen or so, only 16 percent of the Catholics in my sample attended regularly as adults. Sex segregation may be self-perpetuating. In other words, because the soccer stadium is seen as appropriate for men while the Catholic church is associated with women, most men stay away from religious services.

The Predictors of Fandom

Combining all the background information on the men with their fan scores in a multiple regression equation[22]—a statistical technique that measures the independent contribution of each variable while holding all others constant—I learned that the single greatest predictor of fandom is past athletic participation.

Playing soccer is a nearly universal experience for boys in all regions of Brazil. Only seventeen of the two hundred men said they had not played soccer as boys, whereas ninety-eight had played in organized leagues and the remaining eighty-five had played in impromptu neighborhood games. Men who had been on organized teams were twice as likely as those who played on informal neighborhood teams to score within the highest fan category. Contrary to the notion that poor athletes become enthusiastic fans to compensate for their lack of playing skills, only one of the seventeen men who had not played soccer scored in that range. (See table A5 in Appendix 2.) The pattern of organized players being more involved as fans than "pick-up" players holds true for current adult participation as well as for childhood participation on soccer teams. (See table A6 in Appendix 2.)

American studies of fans show that those who have had personal experience with a sport are more likely to be its fans, as adults, than are nonparticipants.[23] My findings refine that generalization: it is not just playing a game, but playing in uniforms in scheduled competitions that addicts people to a sport and predisposes them to high levels of fandom in later life. Playing a sport with full teams, in accordance with rules enforced by a referee, usually in front of an audience, lays the basis for greater empathy with the professional players who operate under the same conditions. Of course, some are drawn to organized sport as young fans wanting to mimic their athlete heroes more closely, but most join as players seeking higher levels of competition, then develop a greater appreciation of the sport and its most excellent players.

This finding has tremendous implications for the role of youth leagues everywhere. We tend to think of "Little Leagues" as training and screening grounds for promising child athletes, determining who is good enough to proceed to the next level of training (in high schools in America and on apprentice teams in the soccer-playing nations). We overlook the importance of youth leagues as training grounds for future fandom for the overwhelming majority who are screened out of the preprofessional track yet want to stay close to the sport they love. Professional sport establishments make a wise investment wherever they support youth leagues. When they permit girls to play too, they potentially double the ranks of future committed fans.

The second-best predictor of fandom is participation in the sport lottery. The lottery activity reported by the two hundred men in my sample is very close to the city average; 86 percent bet at least once a month, and 57 percent bet weekly. Those who play the lottery most frequently and bet the most money are two and a half times as likely to be strong fans as those who place minimum wagers irregularly. (See table A7 in Appendix 2.) The sport lottery serves as the main outlet for the gambling interests of these men—a mere fifteen said they ever bet money with friends, while sixty-five conceded they occasionally wager a beer on a game's outcome. As one man explained, even if you lose you get a beer; it's more social than betting money. The lottery often becomes social too, when people pool their bets. Most lottery pools are made up of six to ten co-workers who jointly discuss the games and select via an odd-man-out scheme wherever they disagree. Some participate in pools with their families or in-laws in addition to placing their own bets.

From my interviews it is clear that level of fandom influences betting interest and vice versa. Those already close to soccer feel they know something that might help them win a lottery and get rich. For others, interest in the sport lottery is the stimulus to be more attentive to the sports section and conversations about the teams.

In addition to a man's past athletic experience and his current lottery participation, four other variables help predict with reasonable accuracy whether he is a weak, average, or strong fan: how often he talks with his friends and neighbors, how religious he is, how often he watches television, and whether he still plays soccer.[24] (See table A8 in Apprendix 2.) Other variables improve the prediction only marginally, if at all.

These findings are limited to fandom of one sport in one cultural setting. Yet here is a provisional answer to the question, "Who is the fan?": the adult male who is well integrated into the society through family, friends, and the media and who has either an economic investment in sport through gambling or a personal investment through organized experience with the game. Integrated people participate in their community and its traditions. For men in Brazil this includes playing soccer as a boy, being a fan as an adult, and betting in the soccer lottery too.

Given that soccer is the only professionalized team sport, it is not altogether surprising that standard demographic information about age, race, education, and occupation does not help to predict levels of fandom, even though these variables usually influence choice of leisure pursuits.[25] With respect to education and occupation, data from an American survey also supported the "the more, the more" hypothesis. Wilensky found that people with the best education and most challenging work are the ones most likely to enjoy creative, satisfying leisure activities.[26] I had no sophisticated measures of work attachment with which to test this notion on my Brazilian sample, but by their self-evaluations the men who reported being dissatisfied with their jobs (35 percent) were no more or less likely to be strong fans. Likewise, those who perform routine or menial tasks are no more drawn by the lure of spectator sport than those with more

variety in their jobs. In a one-sport culture, interest in soccer transcends such societal divisions.

The lack of correlation between fandom and other items is
more surprising. Knowing a man's income does not help predict his
fan score. Whether a man is single or married, with or without
children, affects how much free time and disposable income he has,
yet neither marital nor family status influences fan scores. The youngest men, most likely still to be single, attend Maracanã games
slightly more often, but older, married men rival their fan scores
because of their greater soccer knowledge and media consumption.

Knowing how many hours per week a man works does not
help predict his level of fandom either, though common sense says
it should. After all, there is a marked difference in leisure time
between those in my sample who hold a single job for forty hours
a week, those who work six-day weeks, and those who have second
jobs and work fifty to eighty hours each week.

Another counterintuitive finding is that residential location is
not related to stadium attendance. Maracanã is in Rio's Northern
Zone, as are most factories. Many of the men in my sample live in
northern communities where housing is cheap and close to their
work. Yet as many from hilltop favelas or costly apartments in the
Central Zone or Southern Zone take the time and spend the money
to watch their teams.

Some men from the Southern Zone do use poor transportation
as an excuse for their infrequent visits to the stadium. One young
man elaborated that he would have to catch a bus at 6:00 P.M. to
make an 8:00 P.M. start time, not getting back until 1:00 A.M., and
then would be too tired to get to work by 6:00 A.M. Rather than
jeopardize his job, he goes to Maracanã only when he accompanies
friends going by car. However, most fans who complain about the
long trip to the stadium go anyway. Predictions of sport consumption
based on sheer convenience do not work because the attendance of
strong fans approximates what economists call an "inelastic demand
curve" for their teams. Overcoming obstacles posed by money, family, time, and distance, they show their loyal support by their presence.

Fan Loyalties

I asked the men what team they cheer for, how they came to pick
that team, how long they have supported it, which teams they most
enjoy seeing beaten, and how their loyalties affect their lottery bets.

As I expected from the working-class composition of my sample, Flamengo fans are overrepresented (42 percent) and Fluminense fans underrepresented (11 percent), whereas Vasco (21 percent) and Botafogo fans (16 percent) roughly approximate their representation in the city as a whole; only seven of the two hundred men claimed one of Rio's smaller teams as their own.[27]

Fans were more likely to attribute their team affiliation to family influence than to anything else. One fan said, "I was raised with the Flamengo flag; I knew it before I knew the flag of Brazil." Another said, "I was cheering for Flamengo with my family before I could talk." But many others described families with mixed loyalties. For example, one Botafogo fan said his father is Vasco, his mother is Fluminense, his wife is Flamengo, and his brothers divide their loyalties among Rio's four major clubs.

Of the men who knew their fathers were fans, half cheered for the same team and half for some other team. But more than half the men in my sample either did not know their fathers or did not know whether they had teams. Only 30 percent of the men in my sample were born in Rio; some had come to Rio as children or adults from the nearby Middle States or Europe, where soccer was well developed, but many others were raised in small towns or rural areas in the interior of the Northeastern states, where soccer was less important in their fathers' era and the leisure time for it was a luxury many families could not afford.

A boy could strengthen his connection with his father by supporting the same team, or he could choose to annoy his father by cheering for a hated rival, as one Fluminense did to his Flamengo father. But even boys without fan fathers cheer for a team. They are socialized into fandom by other enthusiastic fans, typically uncles, friends, or neighbors. In a place where it is expected that a male have a team, a boy will choose one early.

Team selection is a complex process. To lay a basis for a thorough structured analysis would require answers to many more questions. What I did learn, however, is that choices often seem haphazard or irrational, as in the case of the man who said his entire family was Flamengo, including his mother, who had given him a Vasco shirt for his tenth birthday; he didn't know why she had given him the shirt, but he had been a Vasco fan ever since.

Many men referred to the tradition of the team, rather than their personal relationships, as the basis for their loyalty: "I'm Portuguese, so of course I'm Vasco"; "I'm black, so I have to be Flamengo—it's tradition"; "I like Fluminense because the players and fans are all gentlemen." Others eliminated teams based on their stereotypes: "I'm not black and I don't live in a favela, so I can't be Flamengo." Some offered personal reasons for their choice: "My team won the first game I ever saw"; "my team won the championship the year I really became aware of professional soccer"; "my favorite player was on that team." Generally, the weaker the fan, the more vague his reason: "I like the colors of the team shirt"; "I like the style of the team shirt"; or simply, "I like my team because it's appealing."

Given the variety of reasons for choosing a team, the homogeneity of fan groups that created club stereotypes is breaking down in modern Rio. Fathers there expect media heroes or peer influence to sway their sons' soccer affections, and they shrug it off as just one more instance of losing control over youngsters. In cities like Belo Horizonte and Pôrto Alegre, where loyalties are split between two major teams and where there are fewer diversions to compete with soccer, rivalries are taken more seriously and fights break out more frequently. Soccer traditions are inextricably linked to family traditions; there, forsaking one's father's team would be taken as a real rejection.

In "melting pot" metropolises like Rio and São Paulo, where Cariocas and Paulistas are mixed with migrants from many other states and countries, traditions are not as deeply rooted as in cities like Belo Horizonte and Pôrto Alegre, where populations are more stable and less diverse. Sport commentator João Saldanha feels that newcomers who adopt a team do not make as strong fans as those who inherit one.[28] At least one psychologist of sport, Arnold Beisser, has suggested the opposite, singling out migrants as having especially strong needs for local fandom to alleviate their loneliness and sense of estrangement.[29] My interviews support both Saldanha and Beisser.

Migrants are introduced to Rio's soccer shortly after arrival. Supportive of Beisser's view, in their first few years in the city, many show interest in a team because they have so few personal ties to occupy their time. But after the period of adjustment (three to five years), interest in soccer wanes. Supportive of Saldanha's view, the men born in Rio and those who came as young children—those who grew up with their team—are more likely to score as strong fans than those who migrated to Rio later in life.

Those who migrated as adults reported that soccer had eased their entry to a strange city, at least a little. More than two-thirds had been following some Rio team since childhood. Because newspapers throughout the country report on Rio's great teams, men were often Flamengo fans as well as fans of their local club. One man from Minas Gerais said he had been a Botafogo fan for as long as he could remember because it was far more popular where he lived than Flamengo or Vasco, though he could offer no reasons for this popularity. Another longtime Botafogo fan explained that he had developed his respect for the club because it starred World Cup players—like Zagalo, Garrincha, and Gerson—that he used to read about in his local paper. Through soccer, these men had a connection to Rio before arrival—a head start in feeling themselves a part of what goes on.

The rest of these men reported that their team affiliation dated from shortly after their arrival in Rio. The reasons for their choices varied widely. Some had been taken to Maracanã Stadium by a relative or workmate and have been cheering ever since for either the winner of that game or their host's team (even if it lost). But most found the choice even easier because of a characteristic of the sporting world—names of popular clubs are borrowed and used elsewhere (just as São Paulo's famous Corinthians took its name from the touring British amateurs). One man told me he became a Flamengo in Rio because he had been a fan of the local Flamengo team in Piauí; another said he cheered the local Vasco team in Sergipe, so he is a Rio Vasco fan too. Others chose Rio teams that shared the colors of their hometown teams. Those who could not make a connection in any of these ways chose Flamengo because "it was so popular; everyone was talking about it."

The migrants who could follow their original hometown team through the newspapers still considered it their number one loyalty. That fan from Minas Gerais, for example, said a Cruzeiro win is still more important to him than a Botafogo win, although he never bets against either team in the lottery. A Bemfica fan from Portugal keeps his tie to his homeland alive by reading about Bemfica every Sunday; an Italian immigrant does the same for his Juventus team in Turin. The unity of the soccer world—including its overlapping names and colors—provides newcomers with a sense of continuity in their lives.

Whether migrant or native, the men in my sample professed loyalty to their clubs. More than 60 percent of the men I talked to said they never place a lottery bet predicting their team will lose. When their team plays against a strong opponent, they use their "win or tie" option on that game; one man said, "when my team loses, I lose." Some spend extra money for a "triple," in effect eliminating the game by checking win, lose, or tie. Lesser fans and pragmatists bet their team to lose when it is in a slump and facing a strong rival.

Their betting principles and their sacrifice of time, money, and comfort to attend games confirm the devotion of the strong fans. Some degree of loyalty of lesser fans is expressed by their lifetime commitment to one team. The question, "How long have you supported your team?" got only three answers: "always," "since I was a child," and "since coming to Rio."

Brazilians rarely switch teams, no matter how disappointing their teams' performance or management. Three respondents had switched before age twelve, but only two of two hundred had switched as adults, and they were both weak fans. In other words, one is not so much a soccer fan as a fan of a particular club. This is true throughout the sporting world, not only Brazil. It is fans' allegiance to a team that makes them put up with stadium crowds week after week. Says British journalist Russell Davies, "There is something so hugely unrealistic about a loyalty that can survive any disaster . . . that one is tempted to think that it is the very pigheadedness of supportership that makes it enjoyable to keep up."[30]

With twelve teams to choose from, switching teams would be easier for the Brazilian fan than for the American who, after abandoning the sole local team, has only televised games of the others. But strong loyalties keep the Brazilian fan from taking advantage of his buyers' market. He would no more think of defecting from his club than of breaking other primordial ties to his kin or ethnic group. Societal values place constraints on disloyalty, as evidenced by the sexist saying, "Changing women is understandable; changing teams shows weakness of character."

Fans' loyalty, in turn, accounts for their intense involvement in club affairs. Economist Albert O. Hirschman says two responses to deterioration in the performance of an organization are exit (leaving), and voice (expressing dissatisfaction to the management).[31] Because loyalty to team detracts from the exit option, fans are forced to use the voice option with determination and resourcefulness, as exemplified by Tarzan's manifesto. On the other hand, knowing that fans have ready access to substitute teams makes management responsive to their voice to reinforce their loyalty. Unlike American fans, who accept that managers' decisions are made according to business tenets, Brazilian fans believe that their directors, like themselves, are motivated by loyalty, not commercial considerations.

Brazilians make sacrifices for their teams. War in progress—even mock war—stirs passions, especially when the enemy is visible and the divisions reinforce primordial sentiments. Even though club stereotypes do not hold true for every fan (I met Portuguese men who did not support Vasco, as well as blacks who were not Flamengo and upper-class men who were), those stereotypes were invoked as fans explained their feelings about their rivals. Several men told me they do not like Vasco because they do not like the Portuguese. One man said he hates Fluminense because it is a racist club. Others expressed the opposite sentiment: they hate Flamengo because they dislike blacks. One characterized Flamengos of any race as "ignorant people without education." Many summed up the overwhelming antipathy for Flamengo as class snobbery, or even class warfare. Traditional rivalries are rooted in the social symbolism of the teams. And they are so strong that 100,000 fans attended a Flamengo vs. Fluminense game even while Fluminense was in sixth place.

Other rivalries are based on current team standings. Realists more than traditionalists, some fans say the rival they most enjoy seeing beaten is the one that most threatens their team's chances for the championship. Often the rivalry is based on one or two recent games where the rival has humiliated one's own team. At the time of my interviews, Botafogo had just shut out Flamengo six to zero. Goading the opposition, Botafogo fans carried banners reading "6 x 0" to the stadium for their next confrontation with Flamengo. Understandably, Flamengo fans wanted revenge.

Personal rivalry, based on playful interaction with friends and family, provided just as many reasons for wanting to see a team lose. One man said, "just to be opposing my son; it's more fun." Many men expressed special animosity toward the Flamengo fans they knew because "they think they own the world after victory" and "they make it unpleasant for everyone." One man complained that the Flamengo fans at work "think their team is the Brazilian Selection"; his complaint was corroborated by his workmate who told me "Flamengo *is* Brazil." Such fanaticism led more than one of my respondents to say he would cheer even a foreign team against Flamengo. Strong anti-Flamengo sentiments often unify opposing fans. One Vasco fan chose his best friend's team, Fluminense, as his second-favorite team for the fun of joining against Flamengo whenever it played either of their teams.

Personality traits probably explain whether a man chooses a friend's or relative's favorite team as his second team or as his special rival. In either case, as long as the mood is playful, a shared experience is the outcome. Strained relations can be the consequence when more is at stake. The 1970 World Cup final between Italy and Brazil was more than a game because either victor would become the first tri-champion and retire the coveted Jules Rimet trophy. São Paulo papers were filled with stories about families splitting for the match; the emotional investment was so great that immigrant fathers cheering for their native Italy sent away sons cheering for their native Brazil.

The conclusion to be drawn from these two hundred interviews is that soccer strengthens social bonds because the rivalry is mostly in fun. Only one person said he exclusively seeks the company of other Flamengo fans at work: "We suffer together when we lose; we're very close." All the others said their social groups include fans of all teams. Only one person lumped soccer with politics and religion as topics to avoid because of people's sensitivities. Nine men described their soccer discussions as "heated," one as "half-heated," and the rest described them as "full of little jokes."

Social integration and fandom are mutually reinforcing; the more one has of one, the more one gets of the other. Socially connected males do not want to be excluded from the most popular conversation. One man admitted reading the sports page because "guys think you're crazy if you know nothing about soccer." Keeping abreast of soccer news can promote exposure to other types of news and other topics of talk. Fandom, then, is both a symbolic manifestation of one's sense of belonging and a support for participation in the community.

Rio's Maracaña Stadium, the largest in the world, holds 220,000 spectators. Players and referee are protected from the fans by a moat ten feet wide. The adjoining covered arena for 30,000 offers perspective. Photo courtesy of Don King Productions.

Fans express their anger after the humiliating early elimination of the Brazilian team from the 1966 World Cup. (*Left*) They hang in effigy the soccer authorities responsible for selecting the players and coach. Photo by Evandro Teixeira. (*Right*) Candles burning over photographs symbolize death to the defeated players. The sign says "Death to the commission—we'll be waiting for you at the airport Thursday." Photo by Odyr Amorim. Both photographs courtesy of Jornal do Brasil.

Street celebration after Brazil eliminates Uruguay in the 1970
World Cup semifinals. Photo by Evandro Teixeira, courtesy of Jornal
do Brasil.

(*Upper right*) Pelé is honored as Sportsman of the Century. Photo courtesy of the Cosmos Soccer Club.

(*Lower right*) After the 1970 tri-championship of the World Cup, President Médici shares the limelight with Carlos Alberto (*left*), the Brazilian team captain, and coach Mario Zagalo. Photo © 1970, Manchete.

(*Left*) The Fluminense team takes the field. Courtesy of the Brazilian Tourism Authority.

(*Right*) The celebration of a Vasco da Gama goal. Courtesy of Agência Globo—Rio de Janeiro.

(*Left*) Flamengo's Organized Teen Fans burn the opponents' flag. Fan support is measured in part by the visibility of team shirts and flags. Photo courtesy of Agência Globo—Rio de Janeiro.

(*Upper right*) Brazilian fans are willing to tolerate discomfort for a good vantage point. Photo courtesy of Agência Globo—Rio de Janeiro.

(*Lower right*) One of the few women in the bleachers gets carried away. Photo courtesy of Agência Globo—Rio de Janeiro.

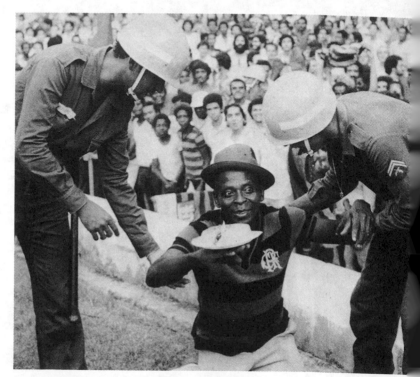

(*Upper left*) Santista, the masseur of Rio's Vasco da Gama team, carrying his voodoo charms onto the field for luck. Photo courtesy of Agência Globo—Rio de Janeiro.

(*Lower left*) Flamengo fan with cake, a spiritualist religious offering, is escorted off the field. Photo courtesy of Agência Globo—Rio de Janeiro.

(*Right*) Brazilians acknowledge the fans' contribution to victory. President of the Flamengo Fan Club, Jayme Rodrigues do Carvalho, his wife, and his son share the honor of a bi-championship trophy with the team captain. Photo courtesy of Jayme Rodrigues do Carvalho.

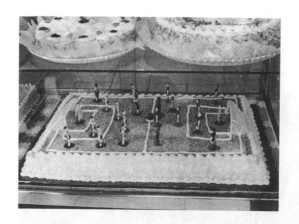

(*Above*) Birthday cake displayed in Copacabana bakery shop.
Photo by the author.

(*Below*) Autobol, a Brazilian invention that combines demolition
derby and soccer. Note the goal-tending car. Photo courtesy of Agência
Globo—Rio de Janeiro.

S / X

The Shared Symbols of a Culture: Its Heroes, Villains, and Ideology

Shared interest in public personalities is an important expression of collective spirit. People who can identify society's leaders, celebrities, and heroes feel assured that they "belong." They also can talk to others with the assurance that their comments about these personalities will be understood. Teams and players, as the focal points of people's interest in sport, are an important source of common symbols. The athletes are the actors at center stage whom others watch and discuss. Focal points for hostility bring people together too, again showing that there can be unity through conflict. This has been the role of scapegoats throughout history, and soccer coaches and referees, as scapegoats, are no exception.

In a nation where virtually all boys grow up playing soccer to the exclusion of other sports, Brazilian men show great admiration for the small percentage who rise to the top and make their living playing the game. Professional players symbolize the ideal of social mobility. They strengthen their fans' faith in an open society and give hope to millions of boys who play the game.

Players also symbolize the special talents and grace of a nation's people. Individual athletes who win the attention of the world sporting community can do as much as winning teams to reinforce the admiration accorded a nation. The stars of Brazilian Selections—first Friedenreich, then Leonidas, later Garrincha—have promoted a positive self-image for their countrymen. The global idolatry of

121

Pelé as the best soccer player in history remains a source of pride for Brazilians.

Players as Public Persons

To get some notion of how soccer players compare with other public personalities as common symbols, I showed twelve photographs to the two hundred working-class men I interviewed in Rio in 1973 and asked each respondent to name as many of the persons pictured as he could.

Overall, the political figures fared poorly. Twenty-four men did not recognize then-President Médici, although his picture was hanging in all public buildings and, as chief of state since 1969, he was regularly featured in television news and the daily papers. Only 32 percent could name Finance Minister Delfim Neto, one of the masterminds of the "Brazilian miracle" and second only to the president in terms of television and press coverage.[1] The image of Richard

Table 1
Results of the Photograph Recognition Test

Public Personality	Percentage Who Recognized Photograph
POLITICIANS	
President Médici	88
Delfim Neto (minister of finance)	32
Richard M. Nixon	59
Chagas Freitas (governor of Rio)	44
ENTERTAINERS	
Regina Duarte (television soap opera star)	60
Chacrinha (popular television comedian)	99
Roberto Carlos (popular singer)	95
SPORTSMEN	
Emerson Fittipaldi (race car driver)	74
Jairzinho (Botafogo star player)	84
Afonsinho (free agent player)	49
Tostão (World Cup veteran)	91
Pelé	99.5

Photos courtesy of *Jornal do Brasil*'s archives (selected with the aid of the sport staff). Photographs were shown in the order listed here.

M. Nixon, as president of the United States, was seen frequently on the front pages of Rio's most respected papers, on television and movie-house news highlights (Nixon was in the news even more than usual when this photograph testing occurred during the early days of the Watergate scandal), yet only 59 percent of the men recognized him. Only 44 percent recognized Chagas Freitas, governor of Rio since 1970, even though his picture appeared regularly in the newspaper he owns, *O Dia*, a crime and sport paper that is the most popular daily among the working class.

Figures from the world of entertainment fared considerably better. Even though only 61 percent of the men reported having television sets in their homes, virtually all reported easy access to television in some family member's or neighbor's home.[2] Roberto Carlos, the most popular singer in all of Latin America, received a 95 percent recognition rating. Chacrinha, a slapstick comedian whose popular prime-time show is aired several times weekly, was recognized by 99 percent of the men. Even Regina Duarte, star of a nightly prime-time soap opera, was named by 60 percent of these respondents—giving her a higher rating than all political figures other than the president.

Television personalities are recognized by so many because Brazilian television offers less diversity than American television audiences get from their three commercial and one public networks, besides numerous local stations, now supplemented by cable television. People in Rio are more likely to watch the same shows, since TV-Globo, the major network, captures 45–50 percent of the viewing audience; none of its several competitors gets more than 10 percent.

From the world of sport, race car driver Emerson Fittipaldi (pictured in street clothes), then in his heyday of bringing glory to Brazil with his world championships, was recognized by 74 percent. All but one person recognized King Pelé—the sole exception being a new migrant from an impoverished town of the Northeast. Tostão, who earned a large share of the credit for the 1970 tri-championship, was named by 91 percent of the men. Tostão was one of the very few players in 1973 to have his image promoted by commercial advertisers. Jairzinho, a star player on the local Botafogo team, also was catapulted to national fame during the 1970 World Cup. (Television cameras captured young Jair kneeling and crossing himself after every goal he made.) Jairzinho was recognized by 84 percent of the men. Afonsinho, a respected but less illustrious Rio player, who recently had press attention for being one of the first to win free-agent status (a player who controls his own contract), was recognized by 49 percent—that is thirty-four more people than knew the influential minister of finance.

Since they have only one national sport, Brazilians do not divide their interests and loyalties among multiple sets of athletes as do fans in the United States. The effectiveness of players as common culture symbols is strengthened by this concentration of attention.[3]

Brazilians are unusual in calling players by snappy nicknames (like Pelé and Tostão), some endearing diminutive form of their first names (Jair becomes Jairzinho; Afonso becomes Afonsinho), or occasionally by their last names (like Rivelino). They are rarely referred to by the lengthy full names that make nicknames essential, and most Brazilians could not tell you that Tostão's real name is Eduardo Gonçalves de Andrade or that Carlos Alberto is Carlos Alberto Torres. This intimacy is not extended to people in other sports (note race car driver Emerson Fittipaldi). The familiarity expressed by nicknames is one of many ways a familylike closeness between soccer player and fan is cultivated in Brazil. Another way is through the newspaper summary of each player's performance in the previous game. In Brazil all players, not just the stars, get the press attention that makes them widely known.

When Brazil gets live coverage of more games, there is every reason to believe that soccer players' importance as cultural symbols will grow as players get added exposure. High-powered zoom lenses will bring star players closer. As more players are used for product endorsements, their recognition quotient will be further enhanced, especially among people who do not follow soccer. With more television exposure, more players will match other television entertainers as common symbols.

The Symbolic Importance of Villains: Coaches and Referees

Whereas star players serve as culture heroes, coaches and referees more often act as scapegoats, unifying the fans in anger. The coach and referee both work on jobs where the opportunity for praise is slim, while censure is virtually assured. On the field, their job performance and delicate judgments are assessed by competitive masses. The soccer machine could not operate without men willing to participate under such adverse conditions. Rarely do partial observers declare that their team lost because the other team played better.

In one respect, the referee suffers more from scapegoating than the coach, who often joins the others in condemning the referee and questioning his eyesight and honesty. But in another respect, try as he might to get the referee to take the blame for his team's loss, the coach is culpable for the seasonal record. Not all referees can be dismissed as thieving or blind. If a team consistently loses, the coach certainly will be replaced.

Virtually all coaches in Brazil are former professional players. Becoming a coach is one way athletes who love the game can remain involved, and coaching is one of the few ways sport provides lasting social mobility for players. Even though sports are not part of the school scene in Brazil, there are many coaching positions because a club's training staff must be large enough to service its youth teams as well as its professional team and its squad of reserves. As in all sports, star players do not necessarily make the best coaches; an average player can be an excellent teacher and strategist. A coach coming out of the players' ranks is not likely to have studied physical education in any formal sense. Within the coaching staff, the physical trainers are far more likely than the coaches to hold university degrees. And it is only in the past twenty years that coaches have accepted professional trainers as partners in building and molding athletes.

Hardaker describes the soccer coach's job perfectly: "Properly done [it] involves long hours, hard work, obsessive commitment, a rather painful dependence on the ability and efforts of other men, and little or no security."[4] No security comes closest to the facts. *Goal Magazine*'s 1971 survey of the English League found that one coach had been fired every two weeks over the prior twenty-five years.[5] For every coach in Rio or São Paulo who succeeds, eleven are doomed to fail. Brazilian directors feel a great deal of pressure from their fans, who assume they have a voice in the preparation of the teams. The easiest way to respond to disappointed fans who want to see evidence of change is to dismiss the coach. The coaches of top professional teams can usually relocate in musical chairs fashion, exchanging positions with equally unsuccessful colleagues in other clubs.

Because of their visibility and the instability in their careers, coaches command an extraordinary amount of media attention and become public personalities in their own right. They can be treated as heroes or as villains, sometimes praised one day and damned the next. One might assume that the apex of a coaching career would be appointment to head the national team. Surprisingly, this is not always the wise coach's view of things. As Pelé explains in his autobiography, training a World Cup team can ruin a coach's career, for it is the coach more than anyone who is blamed for defeat. Being burned and buried in effigy is expected, but coaches are often victims of more than symbolic displays of anger, and the police must be called in to protect family and home from bomb threats or hostile mobs. Such dangers were faced by Mario Zagalo, the coach of the defeated team in 1974, even though the same man had been considered a Brazilian hero in 1970 when he coached his team to its memorable tri-championship victory. Zagalo took the 1970 challenge after two other coaches turned down the opportunity because they believed that the nationalistic emotions wrapped up in the World Cup made it too great a risk.

Threats of injury to the coaches occur irregularly, but risks to the lives and limbs of referees are real and frequent. Stories of referees being shot to death in small-town stadia periodically appear in newspapers in Latin America and Europe. Assaults occur less frequently in major cities, where security measures are tighter. Maracanã's protective moat design has been copied by every major stadium constructed in Brazil and in some other countries as well. Assaults on officials in American sports are extremely rare. When Americans read about those in other countries, they are likely to blame hot Latin and Mediterranean tempers, English hooliganism, or excessive nationalism. But there are structural aspects of the game that better explain the soccer referee's special vulnerability.

Most important, soccer is a team sport where a solitary figure is entrusted with total authority. In soccer twenty-two players on a field some 100 to 130 yards long are judged by one person. The referee is in charge of all aspects of the game, and his decisions are final. He is assisted by two linesmen, one on each side of the field. The referee accepts their judgment if he was not in position to see the action himself, but if he was in position, he can ignore their ruling.[6] Only the referee can stop the action for serious injury, only he can order players off the field, and only he can suspend or terminate a game. The referee is, in fact, the highest authority in the stadium. He can even give orders to the chief of police should he decide evacuation of the stadium is necessary.

There are no checks on the referee's power in soccer. In contrast, in basketball, football, and baseball at least two officials can confer and jointly reach a judgment. Even in tennis, where one official could adequately patrol the small court, the responsibility is shared by two. The presence of other officials guards against abuse of power. But in soccer the audience cannot be assured of that, nor should they be. One highly respected referee admitted to me that there have been rare occasions on which he got carried away with his own power and purposely made a bad call just to show that he was more important than Pelé, the other players, and the governor in the VIP box, all combined. There have been proposals to increase the number of referees to two, but the conservative International Football Association Board continues to reject them.

Besides being the sole authority, the referee is given powers that directly affect the final score in a low-scoring game. It is not a coincidence that in Portuguese the words for "referee" and "judge" are identical. The referee not only cites rule infractions, but must decide if an offense is intentional or unintentional, for only the former is a foul. Fans observe the offense, but they are too far away to make the delicate judgment about intent. The fans may feel that the referee himself was too far away. Hardaker estimates that in an average game a referee runs between seven and eight and a half miles and makes 120 decisions.[7] Obviously it is impossible for him to see more than a fraction of the fouls committed on the huge field; for those he does see, his power to judge intent can be abused.

Because of their solitude and the somewhat arbitrary nature of the penalty situations, soccer referees are more vulnerable to bribery attempts than are officials in many other sports. Fans are always suspicious of partisan motives—whether based on considerations of heart or of wallet. Although a referee's decisions can be influenced by the howling crowds, mounting tensions, or considerations of reputation, the sport is totally dependent on the honesty of its officials.

There is yet another feature of the referee's role that seems peculiar to American sports fans. Like American football, basketball, and hockey, soccer is a time-limited game. It is played in two forty-five-minute halves, separated by a ten- or fifteen-minute break. Yet there is no official clock in most of the grand stadia of Europe or Latin America. The referee is timekeeper in addition to his already extensive list of responsibilities. No time-outs are allowed in the game, but the referee can stop his clock for injuries (again, at his discretion) or when fans threaten to invade the pitch. In other words, only the referee knows for sure when the game will end.

One example from the 1978 World Cup should suffice to demonstrate how fans might think a referee has purposely deprived them of a victory. In the first round of the play-offs, Brazil was tied with Sweden, 1–1, with forty-five seconds left, according to the unofficial clock of the broadcasters. The referee awarded a corner kick to Brazil, which was perfectly executed, then headed in for a winning goal. The crowd went crazy. Then the Welsh referee signaled that the goal did not count because time had already run out. Unlike basketball, there is no concession to plays in process. With victory in hand one second, gone the next, the confused fans and players had nowhere to go to appeal the decision. It is fitting that a culture known for less concern with punctuality than business-oriented America should have their national sport bounded by such an invisible notion of time.

Picture a soccer game: nonstop running, then a carefully executed attack on the goal that comes close, but misses. This happens over and over. Tensions build; frustrations mount. The stadium is filled with two intensely competitive masses. Fans see obvious fouls that occur out of sight of the referee, and fans think they see fouls the referee should have noticed. If the fans seriously question a referee's neutrality or honesty, they may try to attack him during crucial games. Smaller and older stadia have no moats or fences to keep fans at a distance. Only the police offer protection, and hometown police have been known to launch their own attacks, as when partisan stadium police injured visiting Flamengo players in Bahia during the national championship. Of course, far more often fans accuse the referee of incompetence, not dishonesty, and express their hostility through cutting words rather than violent actions. Rio fans reserve a biting accusation for the men in black who inspire their wrath: 100,000 people in Maracanã chant rhythmically, "*Bicha, bicha,*" the derogatory Portuguese slur of "faggot, faggot."

Given such abuses, who becomes a referee and why? In 1974 there were 292,025 referees in the member associations of FIFA, so plenty of men have been willing to assume the role.[8] In Europe referees are part-time amateurs who undergo minimal training. Typically, they share the working-class background of the players. In Latin America, where literacy is required so they can pass a specialized school course, referees are more likely to come from the middle class. Most hold other full-time jobs, some in the liberal professions like law and engineering. There are critics who feel that too much is at stake and that the pace is too fast in big-time professional soccer today to have the game controlled on the field by amateurs.[9] But Hardaker supports amateurism; he fears professionals might compromise impartiality for the sake of career or, worse yet, encourage bribery so they can make a good living before mandatory retirement at age fifty.[10]

Hardaker estimates that it takes ten years to work one's way up from the amateur players' leagues to the professional leagues, so those officiating in first-division games are experienced in spite of their amateur status. Such long training appeals only to the highly motivated, and the incentive is not primarily monetary. Usually referees are not highly paid, considering the physical and mental requirements of their task, in addition to the crowd's abuse. In Europe the referees receive modest fees that range from $35 for a first division game in England to $150 in Spain.[11] In Latin America, where training requirements arc greater, the referee's pay can be a good supplement to an income. In Maracanã Stadium, for example, the referee receives $135 a game plus 1 percent of the gate over $80,000. A referee qualified for first-division matches can earn $10,000 a year on the job. There are even some full-time professional referees in Brazil; twenty international-class referees earn as much as $30,000 a year.

Money in part motivates some people to referee, but most men referee because they love the game of soccer. Many played as amateurs and wanted to play professionally. Officiating is the next best thing—referees are on the field and integral to the action. Non-stop running for ninety minutes is so physically demanding that referees consider themselves athletes. Clearly, many referees enjoy their total power over an important event; at a minimum they like to exercise authority and see the balance of rules as part of the game's beauty and integrity. Most important, the job done right can earn the referee respect and admiration. Armando Marques and Olten Ayres Abreu are prime examples of Brazilian referees highly regarded as skilled and just; they have enjoyed celebrity status similar to that of the players for nearly a decade.

The referee is an essential part of the sports spectacle just like the players. Fans may feel that paying their money at the gate entitles them to have fun by criticizing the referee. Journalists practicing pop psychology say that fans enjoy heaping abuse on the official because it releases their pent-up aggression against authority figures like bosses or fathers. What is clear, however, is the role of the referee helps bring fans closer together. Outside the stadium the controversial nature of some calls sparks endless conversations between strangers and friends alike. Inside the stadium the crowd is united by expressing collective sentiment *against* the referee as much as by shouting encouragement *for* their favorite players. Whether the yell is "thief," "you're blind," or "faggot," harmonizing chants to upset the referee are a time-honored part of the sporting ritual.

The Mobility Ideology

Democratization and professionalization of soccer caused a drastic change in the socioeconomic origins of both players and directors. When teams were affiliated with regatta and cricket clubs, they were composed of foreigners and sons of the local elite and were managed by directors from the same privileged strata. But when the proletarian district clubs run by local leaders were included in the league, the real aristocracy left the established soccer clubs for more exclusive country clubs and jockey clubs, and their place was taken by the city's new successful commercial class. The players from "fine family" backgrounds stayed on the teams as long as less affluent players were paid under the table, but with professionalization they quit rather than be tainted as club employees. Their places were taken initially by players from the growing urban middle class. Over the years, the class level has steadily declined; today it is estimated that more than 80 percent of Brazil's professional soccer players are from the lowest social class.

As the social class of players changed, so did their race. In the chic era of soccer all players were white, and so were their petit bourgeois replacements. But even before professionalism was legalized, some clubs recognized the talents of mulatto and black players. Several years after the mulatto Artur Friedenreich broke the color barrier in 1909, a black player was signed by the America club in Rio, causing a number of teammates to defect to Fluminense. In 1923 Vasco da Gama, which had a policy of nondiscrimination, was promoted to Rio's first division thanks to its predominately nonwhite championship team. In response, some established clubs temporarily broke away from the league.[12] But the dazzling skills of Brazil's blacks and mulattoes ultimately proved irresistible, culminating in the starring role of Leonidas, a black center forward, in Brazil's excellent 1938 World Cup team. Sport historians say it is no coincidence that Brazil challenged Argentine and Uruguayan dominance in South American soccer at precisely the time it admitted nonwhite players to its best clubs.[13]

The elite Fluminense Club was the last to hire black athletes, and that was not until the 1960s. Fluminense's current employee policy reflects the Brazilian pattern of broad social-class prejudice rather than limited racial prejudice. Whether black, brown, or white, the predominately lower-class soccer players are not welcome to mingle with the upper-class members and their daughters at most Fluminense dances or dinners. Brazilian soccer authorities insist there is no racial discrimination in the game today. Blacks and mulattoes are well represented on teams throughout the country, although the CBD cannot report their exact proportions or describe their representation in the coaching profession. There are studies that demonstrate racial prejudice in Brazil; the visibility granted successful nonwhite athletes may falsely dispel accusations of its persistence.[14]

Do Brazilian players, regardless of race, achieve social mobility that lasts beyond their playing career? The myth versus the reality of upward mobility through sport varies from society to society. The Americans adopted the British ideology that games and sport have educational merit and deserve budget and space allocations within schools. The American practice of using high schools and universities as training and screening grounds for professional athletics is thought to be the most important channel of mobility in the United States. Athletic eligibility rules may keep working-class youth in high school and foster better grades; the best athletes receive scholarships for higher education that many could not afford.

Organized sports in colleges and universities are on a small scale or virtually nonexistent in the rest of the world. In Brazil, money and space are too scarce to support anything but minimal physical education programs within the schools. Sport may facilitate upward mobility by leading to a professional career. In Brazil there are 8,300 professional athletes playing soccer,[15] more than three times the number of professional athletes in the United States, even though Brazil's population is only half as large.

But short of a professional career, sport can still lead athletes indirectly to higher educational or occupational attainment than they would otherwise achieve. In Brazil, youth soccer falls under the jurisdiction of the professional division of the club. Players may be developed on three separate teams according to their age: *mirim* for children ten or eleven; *infantil* for youths twelve to fourteen years old; and *juvenil* for boys fifteen to seventeen. The age at which a player can move from juvenile to professional is not prescribed but varies with talent and maturity (e.g., Pelé was placed on the professional roster by age fifteen). These children are preprofessionals; even the youngest children on the mirim team are under the direction of a professional soccer coach and his staff and are legally under contract to serve the club. In exchange for their hard work, these youngsters are often housed by the soccer clubs and given education and health care far beyond their families' means.

A description of the youth soccer program in Rio's Botafogo illustrates the benefits of Brazil's recruitment system for both club and player. Botafogo has eighty children, aged eleven to sixteen, in their *escolinha* (little school). All these talented children are from the lowest social class or belong to families of subsistence-level poverty, who come from the small towns in the interior regions or the mud and cardboard shacks of the slums at the periphery of Brazil's large cities. Although most of Botafogo's youngsters are found in the southern states, a few represent other parts of Brazil. Boys from the metropolitan area are found during "free-play" tryouts (sometimes called "sieve days") held by the club in a different suburb each Wednesday. Volunteer scouts, along with club trainers, pick out promising youths for further testing. Occasionally coaches from nearby small towns bring boys into the club, motivated by goodwill or the hopes of a "bird dog" reward from the club. Once selected, the children work with three physical trainers and a coach and attend exercise and practice sessions three times a week. They are scheduled to play some fifty games during the year, and up to 5,000 spectators may be attracted to the final games of the city championship.

Every boy dreams of being spotted and signed by a professional team. Parents sign over guardianship rights to the clubs and permit their sons to move to the big city, hoping that the boys may have a real chance to escape a humdrum existence. Even if dreams of stardom do not come true, a boy gains a great deal from the training experience: the club pays his expenses and a monthly allowance of $25—roughly half his father's monthly income—and provides often badly needed medical, dental, and nutritional attention. The hundreds of boys taken in by the soccer clubs will also have the opportunity to study in superior big-city schools that can prepare them for white-collar work or higher education.

Although his phenomenal success is extraordinary, the discovery of young Pelé and his initial contact with the Santos Club typify the Brazilian recruitment system.[16] Pelé grew up as the oldest child in a poor family in the small town of Baurú (population 80,000) in São Paulo's interior. After playing with a neighborhood team from the age of ten, the thirteen-year-old Pelé was invited to join the juvenile team of one of the town's two clubs. Former World Cup player Valdemar de Brito, who coached the team before returning to the city, had been so impressed by Pelé's talents that he returned two years later to convince Pelé's parents to allow the boy to play with the Santos Club. Word of young Pelé's talents had traveled far. Already his mother had refused an offer from a Rio club. But Santos was a good deal closer to Baurú and a far smaller city than Rio. Reluctantly, his mother allowed the fifteen-year-old to depart:

> to me you're still a little boy, but everyone else seems to think
> you're grown up. Maybe I'm wrong. Maybe I shouldn't stand
> in your way if this is really a chance for you . . . you were
> never a good student and I don't want you sewing boots for a
> living the rest of your life.[17]

The famous players on the Santos team received him with kindness, and the child prodigy overcame his initial nervousness and performed promisingly on the field. But he was much too small to be placed on the professional team right away. He was fed huge high-protein meals, started on a body-building course of calisthenics, and dewormed. The soccer he played for the juvenile team was impressive, and the club offered him a generous contract—expenses plus $60 a month—enough money to permit Pelé's father to make monthly payments on the family's first house. Though he was still homesick, his love of the game soon won him over as his goals helped secure the state championship for the Santos' juvenile and amateur teams. An accident to the great forward Vasconcelos opened up a place for Pelé on the club's professional team long before anyone expected it. In no time Pelé was the team's leading scorer, basking in glory for a stunned press, and putting behind him all his thoughts of running home to Baurú.

But the stories of the young boys contracted by the teams do not always have happy endings. Sometimes incurable homesickness sends them back to their families, where the best they can hope for is a position on the town team. Sometimes the malnutrition of a lifetime cannot be corrected, and the player will never be strong enough to endure the demanding sport. Sometimes the fast, tough street soccer the child learned cannot be tamed to the rule-bounded, strategic professional game. Sometimes a poor boy from a rural slum cannot adjust to city life. For the young players who do qualify for the juvenile team, training is more rigorous than before, and they are now playing in front of large stadium crowds. Juvenile games are pregame entertainment for the crowds who pour in one or two hours early to secure their places for first division games. Some players never get used to playing in front of huge and demanding audiences. A few of those who do adjust are offered professional contracts with a club after a year or two.

Brazilian coaches and club directors point to the graduates of their "little schools" with pride because they have lived with the young men since they were children. Raising players is more economical than paying signing bonuses and transfer fees to already established stars. The Botafogo coach told me that 75 percent of his 1973 first-string team was "homegrown," including Jairzinho, one of the 1970 World Cup stars. A club like Botafogo can save so much money, in fact, that it can justify expenditures on the great majority of boys who are cut from its teams. Besides, in a traditional paternalistic society helping the poor is just one more service the nonprofit clubs provide for the community. More pragmatically, the development program in part pays for itself; some of those juvenile players who do not make Botafogo's professional team have their contracts sold to one of Rio's minor clubs. The small clubs cooperate because of the low price of the contract and the superior training the player has received in the big club. The player is consoled because he at least has a career in the city. The rest of the juvenile players are given their contracts as a parting gift, and most return to the interior to play on hometown teams.

Sometimes player sales go from the small clubs to the big ones. This is one way the smaller clubs, who receive less at the gate and sell far fewer memberships, can survive. Every few years they will have a young player who has developed into a strong, promising athlete but with whom they are willing to part. They can use the revenue from the purchase of the player contract to stay financially solvent. Such loses may reinforce their inferior status, but the income allows them to purchase the inexpensive contracts of aging athletes from the better clubs and still do reasonably well on the field. In this way the small clubs may act as farm clubs for the larger clubs around the country, not all of which have player-development programs as elaborate and successful as Botafogo's. The protection of the small clubs by the big clubs is partly in appreciation of this service.

Only the affluent clubs can afford to take in loco parentis responsibility for the lives of children. Other clubs range from having no "little school" to having large early training programs like Gremio's clinic for 1,500 children in Rio Grande do Sul. At a minimum, all clubs have juvenile teams (although not all pay salaries to their apprentice players). Here again the Brazilian sport system mirrors the features of European and other Latin training programs. Gardner contrasts the early training of three average soccer players from Brazil, Italy, and England and concludes that "their lives, despite the geographical and cultural distances that separate them, are remarkably similar."[18]

A number of soccer authorities feel that America will never be competitive in the sport until it adopts the "juvenile team" system established in other countries. Roy McCrohan, British soccer coach of the Minnesota Kicks, is one who holds that position. He left his family at seventeen to start his career as a soccer player, and he gave up his son at age sixteen. "We can't get hold of these boys until they are in their 20s. Then it's too late . . . American boys are . . . willing to train hard. . . . Technically, they're not bad, but it's the game situations where their lack of experience shows."[19] Carlos Alberto, who was one of the stars of the New York Cosmos, is another advocate of the apprentice system. He played for Fluminense in Rio from the age of fourteen. As a member of the juvenile team, he practiced with the professionals and had professional coaching. He played preliminary games before huge crowds. When a professional athlete was hurt, he was placed temporarily on the first team. By the time he earned a regular position on the professional team, he already knew his teammates and their approach to the game. By age seventeen, he was a seasoned player.

Mobility in the Metropolis versus the Community

A lesser career playing in one of Brazil's smaller cities can sometimes mean more long-term security than a higher-paying glamorous position on a Rio or São Paulo team. Thousands of players cannot claim riches but do claim that soccer led them from "rags to respectability."

Brazil's major soccer clubs pay a professional wage. Players' salaries on the big Rio teams are now between $800 and $1,000 a month—a very good wage compared with the $100 a month earned by the city's average laborer. In 1973 approximately one hundred soccer stars earned well over $12,000 a year—many in the $20,000 to $40,000 range.[20] Today a few superstars, like Zico of Flamengo, may earn as much as $750,000 a year. In return for their wages, the players must attend daily training sessions and relinquish their freedom before games for what Brazilians call "concentration"—players are confined to club grounds so that the trainers can monitor their eating and sleeping and ensure abstention from sex.[21] Concentration is typically one or two days, but it may be four or five days before a big game and even longer before a championship match. A combination of the training and concentration schedules eliminates opportunities for big-time players to attend a university or hold part-time jobs in preparation for a postsports career.

A professional career typically starts at eighteen and is over between twenty-six and thirty. Unfortunately, the vast majority of players end their careers with no more money in the bank than when they started. The club, paternalistic in many other ways, does not offer investment counseling or budgeting advice. Players living up to their glamorous image squander money faster than they earn it. Worse yet, they rarely escape exploitation by swindlers or poor money managers. Pelé openly admits nearly losing his great fortune not once but twice, by having entrusted his finances to others who proved unworthy.

At about age thirty most players find themselves with few work skills, more debts than cash reserves, and only memories of their brief careers. Many former players say they experienced terrible depression after leaving the game. Unlike American sports, played in seasons, the Brazilian player has no time off to train for a future career or resume a normal identity out of the spotlight. Typically he has trouble adjusting to retirement. He has little choice but to accept a low-level job that is hardly commensurate with his newly acquired middle-class tastes. All too often, players return to the poverty-stricken environment from which they came. The most famous example, perhaps, is the case of Garrincha. A mulatto slum boy who played his way to the top (in spite of a leg deformed by childhood polio) and starred in the 1958 and 1962 World Cups, Garrincha plummeted into obscurity shortly after his less stellar contribution to the unsuccessful 1966 team. An amazing player—some would say the greatest dribbler of all time—Garrincha found himself jobless, living in an urban slum with his wife and eight children. Another player, Maneco, after a brilliant career, could not find a job, fell behind in his rent and was evicted, and killed himself over a $20 debt.

Soccer players in a smaller city like Curitiba (population estimates range from 800,000 to 1,000,000) experience a different kind of career. Curitiba's soccer clubs are not as professionalized as the major clubs in Rio and São Paulo. While Rio players may receive $5,000 to $15,000 or more upon signing a contract, some Curitiba players sign on for nothing—just for the chance to launch a career in sports. The fan can believe the player retains some amateur spirit and fights for the love of his "shirt" (the club's uniform). Only a handful can survive on their playing salaries alone; most supplement their incomes with part-time jobs.

Commensurate with salaries, clubs vary in what they can demand of their players. Examining Curitiba's soccer system is like cutting an archaeological slice through the history of the sport in Brazil, allowing us to draw generalizations about the effect of increasing professionalism. The Coritiba (sic) Football Club, founded by the German colony, is the city's oldest and most professional club. Coritiba plays in the national championship. Because the caliber of competitors is so much better than in the state championship and because of the revenue that comes from playing those extra games (matches against the big Rio and São Paulo clubs are excellent gate draws), the Coritiba team has improved greatly and acquired some excellent players in recent years. It is rapidly becoming a serious contender in the national championship. Coritiba pays salaries high enough that it can demand three or four training sessions a week and enforce one-day "concentrations" before big games.

When I began this research, the fifth club in the first division, Primavera, was barely more than an amateur district club with a social membership of fewer than 500. Because Primavera offered minimal salaries and their players were of necessity fully employed elsewhere, it could demand no more than one training period a week. Furthermore, it had no facilities for "concentration" and had to rely on trust. Insofar as the players for this young district club all lived in the same neighborhood as their directors and fans, they would have had trouble breaking training without being detected, so an honor system worked quite well.

The demands of the other three first-division clubs fall between those of Coritiba and Primavera. Yet even in the most demanding Coritiba Club, players who wish to go to school for vocational training may do so. Student players are virtually nonexistent in Rio and São Paulo; Curitiba averages four university students per club. A mere twenty-five years ago, 90 percent of all players in Curitiba were students, and forty-five years ago the same was true in Rio and São Paulo. The number of students decreases as a club demands more and more time from its players. Four of the six student players I interviewed in Curitiba said they could not continue their schooling were it not for their salaries from the clubs. Without the academic scholarships that young American athletes receive, these players nevertheless are achieving lasting social elevation through sport because of its consequences for their educational achievement.

Aside from the handful of university students, most Curitiba players hold part-time jobs, having both the time and the need to work. In Brazil, as in the rest of Latin America, men commonly hold two jobs, the salary from one being insufficient in the face of their distaste for the notion of working wives. Club directors feel responsible for helping their players secure second jobs, so that athletes can play soccer and still fulfill family obligations. At the time of my interviews, seventeen of thirty players of the Ferroviário Club had other jobs; ten of them were employed by the sponsoring railroad company, which automatically provides a job to any player who wants one.[22]

Professionalization in Brazil decreases the opportunity for occupational sponsorship. In Rio, when a club pays a large salary for the period specified in a player's contract it has fulfilled its obligations to him. In Curitiba affluent directors are more likely to act paternalistically, because formal contractual relationships are not attractive enough to keep the best talent in the club. Sometimes talented players who receive tempting offers from big Rio and São Paulo clubs refuse because less formal occupational sponsorship seems more promising. The best Brazilian goalie of the thirties, Cajú, displayed telegrams offering him fabulous bonuses if he would leave Curitiba. He refused all offers, realizing, even forty years ago, that he would have no time to build a postsoccer career in those cities.

His club in Curitiba arranged a part-time job with the Public Health Department, and he is now its chief administrator. Jobs arranged by club directors are better than jobs ordinarily within the reach of poorly educated men, and such jobs secure a player's economic future far more than a temporary and unpredictable career in sports.

In Curitiba, former players usually escape the adjustment problems of the players in Rio and São Paulo. Few experience the break with reality that accompanies stardom, and most avoid economic crisis. Players study to prepare themselves for new careers or, like Cajú, they work part time, usually continuing in the same jobs full time after retiring from soccer.

Team incentive bonuses in both big and small cities help keep players unified. (Individual bonuses are prohibited.) In the smaller city clubs salaries are typically based on length of service to the team, and turnover is minimal. Unlike the highly developed soccer centers, where the composition of a team can change dramatically over a two-year period, smaller city teams remain stable for as long as five years, and feelings of loyalty are allowed to grow strong. Heitor, a goalie who was lent to a Curitiba club for a year by a popular São Paulo team, commented on the difference:

> The behavior of one player for his teammates is an attitude of friendship—it's like a family here. In São Paulo, it's different. There they are stars. They think they alone were responsible for the victory. Here in Curitiba, there are no stars—only the "shirt" is important.[23]

The "family" feeling, the absence of large ego conflicts, the lesser distractions, and the benefit of social control in a community environment contribute to the recent success of the smaller city clubs. As professionalism takes stronger hold, it is likely that the problems of players in Curitiba will approach those of athletes in Rio and São Paulo. For example, teams from the provincial states that have been admitted to the national championship ask their athletes to play all year long, leaving no time between seasons to prepare for a postsports career. As more travel is required, schooling and part-time jobs are no longer feasible. As the level of expertise and salaries rises, so do the days required for training and concentration. And the game of "musical teammates" will come to the smaller cities as the best provincial players get big-city offers they cannot refuse and as the provincial clubs become wealthy enough to pirate big-city players. The advantages of stability and team solidarity will be lost to the "star system" known in sport centers around the world.

The principal way American athletes protect themselves against backsliding social mobility is by demanding economic security through players' unions. By threatening player strikes, they have secured disability insurance and large pensions based on number of years of service. High-salaried American professionals also often had to declare bankruptcy until players' unions recommended tax accountants and reliable business managers and provided investment services.

Players' unions in Brazil have been largely ineffective. Players are ineligible for government retirement pensions, which require twenty-five years of service; few play for even ten years. The clubs have been unwilling to establish their own pension plans, and they offer no disability insurance. Some clubs give money to an injured player until he can find another job, but such payments are paternalistic largesse, not player rights.

Brazil has a history of weak unions in general, and getting Brazilian athletes to act together has proved difficult. In fact, it is not clear that the Brazilian government would tolerate a players' strike; it has squelched strikes of other unions with less reason. Many players have not supported the National Congress of Athletes or state unions like the Syndicate of Professional Athletes of São Paulo or the Foundation for Professional Athletes' Security in Rio, diluting the strength of their numbers. In addition, the old patron system assumed that relationships between different social classes would be symbiotic rather than adversarial. Individual players, hoping to court sponsorship from club directors, do not want to risk alienating them by banding together with those of their own class to make demands.

Although the degree and duration of social mobility vary with circumstance, soccer has been an important escape route for professional players. Even those who returned to the lower classes after their careers seem grateful for the prestige they acquired during their playing days and for the exposure to Brazilian and foreign cities. One former player told me he was still appreciative that his club has arranged a low-paying job as a public functionary, since otherwise he would have been a bricklayer's assistant. Especially for players from small towns in Brazil's interior, soccer has provided the only hope for a better life.

The Special Symbolic Importance of Pelé

Pelé is the single most recognized figure in Brazil; he is the most written-about person in Brazilian history. Any society is made richer by the presence of heroes, but in places like Brazil, where integration is problematic, symbols that draw people together are especially important. In 1960, when Italian clubs pooled their resources to offer an unprecedented $1 million for nineteen-year-old Pelé's contract, the Brazilian Congress promptly declared the young man a "nonexportable national treasure." A Marplan survey conducted during the 1970 World Cup in Rio showed that 76 percent of the overall population and 82 percent of the lower class agreed that Pelé should not be allowed to play for a foreign team.[24] Pelé and Brazil were synonymous—he belonged to the people. To show their devotion, Brazilians have named streets, babies, a brand of coffee, a candy bar, and a giant stadium after Pelé.

Pelé's fame is of global proportions. He has visited eighty-eight countries, met two popes, five emperors, ten kings, seventy presidents, and forty other chiefs of state. Biographies of Pelé have been translated into more than one hundred languages. The Santos Club exhibited star Pelé in as many as 180 games a year between 1958 and 1974. Unusual stories abound from these travels, the most striking being that the Nigerian-Biafran war was halted for one day to allow Pelé to play a game.

Pelé earned his worldwide fame by breaking nearly every record in the annals of soccer. Ninety-three times he scored three goals in a row during a game; thirty-one times he scored four goals, six times he scored five goals, and once he kicked in eight goals during a game.[25] He is the only player to have scored over one thousand official goals, ninety-seven of which were in international-level play, and he is the only person to have played on four World Cup teams. In twenty years he very rarely disappointed his audiences; in his record 1,362 appearances, he scored a career total of 1,281 goals.

Some tried to explain his talents by pointing to uncommon peripheral vision or his well-placed center of gravity, but Pelé stated simply that his talents were the gift of God. In gratitude, Pelé dedicated himself to humanitarian ideals. After his historic thousandth goal, Pelé wept, "remember the children, remember the poor children."[26]

As role model for youth, Pelé wanted to set a good moral example that would inspire adults as well. Pelé never rushes through a crowd: he gives autographs, flashes his contagious smile for the cameras, and calls fans "player number twelve." He feels that people who support a star have a right to his time; institutions are public property. Pelé has long tolerated a split existence. He refers to himself as both Pelé and Edson (his real name is Edson Arantes do Nascimento). Edson is the private man; Pelé, the hero, belongs to the people.

Pelé knew early that opponents would resort to unclean play if that was the only way to prevent his scoring. In 1962 he was injured early in Brazil's second championship series; in 1966 he was the victim of a brutal attack by triple-teaming opponents; and he risked violence again to give confidence to the 1970 team. Acts of heroism in war usually are not witnessed by the people the soldier represents, but heroism in sport is different. Pelé's dedication to his country could be appreciated directly by the proud Brazilians.

As a man with a common background, Pelé symbolizes the realization of dreams of upward mobility everywhere. The former shoeshine boy, peanut vendor, and fourth-grade dropout returned to his studies and received a university degree during a sporting career that made him one of Brazil's wealthiest men. Some people fear that open spending separates the hero from the poor fans, but no one showed resentment when Pelé built a $1,600,000 mansion. Pelé's leap from rags to riches is taken as evidence of equal opportunity for people of all races. The embrace of kings and presidents makes the whole world look less racist, while the excellent treatment Pelé receives at home belies the existence of racial prejudice in Brazil.

Just as the tri-championship was important as a cultural achievement that merited international front-page recognition, Pelé's undisputed supremacy made Brazilians proud to be Brazilians. They identified his goals as their goals. When Brazil needed national symbols to help unify a divided country, Pelé served as one. When Brazil's self-image needed bolstering, Pelé represented his countrymen and displayed first-rate talent. His travel the world over gave Brazil visibility at a time critical to its national development.

Pelé also rises above nationalism; adoring fans all over the globe mightily cheered him as he scored against *their* national teams. Sport idols are among the few personalities that unite international folk culture. This is one reason multinational corporations like Coca-Cola and Pepsi-Cola are anxious to sign on superstars like Zico and Pelé as roving ambassadors.

On 4 October 1974, Pelé played his farewell game with Santos and retired. When a hero has been a hero so long that he has become an institution, he is granted some sort of "immortality."[27] Yet a hero's image is not inviolate. Pelé tested the durability of his legend in June of 1975 when he came out of retirement and signed a multimillion-dollar contract to play soccer for the New York Cosmos. Brazilians were shocked and angry to think that their humble hero was, after all, only a human who had his price. Some journalists openly accused him of being mercenary. Money alone, however, would not move him. He was talked out of retirement at age thirty-four, in large part, because he missed the game.

Since 1971, Clive Toye, general manager of the Cosmos, and Phil Woosman, commissioner of the North American Soccer League, had been imploring Pelé to bring soccer to the United States. Sport is an important part of the cultural relationship between nations, and the United States had cut itself off by not speaking the same sport language. Henry Kissinger added his stature to the invitation and talked to Pelé and Brazilian government officials. Pelé, and only Pelé, could perform an "international miracle" by bringing soccer to the United States. Through a public relations campaign, Pelé allowed all the Brazilian people to share this mission and the glory that came with its successful completion at his final retirement in October 1977. In a masterly turnabout of mass sentiment, he exchanged his countrymen's scorn for their support.

Pelé accomplished this first by negotiating an estimated $4.5 million contract, establishing the "Brazilian worth" at a figure higher than most could imagine. And he demanded a sport exchange of coaches between the United States and Brazil: American expertise in swimming, basketball, and track would be traded for Brazilian expertise in soccer. He also got Warner Communications, the parent corporation of the Cosmos, to sponsor a soccer school for the poor children of Santos, and he personally set aside funds for their regular schooling as well. As the negotiations came to a close, Pelé's press communiqués stressed one theme: the United States is always exporting technology to Third World nations; now, through Pelé, Brazil will export know-how to the northern superpower. And he got his government's blessing, too. It is through export products that countries promote their names. Pelé's goals would be Brazilian goals.

Satellite transmission brought to Brazilian televisions Pelé's first game with the Cosmos, against Dallas. On the screen Brazilians saw signs displayed throughout the grandstands, with the bilingual message, "Obrigado, Brasil—Thank you, Brazil."

Conclusion:
The Consequences of Sport

People are social animals. The tribal instinct—the need to belong to
something larger than ourselves—is apparent in all societies. In advanced societies sports teams are perfect recipients for human loyalty.
Fans identify themselves with their teams and with other fans who
share their concern. Threats from challenging teams rally our sense
that we are needed, which in turn reassures us that we belong.
Perceiving the team "tribe" as our own makes us proud when it
wins, ashamed when its loses, and hopeful it will win again.

Sport does help connect people in complex modern societies.
The case of soccer in Brazil shows that sport does link people, groups,
towns, cities, and regions into a single national system, as it links
nations into a single world system. Through ever-enlarging circles
of competition, there is a renewed sense of collectivity.

By providing a structure for human loyalty from grass roots
to international levels, soccer reinforces the individual's citizenship
in multiple groups at the same time. The men in my study smiled
as they rattled off the names of World Cup veterans and identified
photographs of their local soccer idols; the mere act of recognizing
common symbols made them feel like "insiders." Cheering a Rio
team reminds these men of their civic pride; cheering the Brazilian
Selection gives them occasion for patriotic sentiment, anthem-sing-
ing, and flag-waving. Recognizing names of foreign clubs and idols—
England's Bobby Charlton, Portugal's Eusebio, Germany's Beck-

145

enbauer, Italy's Chinaglia, and Holland's Cruyff—makes fans feel worldly.

Providing a common focus for people's attention, soccer creates bonds between strangers and strengthens bonds between familiars. Soccer games and the sport lottery are the most talked-about subjects in the city. The men in my study related to their friends, workmates, and neighbors through sport more than through anything else. Families and friends watch the big matches together. Nearly half the men in my sample said they often go to local league games alone and share the event with fellow supporters, who hug one another in spite of being strangers. One's team affiliation is a salient identification in Rio de Janeiro, and the sense of bonding, even communion, with fellow fans is real.

Mass society theorists ask how the diverse elements in both urban centers and the nation can coexist peacefully. Their concern is with society's need to maintain and confirm unity. Sharing such events as the local and national championships, the Brazilian Selection's games, and the sport lottery promotes a collective consciousness. The awareness that so many others are watching the same event makes it an experience above the ordinary, an occasion for togetherness that makes a society greater than the arithmetic sum of its parts.

In contrast, mass culture theorists, concerned with the ultimate destruction of societal diversity, fear a homogenization of personal and political values and cultural heroes—a uniformity rooted in the centralized state, mass education, and the media. In mass culture, the usual differences in attitudes, tastes, and behaviors between the sexes, age cohorts, and socioeconomic classes begin to disappear. Although minority groups still remain strong, racial, ethnic, and immigrant groups begin their slow assimilation, and ties to locality or neighborhood are to a large degree replaced by ties to the metropolis and nation-state.[1]

Paradoxically, by dividing and unifying simultaneously, soccer shows that neither mass society nor mass culture theorists need worry. By giving dramatic expression to the strains between groups and regions, soccer confrontations sustain traditional pluralism, countering cultural homogeneity while accentuating the wholeness of the social system. Soccer clubs break down Rio's urban mass according to meaningful social divisions; their teams symbolically represent the old rich, the modern middle class, the poor, the blacks, the Portuguese, and a number of neighborhood communities. Yet Fluminense, Botafogo, Flamengo, Vasco, and the eight smaller clubs, united in a Rio league, bring their opposing fans together through shared enthusiasm for soccer, the only professionalized team sport.

The structure of sport provides a crisscrossing of multiple loyalties that prevents deep cleavages along any one axis. A Fluminense fan temporarily suspends his opposition to Botafogo when it represents his city in a championship duel against a São Paulo team. A clear-cut victory provides a rare occasion to make public affirmation of citizens' feelings of community, which momentarily suspend divisive team loyalties loaded with primordial sentiment. Regional jealousies are played out in the national championship, but the all-star team makes allies out of opponents. The threatening attacker from a São Paulo rival, now one of the stars of the Brazilian Selection, is cheered by fans in Rio who hate him during the national championship.

Televised Selection games capture very close to 100 percent of the audience throughout Brazil. Backwoodsmen and urbanites, northeastern plantation hands and southern factory workers, men, women, and children know that everyone everywhere in one vast land is supporting the team. The tri-championship remains unparalleled as a source of patriotic pride and global recognition. The paradoxical divide-and-unify achievement of sport is found even at the highest level of competition: the tri-championship sharpened Brazilians' national consciousness as it underscored their valued world membership. The entire Brazilian television audience was linked to fans all over the globe who were also watching the dazzling skills displayed by the World Cup teams.

Who Reaps the Benefits of Sports?

Following soccer in Brazil is not a substitute for primary relationships for alienated outsiders; rather, it is the principal focus of leisure life for men who belong. Well-integrated people follow soccer because it is part of the social scene, and following soccer gives them a knowledge of main events and characters that deepens their sense of integration and confirms their "insider" status.

My survey data show that the more socially connected a man is, the more likely he is to reap the integrative benefits of fandom. In other words, the sense of attachment to society that an individual feels is variable and can be conceptualized as a vicious cycle. Outsiders are left out, while insiders are in a position to be drawn into all central parts of social life.

As we shift from individuals to the level of groups, regions, or societies, whether any integrative benefits can be reaped from sporting conflict becomes dependent on the measure of real conflict between opponents. Goffman suggests that the most engrossing contests are close, but not too close, to reality.[2] Where societies are relatively homogeneous or harmonious, symbolic content in sport is minimized, and the quality of play alone determines the worth of the spectacle. Where societies have numerous or intense internal cleavages, the conflict dramatized is so real that the spectacle is enhanced, but only up to the point where hostilities are so intense that playing together becomes impossible.

Ritualized conflict can reduce hostilities, by giving them free expression, or can stimulate them. Within Northern Ireland, where teams typically represent either Protestants or Catholics, game arrangements reflect the warring hostilities between the two religious factions. Protestant teams refuse to play in Catholic stadia, and Catholic fans must enter Protestant stadia under police guard. A large percentage of the town's police force is needed, equipped with riot gear and trained dogs, and opposing fan groups are separated by barbed wire.[3] The distance between mock war and real war is not great; where animosities run deep, ritual conflict may easily lose its game character and serve as a catalyst for riots and disorder.

Brazil's soccer games are exciting because they express strong primordial loyalties. The symbolic conflicts represent important social cleavages, but the antagonisms are not deep enough to preclude friendly rivalry. For example, racial discrimination has been documented and racial divisions are real, yet Brazilians have the highest miscegenation rate in the world. Race relations in Brazil are such that blacks, mulattoes, and whites coexist without the physical distancing found in the United States. Although social class contrasts are bold and the gap between rich and poor is widening, Brazil has a paternalistic history, and the spirit of noblesse oblige still unifies the upper and lower classes. Foreign ethnic groups were welcomed into the "melting pot" because Brazil needed their skills and labor. Racial, class, and ethnic groups are divided, yet a measure of social cohesion enables them to play together and build an even greater sense of shared interests. Evidence of that cohesion is the rarity of large-scale violence in Brazilian soccer.

The history of international sporting confrontations supports the notion that the most engrossing contests represent primordial loyalties that stir our passions, and patriotic sentiment expresses our broadest loyalty. Millions of Americans who care nothing about the sport were enraptured by the 1980 USA–USSR Olympic hockey game because it was so freighted with nationalistic symbolism. But nations near or at war will be unable to meet on the playing field. After IRA hunger striker Bobby Sands's death, English and Welsh teams canceled games scheduled in Belfast, underscoring the strained relationships. The Arab nations' refusal to play against the Israelis is another case in point. Fighting nations that do agree to meet on the playing field do so at risk of exacerbating the ill will, as in the 1956 water polo match between the USSR and Hungary that took place just after the Soviet invasion of Hungary. Witnesses said the game quickly became warlike as blood flowed into the water while fans shouted insults from the stands.[4] The "Soccer War" between Honduras and El Salvador best illustrates how ritual conflict can lose its game character and how fighting nations—those most in need of the integrative benefits of sport are least likely to get them.

Pluralism versus Unity

A society's level of integration determines whether intergroup conflict can be dramatized playfully, but it is primarily the organization of sporting institutions that determines whether the culture's pluralism or its unity is reinforced through ritualized contests. Sport's paradoxical ability to divide and integrate serves the ends of both pluralism and unity, but not necessarily equally. The particular features of sporting institutions affect which is accomplished to greater extent. Most important, integration is best served in systems emphasizing intercity rivalries, whereas cultural pluralism is strengthened through well-developed intracity rivalries.

Besides the organization of sport, culture, history, climate, technology, and geography also give each sporting system a distinctive flavor and have an impact on the relative emphasis on unity or pluralism. For example, the Puritan ethos still limits American acceptance of gambling. Delaware tried to tie its state-operated lottery to National Football League games, but the commissioner objected strenuously and tried to stop the project in court on the grounds that it would be bad for football's image and would invite game fixing. The $1 billion a week illegal gambling industry already offers plenty of incentive for interference, yet it was not mentioned by the plaintiff.[5] State lotteries in the United States are most typically based on a random-number system. A bettor, whether choosing numbers or drawing them, does not have the benefit of a sociable topic of conversation, as is the case in all the sport lottery countries. In England, for example, eight out of every ten homes receive pools coupons in the mail, and twenty times as many people gamble on soccer games as see them.[6] Whoever you meet, wherever you go, you can safely assume that Britons will join in a talk about good bets for the upcoming games.

A society's level of technology affects both the organization and the impact of its sports. America's earliest baseball leagues were organized within cities, but the first professional league was organized for intercity competition just a few years after the developing railroad network linked the East and the Midwest.[7] Thanks to early network television, regions without professional teams have long been drawn into the national sports competitions; recent technology enables satellites and cables to bring local game coverage of teams like the Atlanta Braves as far as distant Hawaii. America's multi-network television nicely supports our multisports system, but it diminishes the ability of any single sporting event to be an occasion for national communion. The Super Bowl, always one of television's highest-rated spectacles, draws in slightly fewer than half the nation's households. Nothing like the Brazilian Selection games brings everyone in the United States together.

The principal difference between Brazil's system and others in the world is its greater development of intracity rivalries. If sporting systems were placed along a continuum, the United States would be at one extreme, virtually all its professional contests being between cities, and Brazil would be at the other extreme, with its local championship being more important than its national championship. European systems would be intermediate but closer to the United States, and other Latin American systems would be intermediate but closer to Brazil.

In the American sport system, the territorial monopoly given to one professional team in a sport per city makes its inhabitants suspend their internal divisions to support the team that represents them all.[8] Major cities reap integrative benefits not only within but also between themselves, for they are tied to each other through nationwide competitions. Yet the restricted number of franchises creates a situation of contrived scarcity that limits national unification. With only twenty-eight football teams, for example, only twenty of the fifty states are involved in the league games culminating in the Super Bowl. Fans in the other thirty states, freed from local loyalty, can support the season's best professional teams or personal favorites, but they lose the integrative benefit of a team that would tie them together with others in their region by tying that region into the national system.

In the United States, the interests of unification are better served by high-school and collegiate sport, where all towns, cities, and states are represented in the member athletic associations; 465 football teams participate in the National Collegiate Athletic Association competitions, and another 14,740 schools compete at the high-school level.[9] Scholastic sports also promote cultural pluralism because, at that level, intracity and intraregional rivalries are routine and schools often represent important social cleavages. Think of a high-school basketball state championship that pits the best white suburban team against the best black ghetto team, or the national followings attached to school teams with a religious affiliation, like Baptist Baylor University and Catholic Notre Dame.

European soccer is noted for its balance between intracity and intercity competition. Here the goals of pluralism and national integration are served equally. Most European countries contain a number of population and culture centers. When soccer was introduced in the late 1800s, each major city developed three or four first-division teams, as well as a number of lower-division teams, which face each other regularly in league competitions that dramatize local rivalries. But the impetus for a football association stemmed from the desire for a national league competition. European countries, being small, easily developed national championships in which teams traveled, as did many fans, and regional rivalries flourished.

In Latin American countries, which developed as imperial colonies, urbanization and industrialization typically were concentrated in the capital city—in a few cases one other city as well—while the rest of the country remained provincial producers of raw goods. With the introduction of soccer at the turn of the century, the best clubs developed in each major city, so intracity contests offered the highest level of competition. Provincial cities centered their resources on one or two top-level teams that could compete with the major city teams. National leagues were formed early, in every country but Brazil, and regional rivalry found expression. In Latin American cities, intracity rivalries are well developed, and intercity rivalry, although less developed than in Europe, is a long-standing tradition. With modernization, provincial cities are beginning to rival capital cities, and their teams' greater competitiveness reflects this change.

Brazil, far larger than other Latin American countries, has always had numerous population centers. (Ten cities have populations greater than one million.) But the distances between cities were too great and transportation was too poor for the routine travel required for a national league. Air travel enabled the start of the national competition in 1970, but league structures are still organized by states. One consequence of Brazil's variant pattern is the full-blown development of soccer in several states, since each system was independent and not overshadowed by the superior Rio and São Paulo teams. Although the state leagues brought interior cities into regular contact with the wealthy capital, the emphasis was placed on the local rivalry within the major city, with its proliferation of first-division teams. Many social divisions could be represented by these numerous teams, exaggerating the benefits of cultural pluralism. Intracity rivalry also promotes fans' feelings of involvement because each fan group, sensing its solidarity against the others, competes to demonstrate stronger support.

The central position of the soccer clubs in Brazilian community life sustains cultural pluralism by giving people of similar background a place to meet. The clubs, by providing athletic facilities and hosting dances and parties, focus social life for many people in towns and cities. Participating in club events builds family feeling among fans, and volunteering time to its projects brings personal satisfaction and some recognition. Access to team training sessions and victory dances further reduces the distance between fans and their idols. Latin American soccer clubs differ from most European ones by being open to social membership. Fans retain some control over management through voting and through access to directors and their ledgers. Because of their democratic structure, soccer clubs in Brazil really do represent their fans. When supporters say "our team," they mean it.

There are aspects of Brazil's variant pattern that bolster unity more than pluralism. National football associations in Europe and

Latin America concern themselves solely with soccer; Brazil's CBD was a unique organization. The CBD did not have the responsibility of governing a national competition and therefore could oversee all international competition, including the Olympic sports, although soccer remained its primary concern and principal source of revenue. This merging of interests kept amateur sport weak, as evidenced by Brazil's poor showing in the Olympic events under CBD jurisdiction. Not coincidentally, Brazilians do well in volleyball and basketball, two sports with independent federations. Not having the diversity offered by a strong and varied sports system, all types of people are brought together by their mutual interest in soccer.

As the only mass team sport, soccer has a special place in the lives of Brazilians and has become a symbol of national unity and progress. Most athletes channel their energies toward one sport, giving the clubs a huge pool of talent to draw from. The success of the Brazilian Selection, made up of stars from the leading teams of all the major cities, has done more to bring Brazilians together as patriots than perhaps anything else. Soccer players in a single sport system serve as common culture heroes that virtually everyone knows. Superstars like Pelé, as living legends for people all over the globe, have inspired their countrymen to be proud of their Brazilian identity.

The Exception: Sexual Apartheid

Sport transcends social divisions and brings diverse people together—with one important exception: routinely sport separates women from men. Paul Hoch coined the term "sexual apartheid" to describe this near-universal phenomenon.[10] Kate Millett likens sport to "men's house institutions"—rituals that separate males from females and reinforce the values of male supremacy, aggression, competitiveness, and power.[11] Anything that reduces the commonality of experience between the sexes reinforces strong gender distinctions and inhibits communication. Soccer in Brazil is largely sex-segregated, and that has consequences for the experience of growing up male or female and for later-life human relationships.

Chapter 5 described how children who play soccer become adult consumers of that sport as fans; the higher the level of competition, as provided in formally organized games, the greater the likelihood that young players will become fans who give soccer a central place in their lives. Excluded from participating in amateur soccer, Brazilian girls have no personal experience that makes them appreciate professional sport. Until recently, females have been largely excluded as spectators too. Women and girls have stayed away from stadia to "protect their reputations" and have avoided beach soccer and park games because of the coarse language and rowdy crowds.

The soccer scene is changing in ways that reduce sexual apartheid. More teenage girls are joining fan clubs and accompanying boys, without chaperones, to professional games. Pelé has urged the reconstruction of Brazilian stadia to offer more comfort and safety so that more females can participate as fans.[12] But rescinding the law forbidding females to play soccer and encouraging their participation as athletes will bring them to the stadia sooner than will new toilets and more comfortable chairs. Cross-cultural evidence from U.S. camps, schools, and youth leagues shows that girls can be successful soccer players. By defining soccer as a sport that requires "manly endurance," Brazilians have made soccer a test of masculinity. Boys showing no talent or taste for the game fail the test; in a society with few outlets for other sports and activities, the success system for boys is narrow indeed. Similarly, fandom in adulthood demonstrates masculine interests. One must wonder how many Brazilian men go through the motions of fandom more because it is expected of them than because of their continuing attraction to the sport. When more females join the soccer world as players and fans, the association between sport and masculinity will disappear. Some men's interest in soccer will wane as it loses its quality of "masculine preserve," but others will appreciate soccer as an occasion for family togetherness instead of friction.

As it is now, men and women have different interests. The men I talked with insisted that their wives have the church and they have soccer. In traditional parts of Brazil, church is the one place women are trusted to go unescorted. It is a safe world for women, giving them freedom of movement to organize charities, fund-raisers, and social events. Unlike men's interest in soccer, however, women's churchgoing keeps them close to home. The church does not expand their horizon beyond family and neighborhood. While they share worldwide symbols of Catholicism, women's localized activities do little to integrate them into metropolitan or national life.

Patriotic interest in the successful Brazilian Selection has brought many women closer to soccer, as has the introduction of the sport lottery. Although they bet smaller amounts, women play the lottery almost as frequently as men. Many randomly pick their win, lose, or draw bets, but others use the lottery as an occasion to enter conversations about soccer with their husbands and friends. The lottery also provides a new opportunity for female co-workers to informally socialize at work.

Some critics worry that sport consumes too much of men's free time, not only separating them from their wives and children, but also exacerbating the superficialities of male conversation.[13] Does endless sport talk inhibit or preclude other conversations that would promote more intimacy and support between male friends? It would be unfair to blame sport for the nature of male friendships; virtually all male socialization, not just sport, teaches boys to be competitors. Until men want deeper emotional relationships with other men, they will find "fillers" for talks and activities together, whether sport is involved or not. I do suggest, however, that sport fills free time so well that many males may not recognize the limitations of their interactions.

Sport: Support of Status Quo or Push for Change?

Theorists and politicans consider national integration a prerequisite for economic development. National consciousness is an important element of integration, and soccer has made a significant contribution to national pride in Brazil. But we cannot assume that integration is always a good thing. Social order can promote social welfare, but it can also deprive people of their freedom and keep them in their place. Whether we think the power of soccer was used or abused to help Brazil's military regime achieve its nationalistic goals is linked to our political judgment about the nature of social order in that country.

Before evaluating soccer's contribution to stability or change in Brazil, let us think more generally about the familiar criticism that sport acts as an opiate that deflects people's energies from the real sources of conflict in their lives. According to Paul Hoch, sport serves as an opiate in two ways: it creates illusions about individualism by presenting a model in which success depends on hard work and perseverance and distracts attention from organizational bases for blocked mobility; sport also offers a temporary "high," changing nothing that would help people overcome their problems.[14]

Sport publicizes a mobility ideology in every type of modern society; the handful of athletes who reap the highest rewards available in a social system demonstrate some fluidity based on talent and achievement. But does the experience of the few who succeed mislead millions of others, since only a small fraction of those who invest their time and hopes ever reap mobility benefits through professional sport? In the United States, for example, black youths are advised that studying provides a surer escape from poverty, but a number of descriptions of the early lives of black athletes credit dreams of a career in sports as the only thing that kept them away from drugs and delinquency.[15] The opportunities and encouragement for studies are limited for poor Brazilian boys too, especially those in small towns. At a minimum, playing soccer provides one of the few sources of enjoyment and relief from boredom. As a team sport, soccer also provides an arena in which to learn cooperation and competition and, for some, leadership. As the focal point for boys' dreams of a better life, soccer in Brazil keeps hope alive. Thousands of the very best *will* reap health and educational benefits by playing on the nation's apprentice teams, even if they never have a professional career.

Is sport an opiate for fans? Let us acknowledge that sport is not the only thing that deflects people's energy and releases them from either a "pressure cooker" or a boring life. Catholicism and Umbanda offer hopes for spiritual salvation, while samba, television, and movies also help Brazilians forget their troubles. But one need not make the case for surrogate opiates when real drugs surround us. What we know about the markets for alcohol, heroin, cocaine, and marihuana in the United States shows clearly that it is not just the poor or those with routine jobs who seek escape from reality;[16] nearly everybody does, although the means of escape they find acceptable and affordable differ. If spectator sport did not exist, fans would use other routes of escape.

In addition, a competing argument proposes that organizations like soccer fan clubs, samba schools, and Umbanda churches can all serve as a basis for building solidarity among Brazilian workers. Once class consciousness is raised through these social institutions, the potential for collective action can be enhanced rather than diminished by these channels that bring people together. Where political parties and labor unions are suppressed, as in Brazil, soccer's dramatization of the class conflict may be especially important.

Organized sport around the world—not just soccer in Brazil—has both positive and negative effects. Some adolescents do deceive themselves about future playing careers; some adults carry escapism too far, neglecting family or work and, in the most extreme cases, commit murder or suicide for their teams. Rivalries based on primordial loyalties can feed the prejudices of narrow minds. This book has cited instances of resulting small- to large-scale violence. One cannot deny lamentable, even tragic, events related to sports fanaticism, yet this detailed exploration of soccer in Brazil demonstrates that sport more routinely acts as an important constructive social force.

Soccer has promoted real change in Brazil in several ways. Sport's ability to reinforce societal cleavages while transcending them has provided a stage for the "integrative revolution," bringing about a more perfect union between diverse groups of people in a single vast land. By organizing teams representing primordial sentiments into regularized patterns of conflict, soccer ties people together in stable patterns of interaction. Soccer has modernized, rather than obliterated, the roots of ethnocentrism and has therefore helped preserve distinctions within the social system. But, by modernizing them, soccer has harnessed the power of primordial sentiments to bring about civil unity by tying citizens into the society conceived in its broadest terms.

Long before communication and transportation technologies could surmount problems of territorial integration, and before a federal bureaucracy could connect the sprawling country administratively, a network of soccer clubs belonging to a nationwide sports federation united Brazil. The soccer club was often a community's *first* voluntary organization, and even today soccer clubs offer millions of people their *only* experience with grass-roots democracy. For decades, club directories, state federations, and the CBD have brought together men in key sociopolitical and economic positions who form alliances to complement more formal leadership networks.

More recently, Brazil's military regime has consciously manipulated soccer to further its contribution to social welfare and effective political order. The government even used posters of Pelé to induce people to complete their census forms.[17] The national championship and the sport lottery were devised, in part, to stimulate Brazilians' awareness of their own imposing geography. The lottery's enormous profits have been used to support the aged, handicapped, and orphaned and to fund hygiene programs, in addition to financing the construction of parks and public athletic facilities. The Ministry of Education and Culture used these facilities and the lure of sports to attract people in 2,128 municipalities to programs that aimed at eradicating illiteracy while providing recreation.[18] In a country where 76 percent of the men fail the medical exam for the armed services, the programs' effect on physical fitness alone cannot be ignored.[19]

People in developing nations, and not just their governments, want a more influential role in the world system. They have suffered from a "humiliating sense of exclusion" and see citizenship in a respected nation as their "most broadly negotiable claim to personal significance."[20] They want a reason to be proud. Nothing boosted pride in Brazilian citizenship like the tri-championship. In a survey taken right after the 1970 victory, 90 percent of the lower-class respondents identified Brazilian soccer with the Brazilian nation.[21] The glory brought home by the World Cup team was not fleeting. TV-Globo produced a special commemorating the tenth anniversary of the tri-championship. The film features highlights of the game as Pelé tells the story of soccer to a ten-year-old boy, to boost his pride in the nation.

The point that a single sporting event can have a permanent impact can be demonstrated in other ways using other societies.[22] Argentina spent $50 million on installations for television transmission for the 1978 World Cup.[23] A similar telecommunications advance took place in Spain as part of that country's preparation to host the 1982 World Cup. The Spanish government approved a $150 million budget for improvements on its state-owned television. Because of the games, Spain now has permanent production centers, better reception, and an expanded second channel.[24] These contributions to national unification are unmistakable.

Are such enormous expenditures for a sporting event warranted in such poor countries? The Brazilian sport lottery covers only half the expenses of the national team. Are the taxes that pay for the rest justified? Nothing compares with the Brazilian Selection as a basis for collective identity and a focus of solidarity. But its victories also have provided opportunities for propaganda by a repressive military regime.

We can condemn a regime's cruel tactics of social control and restrictions on civil liberties without condemning soccer. Few are fooled by the government's manipulation of sport for its nationalistic goals; it is not "false consciousness" that makes people support their teams. Brazilians want to share both the wealth of a modern nation and the excitement offered by winning soccer teams. If one can promote the other, so much the better. Nor is soccer an opiate that would stop the revolution; a contest that dramatizes real social conflict could not continue in a time of extreme unrest and might even prompt civil disorder. Meanwhile, club divisions, team colors, and fan rituals comfortingly stay the same, as they paradoxically act as a force for social change.

Appendix 1:
The Interview Schedule

Place of Interview:
Date of Interview:

BACKGROUND QUESTIONS:

1. Race:
   ☐ white
   ☐ mulatto
   ☐ black
   ☐ other
2. How old are you?
3. Do you work?
   ☐ yes
   ☐ no
4. What do you do?
5. Do you have any other jobs?
   ☐ yes
   ☐ no (*if no, go to question 7*)
6. What is it?
7. How many hours per day do you work? ____hours
   How many days per week do you work? ____days
8. Would you describe yourself as being ____with your current
   job?
   ☐ very satisfied
   ☐ neither satisfied nor dissatisfied
   ☐ dissatisfied
9. How much do you earn a month?
10. Do you have a savings account?
    ☐ yes
    ☐ no
11. Marital status:
    ☐ married
    ☐ single
    ☐ widowed
    ☐ separated
12. Do you have any children?
    ☐ yes
    ☐ no (*if no, go to question 15*)
13. How many?
    ____girls
    ____boys
14. How many people have their residence in your house?
    ____persons
    ☐ lives alone

15. How many of those people work besides yourself? _____work
Does your wife work?
- ☐ yes
- ☐ no
16. Do you know how to read?
- ☐ yes
- ☐ no
17. Did you go to school?
- ☐ yes
- ☐ no (*if no, go to question 19*)
18. Until what year did you study?
- ☐ primary (1, 2, 3, 4, 5 years)
- ☐ intermediate (1, 2, 3, 4 years)
- ☐ secondary (1, 2, 3 years)
- ☐ university (incomplete/holds degree)
19. Where is your home?
Which district?
20. Have you always lived there?
- ☐ yes (*if yes, go to question 23*)
- ☐ no
21. Where did you live when you were a child?
22. How many years have you been in Rio?
23. Do you, or your wife, have relatives who live in Rio?
- ☐ yes
- ☐ no (*if no, go to question 25*)
24. How many (of your relatives) live in your district?
25. What do you like to do in your free time?
1.
2.
3.
26. What did you do last Saturday and Sunday? With whom?
27. Is there a television set in your house?
- ☐ yes
- ☐ no
If no, where, if anywhere, do you see television?
28. Do you watch television?
- ☐ daily
- ☐ several times a week
- ☐ once a week
- ☐ rarely
- ☐ never
29. Do you go to the movies?
- ☐ several times a week

☐ once a week
☐ once a month
☐ never

30. Do you go to Maracanã Stadium?
☐ most clubs games, and big games between other clubs
☐ most club games
☐ big games of my club and big games between other clubs
☐ only big games of my club
☐ never

31. Do you go to the beach?
☐ daily
☐ two or three times a week
☐ once a week
☐ once a month
☐ never

32. Which of these entertainments do you enjoy most?
☐ television
☐ movies
☐ soccer
☐ beach

33. Have you spoken with any of your friends in the past week?
☐ daily
☐ several times a week
☐ once a week
☐ no (*if no, go to question 35*)

34. What did you talk about?
1.
2.
3.

35. Have you spoken with any of your relatives in the past week?
☐ daily
☐ several times a week
☐ once a week
☐ no (*if no, go to question 37*)

36. What did you talk about?
1.
2.
3.

37. Have you talked to any of your neighbors this past week?
☐ daily
☐ several times a week
☐ once a week
☐ no

38. Do you belong to any social clubs here in Rio?
    ☐ yes   Which?
    ☐ no
39. Do you belong to any neighborhood group?
    ☐ yes   Which?
    ☐ no
    Do you belong to any work group, union, etc?
    ☐ yes   Which?
    ☐ no
40. What is your religion?
    ☐ Catholic
    ☐ Protestant
    ☐ Spiritualist
    ☐ Other
    ☐ Atheist
41. How many times in the past month did you go to church?
    ☐ daily
    ☐ once a week
    ☐ once a month
    ☐ not at all
42. How many times in the past month did your wife (or mother) go to church?
    ☐ daily
    ☐ once a week
    ☐ once a month
    ☐ not at all
43. Do you consider yourself a very religious person, average, or not very religious?
    ☐ a very religious person
    ☐ average
    ☐ not very religious
44. Do you think that praying can influence things like who wins a soccer game?
    ☐ yes
    ☐ no
45. Do you play any sports at the moment?
    ☐ yes
    ☐ no (*if no, go to question 47*)
46. Which sports do you play?
    1.
    2.
    On organized teams?
    ☐ yes

☐ no
Frequency?
47. Did you use to be a sportsman?
    ☐ yes
    ☐ no
    If soccer, organized, or unorganized?
    ☐ organized
    ☐ unorganized
48. Do you bet in the sport lottery?
    ☐ yes
    ☐ no (*if no, go to question 52*)
49. How often do you bet per month?
    ☐ once
    ☐ twice
    ☐ three times
    ☐ four times
50. On the average, how much do you bet?
51. Do you make your own predictions or seek the advice
    of others?
    ☐ alone
    ☐ friends
    ☐ family
    ☐ media, mostly radio and newspapers
    Have you ever pooled your bet with others?
    ☐ yes
    ☐ no
    Have you ever bet against your own team?
    ☐ yes   When?
    ☐ no
52. Does your wife bet in the lottery?
    ☐ yes
    ☐ no (*if no, go to question 54*)
53. Does she understand much about soccer?
    ☐ yes
    ☐ no

QUESTIONS ABOUT SOCCER FANDOM:

54. Do you consider yourself a fan of Brazilian football?
    ☐ yes—fanatic, passionate
    ☐ yes—average
    ☐ no

55. How many times in the past month did you attend a soccer game?
56. Why didn't you go more often?
    (*Those who went to two or more games were asked why they went so often.*)
57. If those games had been televised live, would you go to the stadium or watch at home?
    ☐ stadium
    ☐ watch television
    ☐ neither
58. How many times in the past month did you hear a game on the radio?
    What kind of games did you listen to?
    ☐ most club games, and big games between other clubs
    ☐ most club games
    ☐ big games of my club and big games between other clubs
    ☐ only big games of my club
    ☐ lottery games only
    ☐ Brazilian Selection only
    ☐ never
59. Do you have a favorite soccer club?
    ☐ yes
    ☐ no (*if no, go to question 67*)
    Which is your favorite team?
    ☐ Flamengo
    ☐ Botafogo
    ☐ America
    ☐ Fluminense
    ☐ Vasco
    ☐ Other _____
60. Was your father a fan of the same team also?
    ☐ yes
    ☐ no, cheered a different team
    ☐ no, didn't like soccer
    ☐ don't know
61. What reasons did you have for choosing that team?
    1.
    2.
    3.
62. How many years have you been a fan of theirs?
    If you've ever changed clubs, why?
63. Are you a member of that club?
    ☐ yes; Which activities, social and sporting, do you and your family attend?
    ☐ no; Why not?

64. Do you attend the majority of their games on radio, television, or in the stadium?
  ☐ radio;   Where?
  ☐ television;   Where?
  ☐ stadium
65. Generally, on these occasions, are you alone, with friends, or with members of your family?
  ☐ alone
  ☐ friends; How many?
  ☐ family; What members?
66. (*For those who answered no to question 54*)
  What do you do when you are in a group of men and the conversation turns to soccer?
67. Do you receive most of your sports information by way of radio, newspapers, or friends?
  ☐ radio
  ☐ newspaper
  ☐ friends
  ☐ other _____
68. Do you read a newspaper?
  ☐ yes
  ☐ no (*if no, go to questions 72 and 74*)
  Which newspaper do you read?
  ☐ *O Dia*
  ☐ *Jornal do Brasil*
  ☐ *Correio da Manha*
  ☐ *O Globo*
  ☐ *Jornal dos Sports*
  ☐ Other: _____
69. How often do you read a paper?
  ☐ daily
  ☐ now and then
  ☐ rarely
  ☐ never
70. Which parts of the paper interest you most? Indicate order in which you read them.
  ☐ Brazilian government
  ☐ international news
  ☐ sports news
  ☐ economic news
  ☐ police, crime, accident news
  ☐ religious
  ☐ social column
  ☐ cultural

71. In the sports section, do you read about games in other parts of Brazil?
    ☐ yes
    ☐ no
    ☐ for lottery only
72. Do you know which state Vitoria Football Club is from? (*Bahia*)
    ☐ yes
    ☐ no
    Do you know which state Gremio Football Club is from? (*Rio Grande do Sul*)
    ☐ yes
    ☐ no
73. Do you read the international sports news?
    ☐ yes
    ☐ no
74. Do you know what country Peñarol is from? (*Uruguay*)
    ☐ yes
    ☐ no
    Do you know what country River Plate is from? (*Argentina*)
    ☐ yes
    ☐ no
75. Do you read about other sports?
    ☐ yes; Which?
    ☐ a little
    ☐ no

(*Include the following questions for men who live in the suburbs.*)
76. Does your suburb have a team?
    ☐ yes
    ☐ no (*if no, go to question 78*)
77. Do you attend their games?
    ☐ yes
    ☐ no
    If answer was yes, How often do you attend?
    How many usually attend?
    Who sponsors the team?
78. Does your company have a team?
    ☐ yes
    ☐ no
    If yes, Do you attend their games?
    ☐ yes
    ☐ no
    How does it affect the workers to have their own team?

79. How do you get along with your co-workers who cheer for other teams?
    Do you bet with them about the result of the game?
    Of your closest friends here, are they mostly of the same team, different, or varied?
    ☐ same team
    ☐ different
    ☐ varied
    Do you talk with them about the games?
    ☐ yes
    ☐ no
    If yes, do you talk more before or after the games?
    ☐ before
    ☐ after
    Are these discussions friendly or heated?
    ☐ friendly
    ☐ heated
    Do you remember any occasion on which you fought over a game?
    ☐ yes
    ☐ no
    Which team do you consider your greatest rival?
    Why?

80. Does everyone in your family cheer for the same team?
    ☐ yes
    ☐ no; What happens during games opposing your favorite teams?

81. Does your wife like soccer?
    ☐ yes; Does she attend games, listen to radio, read sports page?
    ☐ no; Does she complain about the time you spend listening or discussing games with your friends?

82. Did you see or hear the final of the last Rio championship—the Flamengo vs. Fluminense of last September?
    ☐ yes
    ☐ no
    If yes, who did you cheer for?
    Why?

83. Did you see or hear the last game of the national championship—Botafogo against Palmeiras (of São Paulo)?
    ☐ yes
    ☐ no
    Who did you cheer for?
    If Palmeiras, or no one, why?

84. What do you think of Flamengo fans?
    (*For Fla fans*)
    I have heard that there are really only two teams in Rio—
    those for Flamengo and those against—why does this attitude
    exist against Fla fans?
85. Did you follow the World Cup games in Mexico in 1970 by
    television?
    ☐ yes; How many?
    ☐ no
86. Did you follow only those games in which Brazil participated,
    or those between other countries as well?
    ☐ only Brazil
    ☐ other countries too
87. Do you remember three names of players from the Selection
    1970?
    ☐ yes; Name three:
    ☐ no; Can't name three
88. Can you tell me what MOBRAL is? (*Adult literacy program*)
    ☐ yes
    ☐ no
    Can you tell me what Itaipú is? (*Hydroelectric plant for Brazil,
    Paraguay, and Argentina*)
    ☐ yes
    ☐ no
    Can you tell me what the Trans-Amazon project is?
    ☐ yes
    ☐ no

Name the people in these photographs:

Can name	Recognizes position but cannot name	Can't name	
☐	☐	☐	89. *The president of the Republic of Brazil— Médici*
☐	☐	☐	90. *The secretary of the treasury—Delfim Neto*
☐	☐	☐	91. *The president of the United States—Richard Nixon*
☐	☐	☐	92. *The governor of Rio— Chagas Freito*

☐ ☐ ☐ 93. *Popular television actress—Regina Duarte*

☐ ☐ ☐ 94. *Most popular singer— Roberto Carlos*

☐ ☐ ☐ 95. *Popular television comedian—Chacrinha*

☐ ☐ ☐ 96. *Race car champion— Emerson Fittipaldi*

☐ ☐ ☐ 97. *One of Rio's top soccer stars—Jairzinho*

☐ ☐ ☐ 98. *Lesser-known Rio player—Afonsinho*

☐ ☐ ☐ 99. *Very famous Cup player from Minas, just bought by Rio team—Tostão*

☐ ☐ ☐ 100. *Pelé*

Appendix 2:
The Predictors of Fandom

Table A1
Relationship between Social Contact with Friends and Neighbors
and Fandom

Fandom Level	Social Contact		
	Low	Medium	High
Weak fan	44%	24%	17%
Average fan	49	52	44
Strong fan	7	24	39
Total	100%	100%	100%
$(N)^a$	(39)	(84)	(77)
	Tau b^b = 0.256, $p < .001$		

Note: This measure of social contact combines answers to separate questions about
conversations with friends and neighbors during the previous week.

$^a N$ = number of respondents in that category.

^{b}Kendall's tau b is a widely used measure for rank-ordered correlations. Even
though these figures are based on a nonrandom sample, tests of significance are
presented in the following tables for those who find it helpful to see them.

Table A2
Relationship between Television Viewing and Fandom

Fandom Level	Television Viewing		
	Low	Medium	High
Weak fan	40%	21%	24%
Average fan	43	60	36
Strong fan	18	19	40
Total	100%	100%	100%
(N)	(33)	(95)	(72)
	Tau b = 0.170, $p < .01$		

Table A3
Relationship between Newspaper Reading and Fandom, Controlling for Formal Education

| | Years of Formal Education | | | | | | | | |
| | 5 or Fewer | | | 6–9 | | | 10 or More | | |
Reads Newspaper	Weak Fan	Average Fan	Strong Fan	Weak Fan	Average Fan	Strong Fan	Weak Fan	Average Fan	Strong Fan
Rarely	47%	15%	12%	40%	20%	0%	0%	15%	0%
Once a week	37	52	25	35	26	22	50	31	
Daily	16	33	63	25	54	78	50	54	82
Total (N)	100% (91)	100%	100%	100% (73)	100%	100%	100% (34)	100%	100%

Tau b = 0.342, p < .001   Tau b = 0.377, p < .001   Tau b = 0.222, p < .01

Table A4
Relationship between Religiousness and Fandom

Fandom Level	Not Religious	Average	Religious
Weak fan	19%	17%	45%
Average fan	46	60	39
Strong fan	35	23	16
Total	100%	100%	100%
(N)	(93)	(58)	(49)

Tau $b = -0.207, p < .001$

Note: Religiousness is measured by a combination of frequency of church attendance and the individual's self-identification as devout, average, or nonreligious.

Table A5
Relationship between Childhood Soccer Participation and Current Adult Fandom

	Boyhood Experience with Soccer		
Fandom Level	Did Not Play	Played Pick-up	Played in Organized League
Weak fan	71%	32%	10%
Average fan	23	48	54
Strong fan	6	20	36
Total	100%	100%	100%
(N)	(17)	(85)	(98)

Tau $b = 0.334, p < .001$

Table A6
Relationship between Current Soccer Participation and Fandom

	Adult Amateur Involvement		
Fandom Level	None	Plays Pick-up	Plays in Organized League
Weak fan	40%	18%	3%
Average fan	38	53	65
Strong fan	22	29	32
Total	100%	100%	100%
(N)	(87)	(76)	(37)

Tau b = 0.233, p < .001

Table A7
Relationship between Sport Lottery Betting and Fandom

	Betting Activity		
Fandom Level	Low	Medium	High
Weak fan	39%	20%	17%
Average fan	47	52	47
Strong fan	14	28	36
Total	100%	100%	100%
(N)	(66)	(56)	(78)

Tau b = 0.234, p < .001

Note: Betting is measured by a combination of frequency and amount of lottery bets.

Table A8
Final Regression Analysis of Fandom on Background
Characteristics

Independent Variable	Regression[a] Coefficient B	Standardized Regression Coefficient β
Past athletic activity	.769 (.174)	.273
Betting interest	.324 (.088)	.223
Social contacts	.193 (.059)	.192
Religiousness	−.296 (.102)	−.171
Television viewing	.188 (.082)	.136
Current athletic activity	.186 (.088)	.104

Constant = 1.114
$R^2 = 0.38$
Standard error B in parentheses

[a]The regression coefficient stands for the expected change in Y (fandom) of one unit of X_1 (first independent variable) when X_2, X_3, X_4 ... X_n are controlled or held constant.

Notes

Chapter One

1. Heywood Hale Broun, speaking at a Yale University Forum, spring 1974.

2. Louis Harris and Associates, Study no. 2153 (January 1972).

3. Edward Shils, *Center and Periphery: Essays in Macro-Sociology* (Chicago: University of Chicago Press, 1975).

4. Anatol Rapoport, *Fights, Games, and Debates* (Ann Arbor: University of Michigan Press, 1960).

5. Georg Simmel, *Conflict and the Web of Group-Affiliation*, trans. Kurt H. Wolff (New York: Free Press, 1955), pp. 34–35.

6. Max Gluckman, "How Foreign Are You?" *Listener*, 15 January 1959, pp. 99–102.

7. Pete Axthelm, "Of Sports and Patriotism," *Newsweek*, 10 March 1980, p. 69.

8. Michael Roberts, "The Vicarious Heroism of the Sports Spectator," *New Republic*, 23 November 1974, p. 17.

9. Richard Henshaw, *The Encyclopedia of World Soccer* (Washington, D.C.: New Republic Books, 1979), p. xii.

10. I learned about the political representation of Israeli teams from Ephram Yuchtman-Yaar, visiting professor of sociology at Columbia University, August 1978.

11. See chapter 10 in Immanuel Wallerstein, *The Capitalist World Economy* (Cambridge: Cambridge University Press, 1979).

12. Clifford Geertz, "The Integrative Revolution: Primordial Sentiments and Civil Politics in New States," in *Old Societies and New States: The Quest for Modernity in Asia and Africa*, ed. Clifford Geertz (Glencoe, Ill.: Free Press, 1963), pp. 105–57.

13. Ibid., p. 156.

14. Barbara Ward, *Five Ideas That Changed the World* (New York: W. W. Norton, 1959).

15. Janet Abu-Lughod and Richard Hay, Jr., *Third World Urbanization* (Chicago: Maaroufa Press, 1977).

16. Henshaw, *World Soccer*, pp. 90–105.

17. This section was inspired by the classic essay on sociability in *The Sociology of Georg Simmel*, trans. and ed. Kurt H. Wolff (New York: Free Press, 1950), pp. 40–57. Although Simmel did not address sport directly, it clearly provides the satisfactions of what he calls the "play forms of association," where people have no ulterior motive for their interaction, where they suspend personal moods and status differentials for the sheer fun of social conversation that has no real consequences.

18. Statement by Bill Veeck, president and owner of the Chicago White Sox baseball team, during an interview with Janet Lever and Stanton Wheeler, fall 1977.

19. Frederick Exley, *A Fan's Notes* (New York: Random House, 1968).

20. Michael Novak, *The Joy of Sports* (New York: Basic, 1976), p. 144.

21. *Jornal do Brasil*, 23 June 1970.

22. Janet Lever and Stanton Wheeler, *Experience of Sport*, in preparation.

23. Christopher Lasch, *The Culture of Narcissism: American Life in an Age of Diminishing Expectations* (New York: W. W. Norton, 1978), p. 5.

24. Gregory P. Stone, "American Sports: Play and Display," *Chicago Review* 9 (fall 1955):83–100.

25. Clifford Geertz, "Deep Play: Notes on the Balinese Cockfight," in *The Interpretation of Cultures* (New York: Basic Books, 1973), pp. 412–53.

26. Robert Lynd and Helen Lynd, *Middletown* (New York: Harcourt, Brace, and World, 1929), p. 485.

27. Ibid., pp. 84–85.

28. Gregory P. Stone, "Sport as a Community Representation," in *Handbook of Social Science of Sport*, ed. Gunther Luschen and George Sage (Champaign, Ill.: Stipes, 1981).

29. Lever and Wheeler, *Experience of Sport*.

30. Frank Manning, *Black Clubs in Bermuda* (London: Cornell University Press, 1973).

31. Jane Jacobs, *Death and Life of Great American Cities* (New York: Vintage, 1961).

32. Emile Durkheim, *The Elementary Forms of the Religious Life*, trans. Joseph Ward Swain (London: George Allen and Unwin, 1915).

33. Perhaps as a recognition of the likeness of totemism and sport, many teams in the United States, from Little League up to the major leagues, have adopted animals as their emblems.

34. Johan Huizinga says, in his classic work *Homo Ludens: A Study of the Play Element in Culture* (Boston: Beacon Press, 1955), p. 8: "Play is

not 'ordinary' or 'real.' . . . In all its higher forms . . . [it] always belongs to the sphere of festival and ritual—the sacred sphere." And Paul Weiss adds that sports, as bounded events, are framed by ceremonies that give them a religious aura and are played by athletes who are thought to have something of the divine in them. See Paul Weiss, *Sport: A Philosophic Inquiry* (Carbondale: Southern Illinois University Press, 1969), pp. 152–53.

35. According to M. I. Finley and H. W. Pleket in *The Olympic Games: The First Thousand Years* (London: Chatto and Windus, 1976), p. 106, civic pride was a crucial motivator for the original Olympics. An estimated 40,000 spectators witnessed the games. City patrons provided the money needed to prepare an athlete for competition and to reward him when victorious; "the herald proclaimed the name of our city while he was crowned."

36. Michael Roberts, *Fans! How We Go Crazy over Sports* (Washington, D.C.: New Republic Books, 1976), p. 30.

37. Randall Collins, *Conflict Sociology* (New York: Academic Press, 1975).

38. *New York Daily News*, 23 August 1981, p. 17.

39. Don McLeese, "Sport: Report from Iron City," in Chicago's *Reader*, 19 October 1979, p. 12.

40. Bill Veeck, with Ed Linn, *Veeck as in Wreck* (New York: Ballantine, 1976), p. 120.

41. Novak, *Joy of Sports*, p. 143.

42. Ward, *Five Ideas*.

43. Geertz, "Integrative Revolution."

44. This is really Simmel's point that social peace comes from the intricate web of our conflicting loyalties. See *Conflict and the Web of Group Affiliations*, trans. Kurt H. Wolff (New York: Free Press, 1955).

45. Paul Gardner, "The Agony of the Feet," *Village Voice*, 17 July 1978, p. 19.

46. Martin A. Jackson, "Britain's Royal Family—Seasoned TV Performers," *New York Times*, 19 July 1981, p. 27.

47. Ibid.

48. Edward Shils and Michael Young, "The Meaning of the Coronation," *American Sociological Review* 1 (1953):80.

49. Estimate from television authorities provided by Dr. Helmut Kaser, general secretary of FIFA, in correspondence dated 1 October 1979.

50. Lowell Miller, "World Cup—or World War?" *New York Times Magazine*, 21 May 1978, pp. 20-22, 63–69.

51. Olympic television audience estimate comes from *The Guinness Book of World Records*, 1979 edition.

52. "TV's *Dallas*: Whodunit?" *Time*, 11 August 1980, pp. 60–66.

53. See Howard L. Nixon II, *Sport and Social Organization* (Indianapolis: Bobbs-Merrill, 1976).

54. For examples of each, see Weiss, *Sport: A Philosophic Inquiry*; Novak, *Joy of Sports*; and Lasch, *Culture of Narcissism*.

Chapter Two

1. Monique Berlioux, director of the International Olympic Committee, provided information on the Olympic movement, correspondence dated 18 October 1979.

2. The translation of FIFA's title is the International Federation of Association Football, not the International Federation of Football Associations, as it often appears.

3. Dr. Helmut Kaser, general secretary of FIFA, informed me (personal correspondence of 1 October 1979) that Rhodesia is a member association but cannot play soccer because of the United Nations Security Council ruling that no Rhodesian passport holder will be permitted to enter any United Nations country. South Africa was expelled from FIFA in 1976 after the adoption of a statutory provision to exclude any national association that tolerated competition marked by discrimination. Seven new national associations have applications for membership pending: Cape Verde, Equatorial Guinea, Angola, Guinea Bissau, Cayman Islands, Belize, and Seychelles.

Paul Gardner remarks on the similarity between FIFA's biannual congressional meetings and a United Nations General Assembly meeting: delegates from an almost equal number of countries use headphones for simultaneous translation. See Paul Gardner, *The Simplest Game: The Intelligent American's Guide to the World of Soccer* (Boston: Little, Brown, 1976), pp. 120–23.

4. Alex Yannis, *Inside Soccer* (New York: McGraw-Hill, 1980).

5. According to John Arlott, *The Oxford Companion to Sports and Games* (St. Albans: Paladin, 1977), the United States entered its first World Cup in 1930 in Uruguay, and it reached the semifinals. Four years later in Italy, a U.S. team was eliminated in a preliminary round. The last World Cup the United States entered was 1950 in Brazil, where its team, believe it or not, beat the powerful British team 1-0 in an early round. This event is considered one of the greatest upsets in soccer history, yet it received very little attention from the American public, which passed up this early opportunity to join the world soccer community.

6. Yannis, *Inside Soccer*, p. 2.

7. Claude Lévi-Strauss, *The Savage Mind* (London: University of Chicago Press, 1966), p. 32.

8. Paul Fussell, *The Great War and Modern Memory* (New York: Oxford University Press, 1975), pp. 26–27. My thanks to Professor Albert O. Hirschman for sending me this reference.

9. Pete Axthelm, "Of Sports and Patriotism," *Newsweek*, 10 March 1980, p. 69.

10. Miller, "World Cup—or World War?" pp. 20, 63.

11. Ibid., p. 64.

12. George Orwell, "The Sporting Spirit," in *Shooting an Elephant* (London: Secker and Warburg, 1950), p. 195.

13. Michael Roberts, *Fans! How We Go Crazy over Sports* (Washington, D.C.: New Republic Books, 1976), pp. 33–34.

14. Ibid., p. 183.

15. R. J. Pickering, "Cuba," in *Sport under Communism: The U.S.S.R., Czechoslovakia, the G.D.R., China, Cuba*, ed. James Riordan (London: C. Hurst, 1978).

16. Cited in Roberts, *Fans!* p. 188.

17. Ibid., p. 186.

18. From the *Playboy* interview, October 1976, p. 86.

19. Cycling can be considered a team sport, but since the first three riders placed are individually awarded, regardless of their country's team standing, I have listed it with the individual sports. The International Cyclist Association, founded in 1892, still sponsors amateur and professional races that inspire enthusiasm in several Western European nations. See Arlott, *Sports and Games*. Real aficionados understand auto racing as a team sport, appreciating the crucial role of the mechanics and pit crew, but the fact that only the driver is known by name reflects the individual character of the sport.

20. Arlott, *Sports and Games*.

21. In 1862 J. C. Thring published ten rules for what he called "the simplest game." See also Gardner, *Simplest Game*.

22. For an excellent description of the evolution of a new game to fit a new culture, see David Riesman and Reuel Denney, "Football in America: A Study in Culture Diffusion," *American Quarterly* 3 (1951): 309–19.

23. The myth that baseball was invented by Abner Doubleday in 1839 at Cooperstown, New York, has no basis in fact. See Arlott, *Sports and Games*, p. 50.

24. Recently a professional volleyball league was started on the West Coast of the United States, but volleyball is still an amateur sport in the rest of the United States and in other countries. Membership figures for the two international federations come from Arlott, *Sports and Games*.

25. Ibid.

26. Ibid.

27. Ibid.

28. Ibid.

29. Gardner, *Simplest Game*, p. 124.

30. Arlott, *Sports and Games*, p. 458.

31. James Walvin, *The People's Game: A Social History of British Football* (London: Allen Lane, 1975), p. 161.

32. Lincoln Allison, "Association Football and the Urban Ethos," in *Manchester and São Paulo: Problems of Rapid Urban Growth*, ed. John D. Wirth and Robert L. Jones (Stanford: Stanford University Press, 1978).

33. Ibid.

34. Walvin, *People's Game*, p. 53.

35. Ibid.

36. Allison, "Association Football."

37. Walvin, *People's Game*.

38. Sport sociologist Peter McIntosh claims that the distinction between professional and amateur reflects the class structure of Victorian England: "The word 'amateur,' French in origin, was first used to refer to aristocratic collectors and connoisseurs of the fine arts. Because of the association of sport and social respectability, the word was transferred to sport in the 19th century and the terms amateur and gentleman became interchangeable." See Peter McIntosh, "The British Attitude to Sport," in *Sport and Society*, ed. Alex Natan (London: Bowes and Bowes, 1958), p. 20.

39. Gardner, *Simplest Game*.

40. Ibid.

41. Her Majesty the Queen serves as a patron and the Duke of Kent as president of England's Football Association. All of its ten honorary vice presidents are Sirs, Lords, or Right Honorables. See Peter Douglas, *The Football Industry* (London: George Allen and Unwin, 1973).

42. Walvin, *People's Game*.

43. Gardner, *Simplest Game*.

44. Allison, "Association Football," pp. 215–16.

45. See Walvin, *People's Game*, chap. 5, "England's Most Durable Export," for rich details on the spread of the game.

46. Arlott, *Sports and Games*.

47. Gardner, *Simplest Game*, p. 113.

48. Arlott, *Sports and Games*.

49. Mario Filho, *O negro no futebol brasileiro* (Rio de Janeiro: Civilização Brasileira, 1964).

50. Antonio Euclides Teixeira, "A isto se chama religião," *Realidade* (July 1967).

51. Gardner, *Simplest Game*.

52. Arlott, *Sports and Games*.

53. Gilberto Freyre, cited in Gardner, *Simplest Game*, p. 13.

54. Warren Hoge, "In Brazilian Soccer, Zico Is Taking up Where Pelé Left Off," *New York Times*, 5 July 1981, p. S7.

55. Gardner, *Simplest Game*, p. 13.

56. Yannis, *Inside Soccer*.

57. Walvin, *People's Game*.

58. Ibid.

59. Ibid.

60. Harris Survey, release dated 19 January 1978.

61. Lowell Miller, "The Selling of Soccer-Mania," *New York Times Magazine*, 28 August 1977, pp. 12–24, 38.

62. Ibid.

63. From *Body of Iron, Soul of Fire*, film sponsored by the American Express Group and shown by the National Park Service at the Statue of Liberty.

64. According to Gardner, *Simplest Game*, the detailed running of FIFA is done by the general secretary, the Executive Committee, and ten standing committees (viz., finance, referees, medical, World Cup, players, press, amateurs, technical, disciplinary, and emergency committees).

FIFA's current president and past president of Brazil's CBD, João Havelange, has never been paid for his decades of service to soccer. His is a charitable contribution to the game. According to my Rio informants, he lives on the income produced by his private bus company.

65. Alan Hardaker, *Hardaker of the League* (London: Pelham Books, 1977).

66. I am quoting from an uncited source from a British soccer magazine that Ian Taylor sent to me several years ago.

67. Gardner, *Simplest Game*, p. 113.

68. Douglas, *Football Industry*.

69. Gardner, *Simplest Game*.

70. Miller, "Selling of Soccer-Mania."

71. Yannis, *Inside Soccer*.

Chapter Three

1. Charles Wagley, "Regionalism and Cultural Unity in Brazil," in *Contemporary Cultures and Societies in Latin America*, ed. D. B. Heath and R. N. Adams (New York: Random House, 1965), pp. 124–36.

2. Ibid.

3. *Encyclopedia Americana*, 1978 ed., 4:454–63.

4. Wagley, "Regionalism and Unity."

5. Many people still refer to Brasília as "Kubitschek's Folly." It is estimated that more than $100 billion was spent on the new capital. Expenditures of that magnitude not only added fuel to already raging inflation but were considered immoral by many critics, who thought the money would have been better spent on Brazil's poor. So far Brasília has failed to attract enough commerce and industry to draw in labor and relieve population pressures from the South. On the weekends, when civil servants and politicians stream out to Rio, it stands stark and empty like a space-age ghost town.

6. See A. Bradford Burns, *Nationalism in Brazil: A Historical Survey* (New York: F. A. Praeger, 1968).

7. See Peter Fry, "Two Religious Movements: Protestantism and Umbanda," in *Manchester and São Paulo: Problems of Rapid Urban Growth*, ed. J. D. Wirth and R. L. Jones (Stanford: Stanford University Press, 1968).

8. Ibid.

9. Peter Flynn, "Sambas, Soccer, and Nationalism," *New Society*, 19 August 1971, pp. 327–30.

10. Ibid., p. 328.

11. Anthony Leeds and Elizabeth Leeds, "Accounting for Behavioral Differences: Three Political Systems and the Response of the Squatters in Brazil, Peru, and Chile," in *The City in Comparative Perspective*, ed. John Walton and Louis H. Masotti (New York: Wiley, 1976).

12. Flynn, "Sambas, Soccer, and Nationalism."

13. Albert Goldman, *Carnival in Rio* (New York: Hawthorn Books, 1978).

14. Robert Harvey, "The Three Brazils," *Economist*, 31 July 1976.
15. Richard Henshaw, *The Encyclopedia of World Soccer* (Washington, D.C.: New Republic Books, 1979).
16. Julio Mazzei and Mauro S. Teixeira, *Cultura, Educação, Educação Fisica, Esportes, Recreação*, 2d ed. (São Paulo: Fulgor, 1976), 1:252.
17. The following sports also fall under its dominion: spear fishing, deep-sea fishing, swimming, crew, diving, water polo, archery, track and field, baseball, boche ball, bowling, cycling, salon soccer (indoors), gymnastics, weight lifting, quoits, handball, squash, hockey, pentathlon, and table tennis.
18. Hunter Davies, *The Glory Game* (New York: St. Martin's Press, 1972), p. 89.
19. Anthony Leeds, "Brazilian Careers and Social Structure: A Case History and Model," in *Contemporary Cultures and Societies of Latin America*, ed. D. B. Heath and R. N. Adams (New York: Random House, 1965), pp. 379–404. I thank Tom Flory for pointing out the application of Leeds's model to soccer directors.
20. The departments are similar to those within the soccer clubs: administration, finance, professional soccer, aquatic sports, and amateur-level sports.
21. Thomas E. Skidmore, *Politics in Brazil: 1930–1964* (New York: Oxford University Press, 1967).
22. Robert W. Shirley, "Legal Institutions and Early Industrial Growth," in *Manchester and São Paulo: Problems of Rapid Urban Growth*, ed. J. D. Wirth and R. L. Jones (Stanford: Stanford University Press, 1968).
23. Peter J. Reichard, "The Price of Progress in Brazil," *New Leader*, 13 May 1974.
24. Harvey, "Three Brazils."
25. Sylvia Ann Hewlett, *The Cruel Dilemmas of Development: Twentieth Century Brazil* (New York: Basic Books, 1980).
26. By 1981 the minimum wage had been raised only to $76.02 (5,-789 cruzeiros).
27. From unclassified document A-114, produced by the United States Department of State, 17 July 1973.
28. *Latin American Political Report*, 2 June 1978, p. 161.
29. Not only right-wing politicians use this ploy to court popularity; Chile's communist president Salvador Allende sent congratulatory telegrams to the popular Colo-Colo team.
30. I gratefully acknowledge the receipt of materials from Mr. W. Baumann, secretary general of INTERTOTO, Basel, Switzerland, 16 January 1979. The nations that belong to INTERTOTO are: Algeria, Austria, Brazil, Bulgaria, Czechoslovakia, Denmark, Finland, Greece, Hungary, Holland, Israel, Italy, Morocco, Norway, Poland, Portugal, Rumania, Spain, Sweden, Switzerland, Turkey, West Germany and Yugoslavia. Although the nations are not members, similar public companies are run in most Latin American countries, Nigeria, the Sudan, the German Demo-

cratic Republic, and the Soviet Union. The lucrative English soccer pools are run by private companies.

31. Detailed information on the utilization of sport lottery profits was taken from the *Onzième Conférence des Directeurs de l'INTERTOTO (1976 à Madrid)*. Minutes of this meeting were translated for me by Anne Moreau.

32. Figures provided by Afro Furtado de Carvalho, superintendent of lotteries, in personal correspondence, 17 March 1978.

33. Phrase attributed to Zico, considered the greatest Brazilian player today. Quoted by Warren Hoge, "In Brazilian Soccer, Zico Is Taking up Where Pelé Left Off," *New York Times*, 5 July 1981, p. S7.

34. My translation of the text of Médici's speech as it appeared in the *Jornal do Brasil*, 21 June 1970, p. 5.

35. Pelé, with Robert L. Fish, *My Life and the Beautiful Game: The Autobiography of Pelé* (New York: Doubleday, 1977), p. 58.

36. Robert M. Levine, "Sport and Society: The Case of Brazilian *Futebol*," unpublished paper, p. 28.

37. Flynn, "Sambas, Soccer, and Nationalism," p. 329.

38. Marplan survey number 160, conducted for the *Jornal do Brasil* in June 1970. I thank Werlington Deslandes for his cooperation in locating this and subsequent Marplan findings.

Chapter Four

1. *Encyclopaedia Britannica*, 1974 ed., vol. 15.

2. Alejandro Portes and John Walton, *Urban Latin America: The Political Condition Above and Below* (Austin: University of Texas Press, 1976).

3. Janice E. Perlman, *The Myth of Marginality: Urban Poverty and Politics in Rio de Janeiro* (Berkeley: University of California Press, 1976).

4. For example, London now has four first-division league teams, with seven more lower-division teams within a twenty-mile radius of the city; there are seventeen professional clubs in the Manchester area. From an interview with Geoff Miller of the Associated Press London Office, conducted by Stanton Wheeler and myself in November 1978.

5. Soccer clubs are the principal, but not the sole, providers of recreational and amateur sport. Expensive country clubs also enter teams of children and adolescents in citywide competitions, especially in elite sports like crew and water polo. At the adult level, the soccer clubs' amateur teams compete in city leagues along with teams from large factories, banks, utility companies, and commercial houses that often have their own training facilities. Businesses that sponsor teams have motives beyond the physical fitness of the participants. As the manager of an instant-coffee factory explained to me, a soccer team bonds his workers (players and spectators both) and instills pride for the factory when they win a game. Management reasoned that greater identification with the factory would boost the workers' morale and make them more produc-

tive. Although he had no records to prove his point, the manager asserted that absenteeism had declined since the introduction of the team.

6. Brazilians dismissed the testimony of American women who protested that they had played soccer as children (while boys played manly football) as evidence that American soccer is quite a different game.

7. Federação Paranaense de Futebol, Boletim Oficial no. 024/81, Resoluçoes Tomadas em 13 de Março, 1981. I thank José Augusto Ross for researching this legislation for me.

8. Soccer clubs in England and most of Europe are organized on the model of the British limited public company. Membership clubs are more common in Latin American and Iberian countries. Well-known examples of social membership clubs in other countries include River Plate, Argentina's wealthiest club, and Real Madrid in Spain. The latter club is housed on a forty-acre site that includes a complex of tennis courts, four swimming pools, basketball arena, track and field stadium, skating rink, soccer fields, and restaurant.

9. Alan Hardaker, *Hardaker of the League* (London: Pelham Books, 1977), p. 68.

10. Marplan survey number 160 (1971) broke down the Rio population's loyalties as: Flamengo (31%); Fluminense (24%); Vasco da Gama (18%); Botafogo (16%); all others combined (6%); no team declared (5%).

11. The special excitement of intracity matches is not unknown to professional sport in the United States, it is just exceedingly rare. Before the Giants and the Dodgers moved to California, New York had three baseball teams. The most famous "subway series" (a World Series championship involving two teams from the same city, so that public transportation enables both fan groups to be present for all games) was in 1951, when the Giants beat the Dodgers for the National League title and faced the American League champion Yankees in the World Series. New York newspapers had stories of fan loyalties splitting the city down the middle. Although there has not been a "subway series" since the 1950s, the possibilities for one still stir the imagination of American fans.

Although rare in the world of professional sport, intracity and intrastate rivalry is common at the amateur level in the United States. High-school football and basketball games often result in brawls between fan groups or vandalism by the visitors. Many of the most intense college rivalries are based on regional proximity: USC vs. UCLA, Georgia vs. Georgia Tech, Michigan vs. Michigan State, Texas vs. Texas A. & M., to name but a few. Americans are familiar with enough examples to recognize these sporting encounters as particularly tense and engaging for athletes and fans alike.

12. I thank sports commentator João Saldanha for pointing out this unintended effect of the sport lottery. (Personal interview on 13 May 1973.)

13. From Marplan survey number 183 of six hundred Rio residents.

14. Knowledgeable fans are most likely to win when the week's games have logical outcomes. When this occurs there are a large number

of winners, because so many people in Brazil know their soccer. Prize money is consequently small and not newsworthy. When many outcomes are illogical, on the other hand, it is only the soccer-naive, who make their choices randomly, who win. A very few will be lucky enough to pick the winning combination and get enormous sums of money and widespread press coverage.

15. Information on sport dailies around the world was provided by Mr. Edouard Seidler, director of *L'Equipe*, France's famous sports daily, in a personal interview (November 1978). There are four sports dailies in Italy which emphasize regional news; two each in Spain and Belgium, and one each in France, Israel, Argentina, and Mexico. Germany's *Kicker* comes out four times a week; Switzerland has several weekly sports papers; and Japan has a daily newspaper that mixes sport with entertainment news and excludes political, crime, and economic reports. All Eastern European countries have daily sports papers—although some emphasize scores more than stories—and *Sovietski Sport* (in the USSR) has the distinction of having the world's highest circulation for a sports paper, with sales of four million after major events. *Sovietski Sport* circulation figures were found in the *Europa Yearbook: World Survey, 1979.*

16. Information on *Jornal dos Sports* provided by its director on 13 April 1973.

17. France's *L'Equipe* is the most respected sports daily in the world (it started the tradition of being printed on colored paper). Sold in thirteen countries, *L'Equipe* covers international sport, not just French sport. The events it created and promoted are among the most exciting competitions in the sporting world: the Bicycle Tour de France, the Auto Tour de France, the Motorcycle Tour de France, Twenty-four Hours at Le Mans, World Cup Skiing, World Cup Yachting, and the European Cup (the club championship in soccer).

18. This figure is remarkably similar to the 17 percent of news space devoted to sport in the *Chicago Tribune* sampled in 1975. From Janet Lever and Stanton Wheeler, "*The Chicago Tribune* Sportspage, 1900–1975," forthcoming.

19. Ibid. Fewer than 1 percent of all stories sampled concerned fans.

20. Information provided by Sr. Helio Costa of TV and Radio Globo (Starlight Communications in New York City) in a personal interview, June 1978.

21. From an interview with Alec Weeks, the head of soccer programming at the BBC, conducted by myself and Stanton Wheeler in November 1978.

22. I tallied the number of doormen listening to radio broadcasts in two residential neighborhoods (Copacabana and Ipanema) during three successive city league games.

23. Soccer "permeates" other environments too. My colleague Janet Abu-Lughod told me that in Cairo, Egypt, one can tell which soccer team won by the pattern of honking horns.

24. Pelé, with Robert L. Fish, *My Life and the Beautiful Game: The Autobiography of Pelé* (New York: Doubleday, 1977), p. 50.

25. Sports commentator João Saldanha, in an interview on 13 May 1973, related this statistic. The five matches with enormous followings are: Flamengo vs. Fluminense in Rio; Corinthians vs. São Paulo in São Paulo; Cruzeiro vs. Atlético in Belo Horizonte; Bahia vs. Vitoria in Salvador; and Gremio vs. Internacional in Pôrto Alegre.

26. Data provided by Roberto Diniz Seabra of the Confederação Brasileira de Futebol, letter of 26 October 1981.

27. Stadia with capacities exceeding 100,000 are in Rio de Janeiro, São Paulo, Belo Horizonte, Curitiba, Pôrto Alegre, Salvador, and Maceió. Stadia in Belém and Fortaleza are being enlarged to hold 120,000 spectators apiece. Information on Brazilian stadia supplied by the CBD bulletin "Extra 6," 1973. Comparable U.S. figures were drawn from *Reader's Digest 1977 Yearbook and Almanac* (New York: W. W. Norton, 1977).

28. Warren Hoge, "In Brazilian Soccer Zico Is Taking up Where Pelé Left Off," *New York Times*, 5 July 1981, p. S7.

29. The structure of the new Confederação Brasileira de Futebol and the support of amateur sports were explained to me by the chief of its Technical Department, Roberto Diniz Seabra, in personal correspondence dated 26 October 1981.

Chapter Five

1. From my interview with Armando Nogueira, 5 September 1973.

2. Ibid.

3. Lowell Miller, "World Cup—or World War?" *New York Times Magazine*, 21 May 1978, pp. 20–22, 64–69.

4. Michael Roberts, *Fans! How We Go Crazy over Sports* (Washington, D.C.: New Republic Books, 1976), p. xi.

5. Armando Nogueira, *Bola na rede*, 2d ed. (Rio de Janeiro: José Olympio, 1974), p. 130.

6. See Rolf Meyersohn, "Television and the Rest of Leisure," *Public Opinion Quarterly* 32 (spring 1968):102–12; Lillian B. Rubin, *Worlds of Pain* (New York: Basic Books, 1976); and Sebastian de Grazia, *Of Time, Work, and Leisure* (New York: Anchor, 1964).

7. This sample's responses resemble those found by Marplan survey number 183, which showed that 87 percent of Rio men said they go home directly after work.

8. Most of the men in my sample, 156 of 200, worked at a place that sponsored at least one soccer team. The multinational drug company where I interviewed had paid all expenses to send its team to Argentina and Uruguay to play teams from its factories there. The Brazilian team had just won the corporation's South American championship, and all employees were given a Carnival party to celebrate the victory. Employees agreed that the team had made them proud of their workplace and that they enjoyed being let out of work early on game days when the team

played on the factory grounds. The players said they would be forever grateful for the opportunity to travel to foreign lands.

9. "Work" was the topic of conversation mentioned by 21 percent, and "women" were cited by another 10 percent. All other answers received less than a 10 percent response.

10. We assume that the more someone cares about a team, the more time or money or both he spends following it. My talks with these two hundred men mostly confirmed this assumption, but there were exceptions. One man told me that he gets too emotional watching his team, so he avoids their games at the stadium. Another young man, a janitor, said he no longer listens to his team's games because he broke his radio by throwing it against the wall in a fit of anger during a game. Not being able to afford a new radio for each game, he considers it safer to wait and buy a newspaper to see if his team won.

11. I inquired about the home base of the following teams: Vitoria from Bahia, Gremio from Rio Grande do Sul, Peñarol from Uruguay, and River Plate from Argentina.

12. Arnold R. Beisser, in *Madness in Sports* (New York: Appleton-Century-Crofts, 1967), suggests that it is the lonely who are most likely to need the surrogate kinship that sport produces. Gregory P. Stone, in "Sport as a Community Representation," also links the need for identification with community through sport to those who have few objective ties.

13. See Morris Axelrod, "Urban Structure and Social Participation," *American Sociological Review* 21 (1956):13–18. For an expression of concern that the old-style community is lost in modern society, see Louis Wirth's pivotal essay, "Urbanism as a Way of Life," *American Journal of Sociology* 44 (July 1938):1–24.

14. The measure of family ties was produced by combining information from three items: how many relatives reside in Rio, how close they live to the subject, and how often he speaks with them. To a large extent, contact with relatives depends on proximity of residence. Families are broken up as cousins move far across a sprawling city, because the working class cannot yet afford the luxury of telephones to cut the distance barrier. Telephone lines are in short supply in Rio and must be purchased outright for $1,000 before one can hook up and pay monthly usage fees to the telephone company.

15. See Albert Hunter, *Symbolic Communities: The Persistence and Change of Chicago's Local Communities* (Chicago: University of Chicago Press, 1974). Hunter's data suggest that objective ties and subjective ties (symbolic attachment to locale) are also directly related; he reports that those most likely to express strong local sentiments for their Chicago neighborhoods are whites of higher social class who have lived in an area for a long time and who have many friends inside that area.

16. Frederick Exley, *A Fan's Notes* (New York: Random House, 1968); Neil Offen, *God Save the Players* (Chicago: Playboy Press, 1974).

17. Meyersohn, "Television and Leisure."

18. One alternative explanation for the "the more, the more" direction of the data is rooted in the methodological problem of "yea-saying" (respondents answering questions in the affirmative to show cooperation with the investigator). Given the patterns of yeses and nos by my respondents, I have no reason to believe that "yea-saying" occurred and was wrongly interpreted as integration. For example, many beach enthusiasts are not movie enthusiasts. The weakly positive relationship between fandom and both beach-going and movie-going is in the direction supportive of the "the more, the more" hypothesis, but the pattern between the variables shows that people do select from leisure alternatives.

19. Information from Marplan surveys numbers 107–13.

20. Marplan survey number 183, March 1972.

21. Claude Lévi-Strauss, *The Savage Mind* (Chicago: University of Chicago Press, 1966).

22. Two principal advantages of this statistical procedure are that it can handle large numbers of variables simultaneously and that when introduced with variables that bear little relation to one another, as in this case, it can order their importance. This technique is more refined than the cross tabular presentations not only because it controls for extraneous variables but also because the uncondensed versions of both the dependent variables and the independent variables are used (that is, respondents' fan scores ranged from 7 to 21, instead of being grouped as weak, average, and strong).

23. See Barry D. McPherson, "Sport Consumption and the Economics of Consumerism," in *Sport and Social Order: Contributions to the Sociology of Sport,* ed. Donald W. Ball and John W. Loy (Reading: Addison-Wesley, 1975), pp. 239–75.

24. Of the total variation in fandom, 38 percent is predictable using the six dimensions named above. That is considered quite a respectable figure, since fandom is a complex phenomenon about which we have little empirical knowledge. Obviously, there is much left to learn on the subject.

25. Although standard demographic variables usually are related to leisure patterns and other activities (see Meyersohn, "Television and Leisure"), other studies have found that integration measures are better predictors. For example, Burstein found that information about respondents' mass media consumption was better than age, sex, and social class as a predictor of political involvement. In the five countries he examined, the greater one's media ties, the greater was one's political participation—that is, Burstein's data also support the "the more, the more" hypothesis. See Paul Burstein, "Social Structure and Individual Political Participation in Five Countries," *American Journal of Sociology* 77 (May 1972):1087–1110.

26. See Harold L. Wilensky, "Mass Society and Mass Culture: Interdependence or Independence?" *American Sociological Review* 29 (April 1964):173–97.

27. The 6 percent of my sample that declared no favorite team is almost identical to the findings of Marplan survey number 160 (1971),

which found only 5 percent of Rio residents claiming no team. See chapter 4, note 9, for the distribution of other team affiliations.

28. From my interview with João Saldanha on 13 May 1973.

29. Beisser, *Madness in Sports.*

30. Russell Davies, "Workers' Playtime," *Times Literary Supplement,* 31 January 1975, p. 105.

31. See Albert O. Hirschman, *Exit, Voice and Loyalty* (Cambridge: Harvard University Press, 1970). I thank Professor Hirschman for pointing out the relevance of his argument to the fan situation in Brazil.

Chapter Six

1. Delfim Neto is now Brazil's minister of planning.

2. Television antennas are plentiful on the roofs of the hilltop favelas. Many poor people are able to make the monthly payments on the sets by charging their visitors a small admission fee, which at times includes popcorn or other light refreshments.

3. For an impressionistic comparison, my students in two 1977 sociology of sport courses showed a set of roughly equivalent pictures to 245 men in the Chicago area. The 68 men with highschool education or less are the most comparable to my Brazilian sample. Overall, those Americans scored higher on the political figures, reflecting their higher level of education and the more advanced state of television news programming: President Carter (97%); Henry Kissinger (85%); Leonid Brezhnev (27%); and Governor James Thompson of Illinois (62%). In the entertainment world, the American scores are somewhat lower, reflecting the greater number of television channels as well as artists to choose from: Carol Burnett (89%); Red Skelton (66%); Frank Sinatra (68%); John Denver (64%). The considerably lower recognition of characters from the sports world reflects the diffusion of interests permitted by the American multisports system: Olympic medalist Bruce Jenner (41%); Chicago baseball player Ernie Banks (64%); Chicago basketball player Norm Van Lier (40%); Chicago hockey player Bobby Hull (56.5%); football superstar Joe Namath (79.5%); and world-famous boxer Muhammed Ali (95%).

This photograph test was conducted during football season. I thank my students for their cooperation on this class project, and I thank Al Wulf of United Press International for lending me the photographs of these American public personalities.

4. Alan Hardaker, *Hardaker of the League* (London: Pelham Books, 1977), p. 162.

5. Peter Douglas, *The Football Industry* (London: George Allen and Unwin, 1973), p. 30.

6. According to John Arlott, *The Oxford Companion to Sports and Games* (St. Albans: Paladin, 1977), International Ice Hockey Federation matches are controlled by two referees, but under the rules of the National Hockey League of North America there is only one referee, who is assisted by two linesmen invested with the authority to call offside infrac-

tions. In rugby the two "touch judges" that assist the referee also have more power than soccer linesmen.

7. Hardaker, *Hardaker of the League*, p. 201.

8. Richard Henshaw, *The Encyclopedia of World Soccer* (Washington, D.C.: New Republic Books, 1979).

9. Arthur Hopcraft, *The Football Man* (London: Cox and Wyman, 1968).

10. Hardaker, *Hardaker of the League*.

11. Paul Gardner, *The Simplest Game: The Intelligent American's Guide to the World of Soccer* (Boston: Little, Brown, 1976).

12. Henshaw, *Encyclopedia of Soccer*.

13. Arlott, *Sports and Games*.

14. Carl N. Degler, *Neither Black nor White: Slavery and Race Relations in Brazil and the United States* (New York: Macmillan, 1971).

15. From information provided by Roberto Diniz Seabra of the Confederação Brasileira de Futebol in correspondence dated 26 October 1981.

16. Pelé, with Robert L. Fish, *My Life and the Beautiful Game: The Autobiograpy of Pelé* (New York: Doubleday, 1977).

17. Ibid., p. 109.

18. Gardner, *Simplest Game*, p. 108.

19. From "Sweet Sixteen: An Age for Future Soccer Stars to Leave Home," *Minneapolis Star*, 5 June 1979, p. 12C.

20. From research reported in the *Jornal do Brasil*, 18 September 1973, section B, p. 1.

21. Gardner, in *The Simplest Game*, points out that the "concentration" period is common in both Italy and Brazil, but not in England.

22. Since I conducted my original research, the name of this club has been changed to Colorado.

23. Janet Lever, "Soccer as a Brazilian Way of Life," in *Games, Sport, and Power*, ed. Gregory P. Stone (New Brunswick: Transaction Books, 1972), pp. 138–59.

24. From Marplan study number 145, conducted after the 1970 World Cup.

25. Harvey Frommer, *Sports Roots* (New York: Atheneum, 1979).

26. Peter Bodo and David Hirshey, *Pelé's New World* (New York: Norton, 1977), p. 38.

27. Orrin E. Klapp, *Symbolic Leaders: Public Dramas and Public Men* (Chicago: Aldine, 1964).

Chapter Seven

1. Harold L. Wilensky, "Mass Society and Mass Culture: Interdependence or Independence?" *American Sociological Review* 29 (April 1964):173–97.

2. Erving Goffman, "Fun in Games," in *Encounters: Two Studies in the Sociology of Interaction* (Indianapolis: Bobbs-Merrill, 1961).

3. I thank John Conroy, who has written articles on Northern Ireland, for talking with me in October 1981 about the impact of the conflict there on soccer rivalries.

4. Michael Roberts, *Fans! How We Go Crazy over Sports* (Washington, D.C.: New Republic Books, 1976).

5. "Sports Betting Is Big Business," *St. Louis Post-Dispatch*, 26 December 1980.

6. James Walvin, *The People's Game: A Social History of British Football* (London: Allen Lane, 1975).

7. See John R. Betts, "The Technological Revolution and the Rise of Sport, 1850–1900," *Mississippi Valley Historical Review* 40 (1953):231–56.

8. The present exceptions are New York's two basketball and two ice hockey teams that regularly meet each other in league play. New York, Chicago, and Los Angeles also each have more than one football or baseball team in their metropolitan areas, but these teams belong to separate leagues or divisions and would meet only in the rare event that each made the championship play-off.

9. "The Sports and Recreational Programs of the Nation's Universities and Colleges," Report no. 4, an NCAA publication based on data from 1971–72; "1976 Sports Participation Survey," compiled by the National Federation of State High School Associations.

10. Paul Hoch, "School for Sexism," *Rip off the Big Game: The Exploitation of Sports by the Power Elite* (New York: Doubleday, 1972), pp. 147–66.

11. Kate Millett, *Sexual Politics* (New York: Doubleday, 1970).

12. Warren Hoge, "In Brazilian Soccer, Zico Is Taking up Where Pelé Left Off," *New York Times*, 5 July 1981, p. S7.

13. These questions were raised by Jay Coakley, sport sociologist at the University of Colorado at Colorado Springs, during a telephone conversation with me (July 1980). These issues are also discussed in Donald F. Sabo, Jr., and Ross Runfola, eds., *Jock: Sports and Male Identity* (Englewood Cliffs, N.J.: Prentice-Hall, 1980).

14. Hoch, *Rip off the Big Game.*

15. Pete Axthelm, *The City Game* (New York: Harper and Row, 1970); Rich Telander, *Heaven Is a Playground* (New York: St. Martin's Press, 1976); Bill Bradley, *Life on the Run* (New York: Quadrangle, 1976).

16. See "Cocaine: Middle Class High," *Time*, 6 July 1981, pp. 56–63, and "Middle Class Junkies," *Newsweek*, 10 August 1981, p. 63.

17. Peter Flynn, "Sambas, Soccer, and Nationalism," *New Society*, 19 August 1971, pp. 327–30.

18. *Banco Real Economic Letter* (July 1978), p. 2.

19. J. A. Pires Gonçalves, *Subsídios para implantação de uma política de desportos* (Brasília, 1971).

20. Clifford Geertz, "The Integrative Revolution: Primordial Sentiments and Civil Politics in New States," in *Old Societies and the New*

States: The Quest for Modernity in Asia and Africa, ed. Clifford Geertz (Glencoe, Ill.: Free Press, 1963), p. 108.

21. Marplan survey number 160.

22. For discussions of the more general contribution of sporting institutions to the trinity of national development, integration, and pride, see James Riordan, ed., *Sport under Communism: The U.S.S.R., Czechoslovakia, the G.D.R., and Cuba* (London: C. Hurst, 1978); Ian Taylor, "Social Control through Sport: Football in Mexico," paper delivered to the Law and Politics of Deviance Group, British Sociological Association Annual Conference, 1971; and Gabriel Escobar, "The Role of Sports in the Penetration of Urban Culture to the Rural Areas of Peru," Kroeber Anthropological Society Papers, no. 40, pp. 72–81.

23. *Banco Real Economic Letter* (July 1978), p. 5.

24. *Variety*, 30 July 1980, p. 54.

Index